THE WORKS OF SHAKESPEARE

EDITED FOR THE SYNDICS OF THE
CAMBRIDGE UNIVERSITY PRESS
BY
JOHN DOVER WILSON

KING HENRY THE EIGHTH

EDITED BY
J. C. MAXWELL

KING HENRY
THE EIGHTH

CAMBRIDGE

AT THE UNIVERSITY PRESS

1969

PUBLISHED BY
THE SYNDICS OF THE CAMBRIDGE UNIVERSITY PRESS
Bentley House, 200 Euston Road, London, N.W. 1
American Branch: 32 East 57th Street, New York, N.Y. 10022

© CAMBRIDGE UNIVERSITY PRESS 1962

Standard Book Number:
521 07538 6 clothbound
521 09481 X paperback

First published 1962
First paperback edition 1969

First printed in Great Britain at the University Press, Cambridge
Reprinted in Great Britain by Hazell Watson & Viney Ltd,
Aylesbury, Bucks

CONTENTS

CONTENTS

PREFATORY NOTE

I am once again indebted to Mr. J. C. Maxwell for relieving me of a burden, my relief being all the greater that *Henry VIII* happens to be the last play in the First Folio to be dealt with in this edition and a play I find less interesting than any other in the Folio. Indeed, its chief interest to me is the question of authorship. I cannot enough admire the way this is handled in the following Introduction; for its cogency, its neatness (not a word too much or too few), and— I would dare to add—its finality; while I find the section on the play equally satisfying.

J. D. W.

INTRODUCTION

I. Date and Authorship

It is now agreed by all scholars that *Henry VIII* is of later date than any other play in the Folio: *The Two Noble Kinsmen* may well be later.[1] The performance on 29 June 1613,[2] in the course of which the Globe Theatre was burned down, need not have been the very first,[3] but Sir Henry Wotton's description of the play as new is scarcely consistent with its having been more than a few months on the stage. On the other hand, as Foakes points out,[4] Thomas Lorkin's letter written the day after the fire, referring without explanation to 'the play of Hen: 8', suggests that it was not completely unknown to his correspondent—though too much stress cannot be placed upon a single definite article in a hastily written letter.

It has long been conjectured that the play had a certain measure of topicality in 1613. Its culmination in the baptism of Elizabeth would have made it a suitable play for the occasion of the marriage of James's daughter, Princess Elizabeth, to Prince Frederick, the

---

[1] In the most recent study, Paul Bertram dates *The Two Noble Kinsmen* early November 1613 (*Shakespeare Quarterly*, XII (1961), 30).

[2] For contemporary descriptions, see E. K. Chambers, *William Shakespeare* (1930), II, 343–4 (Wotton's letter only) and *Elizabethan Stage* (1923), II, 419–23. The New Arden edition by R. A. Foakes (1957) has fresh texts of the letters of Thomas Lorkin and John Chamberlain.

[3] I see little force in Aldis Wright's argument (Clarendon edition (1891), p. xxi) that such an accident was not likely to happen except at a first performance.

[4] New Arden edition (1957), p. xxviii.

Elector Palatine, on 14 February 1613. Malone, who believed the play to be of Elizabethan origin,[1] none the less suggested that the marriage might have been the occasion for its revival, James Spedding thought the completion of the play may have been hastened on for this event,[2] and a number of later scholars have held similar views. The most recent supporter has been R. A. Foakes in his New Arden edition of 1957.[3] He points out that the identity of name between the Princess and the great Queen was exploited in pamphlets and sermons of the time,[4] as were the biblical echoes which are prominent in the final scene.[5] I think that he slightly underestimates the damage done to this theory by the fact that, though the records of court performances before the Princess and the Elector include five plays by Shakespeare, *Henry VIII* is not among them;[6] and not much can be built on the possibility that it was the play to have been acted on 16 February which 'lapsed contrarie, for greater pleasures [in the form of a masque] were preparing'.[7] I think that the theory must remain, on present evidence, what it has always been—attractive, intrinsically plausible, but unproved and probably unprovable.

The play as we know it, then, pretty certainly belongs to 1613, and earlier speculations, to be discussed below (pp. xiii–xiv), that it was originally written in substantially its present form in honour of Queen Elizabeth before her death, have not survived the systematic study of the development of Shakespeare's verse. But the question whether it is related to any earlier play on the same

---

[1] See below, p. xiv.   [2] See below, p. xxv.
[3] Pp. xxviii–xxxiii.   [4] Pp. xxx–xxxi.
[5] Pp. xxxi–ii.
[6] E. K. Chambers, *William Shakespeare* (1930), II, 343.
[7] Cited by Foakes, p. xxxiii.

subject must be raised. The only known play to be cited by a responsible scholar is the anonymous *Buckingham* recorded by Henslowe in 1593.[1] E. K. Chambers suggested this, but with diminishing confidence as time went on. In his 'Red Letter' edition of *Henry VIII* (1908), at a time when he was reluctant to attribute to Shakespeare any share in the Folio text, he suggested that *Buckingham* might have been an early Shakespearian version, and that knowledge of its existence might have been a reason for the inclusion of the present version in the Folio, even if it were completely non-Shakespearian.[2] In 1923, he still referred to *Buckingham* as 'a title which might fit either *Richard III* or that early version of *Henry VIII*, the existence of which, on internal grounds, I suspect',[3] though he had by this time reverted to the more orthodox view of *Henry VIII* as a Shakespeare–Fletcher collaboration.[4] In 1930, all he was prepared to say by way of introduction to the mention of *Buckingham* was: 'The reversion to the epic chronicle at the very end of Shakespeare's career is odd. I have sometimes thought that an earlier play may have been adapted';[5] and he now regarded *Richard III* as a more likely identification for *Buckingham* than any version of *Henry VIII*, though in the section on *Richard III* even this identification is cautiously described as 'not...inconceivable'.[6] I very much doubt whether *Buckingham* had any connexion with any Shakespeare play at all.

[1] *Henslowe's Diary*, ed. W. W. Greg (1904–8), II, 158; ed. R. A. Foakes and R. T. Rickert (1961), p. 20.
[2] Pp. 11–13; reprinted in *Shakespeare, a Survey* (1925), pp. 320–2.
[3] *Elizabethan Stage*, II, 95.   [4] *Ibid.* II, 217.
[5] *William Shakespeare*, I, 497.
[6] *Ibid.* I, 303.

If there is general agreement about the date of *Henry VIII*, this is very far from true about the authorship. The first writer who is on record as detecting stylistic peculiarities in the play is Richard Roderick, in a set of 'Remarks' first published in the sixth edition of Thomas Edwards's *Canons of Criticism* (1758). Roderick did not challenge Shakespeare's authorship, and he did not notice any disparity between different scenes: indeed he explicitly asserted 'that the measure throughout this whole Play has something in it peculiar',[1] and his first examples are drawn from the clearly Shakespearian opening scene. He singled out the frequency of unstressed endings, and invited the reader to 'read aloud an hundred lines in any other Play, and an hundred in This; and, if he perceives not the tone and cadence of his own voice to be involuntarily altered in the latter case from what it was in the former; I would never advise him to give much credit to the information of his ears'.[2] He also noted 'that the emphasis, arising from the sense of the verse, very often clashes with the cadence that would naturally result from the metre'.[3] The examples of this which he cites from Act 5, scene 5, are not very happily chosen, and include reversals of normal stress that could easily be paralleled elsewhere in Shakespeare, but he does hit upon an eminently Fletcherian passage from this scene.

It is hard to say whether Roderick deserves much credit as a pioneer. If he picks upon one Fletcherian passage, he also treats as characteristic of the special metre of this play, because of their feminine endings, lines that are perfectly unremarkable (1. 1. 3, 4, 8, 10). Perhaps the most that can be said for him is that his ear was, at least spasmodically, better than his powers of analysis.

---

[1] P. 263.   [2] P. 264.   [3] P. 265.

Johnson certainly seems to have had no misgivings about the play, and lavishes some of his highest praise on Act 4, scene 2: 'This scene is above any other part of *Shakespeare's* tragedies, and perhaps above any scene of any other poet, tender and pathetic, without gods, or furies, or poisons, or precipices, without the help of romantic circumstances, without improbable sallies of poetical lamentation, and without any throes of tumultuous misery'. But as early as Theobald the view had been current that the play was first produced in the reign of Queen Elizabeth, so that the references to King James must have been added later. Theobald and Johnson assumed that Shakespeare himself added these lines (5. 5. 39–55), which are bracketed in Johnson's edition; but the way was open to suggestions of another hand.

In his 'Attempt to ascertain the Order in which the Plays attributed to Shakspeare were written', first published in the first volume of Steevens's edition of 1778, Malone, accepting the Elizabethan dating for the original version, raised the question of its integrity. He quoted Johnson's suggestion that the prologue might be by Ben Jonson, and added that Farmer 'thinks he sees something of Jonson's hand, here and there, in the dialogue also'.[1] Later, he took up Roderick's remarks on metrical peculiarities, and quoted Steevens as thinking that these peculiarities might come from Ben Jonson (to whom, it may be added, they have not the

[1] P. 315. It may be worth while to insert a warning against the statement of R. W. Babcock, *The Genesis of Shakespeare Idolatry* (1931), p. 17, that Thomas Davies 'threw out *Henry VIII* in 1784'. This arises from a careless reading of Davies's statement (*Dramatic Miscellanies* (1784), I, 339) that Malone and Steevens 'suspect, with reason' that the Prologue was 'not entirely the work of Shakespeare'.

slightest affinity). He himself left it an open question whether the 'peculiarities' really existed.[1]

Both he and Steevens had second thoughts on the matter. In 1790, Malone, commenting on Johnson's note on 5. 5. 39 ff., wrote, 'I suspect these lines were added in 1613, after Shakspeare had quitted the stage, by that hand which tampered with the other parts of the play so much, as to have rendered the versification of it of a different colour from all the other plays of Shakspeare'.[2]

He was apparently now more confident that there were peculiarities, but less confident that they could be attributed to Jonson, than he had been twelve years earlier. Steevens had also shifted his position, for in commenting on the above remarks he wrote that he found Roderick's examples 'undecisive'; that Shakespeare might himself have 'intentionally deviated from his usual practice of versification'; and finally, and more damagingly to the theory he had previously espoused, 'if the reviver of this play (or tamperer with it, as he is styled by Mr Malone,) had so much influence over its numbers as to have entirely changed their texture, he must be supposed to have new woven the substance of the whole piece; a fact almost incredible'.[3] He did however, continue to attribute 'the lines under immediate consideration' (5. 5. 39–55) to Jonson. These rather vague speculations were as far as theories of non-Shakespearian material in *Henry VIII* had got by the time of the 1821 Variorum edition.

For the next thirty years, it was the question of date that chiefly concerned scholars. All this was changed when in 1850 James Spedding posed the question, 'Who

---

[1] P. 317.
[2] Quoted in Steevens's 1793 ed., XI, 202.
[3] *Ibid.*

wrote Shakspere's *Henry VIII*?'[1] Spedding's analysis
gave to Shakespeare only Act 1, scenes 1–2, Act 2, scenes
3–4, Act 3, scene 2, lines 1–203 and Act 5, scene 1 (the
last, in his view, 'altered'). Samuel Hickson at once
made known the exact agreement of his division of the
play, independently arrived at, with that of Spedding,[2]
and Spedding then revealed that the suggestion of
Fletcher's hand had first been made to him by Tennyson.[3]

Spedding's theory was naturally a shock to some
traditional evaluations. Indeed, if Halliwell-Phillipps
is to be believed, 'students who belong to an older
school are literally petrified by the announcement that
Wolsey's farewell to all his greatness, as well as a large
part of the scene in which it occurs, are henceforth to
be considered the composition of some other author'.[4]
But in the second half of the nineteenth century
Fletcher's share in the play came to be generally
accepted. The new theory that was then advanced was
that the 'Shakespearian' parts were not in fact by
Shakespeare. The claims of Massinger were argued by
Robert Boyle in the *Transactions of the New Shakspere
Society* (1885), I, 10, and were still being urged by
H. Dugdale Sykes, *Sidelights on Shakespeare*, in 1919,
though W. E. Farnham had shown how completely
divergent *Henry VIII* was from Massinger's plays in
its use of colloquial contractions.[5] Even such a scholar

[1] *Gentleman's Magazine*, August 1850. My quotations
are from the reprint in *Transactions of the New Shakspere
Society*, I, 1 (1874), Appendix, pp. 1*–20*.

[2] *Notes and Queries*, II (24 August 1850); he added
stylistic confirmation of Fletcher's hand in III (18 January
1851).

[3] *Gentleman's Magazine* (October 1850), p. 381.

[4] *Outlines of the Life of Shakespeare* (ed. 2, 1882), p. 304.

[5] *P.M.L.A.* XXXI (1916), esp. p. 351.

as Aldis Wright, in the Clarendon edition of 1891, regarded Boyle as having made out a good case against Shakespeare, if not an adequate one for Massinger (p. xxiv). During the present century there has been a notable revival of belief in Shakespeare's undivided authorship, though further evidence for Fletcher has been adduced, especially by A. H. Thorndike[1] and A. C. Partridge.[2]

After this historical survey, it is now time to turn to the merits of the argument. It would be fatuous to make spurious claims to a balanced impartiality, and I had better say straight away that I think the case for joint authorship is as fully established as such a case ever can be on purely internal evidence. It may be that minute analysis will yield new arguments—and equally, that it may reveal things about the play which tell against joint authorship [3]—but it seems unlikely that those who have not been convinced by the arguments already available will be convinced by any new ones. (What I hope may become clearer in the course of time is the method of collaboration, which I believe to be almost entirely a matter of conjecture up to now.) [4]

I think that a good deal of harm has been done to the case for joint authorship by the loose use of the blanket term 'disintegration' and so I shall first set out the main differences, as I see them, between *Henry VIII* and all the other plays of disputed authorship in the Folio.[5]

[1] *The Influence of Beaumont and Fletcher on Shakespeare* (1901).
[2] *The Problem of 'Henry VIII' Reopened* (1949).
[3] Some of these are noted by R. A. Foakes, New Arden edition (1957), esp. p. xxii.   [4] See below, pp. xxv–xxvii.
[5] One red herring deserves no more than a footnote. The fact that untenable claims were later made for Massinger's authorship of the non-Fletcherian parts of *Henry VIII* has no bearing on Spedding's arguments for Fletcher's share.

It is natural to think of the controversy about *Henry VIII* in connexion with the controversy about Shakespeare's earliest history plays. It is, of course, by no means universally accepted, even today, that the *Henry VI* plays are Shakespeare's unaided work. But, conceding for the sake of argument that they are, is there any close parallelism with *Henry VIII*? Believers in Shakespeare's exclusive authorship of *Henry VI* have justifiably made play with the failure of disintegrators to agree among themselves, and with their rash and unsystematic use of parallel passages as evidence of authorship. But there is nothing like this about *Henry VIII*. Spedding named Fletcher's as the second hand, and specified the scenes for which he believed him to be responsible. Hickson had arrived at exactly the same division,[1] and subsequent separatists have mostly accepted it unchanged as far as those scenes are concerned, though, as we have seen, there has been some (but diminishing) disagreement about the 'non-Fletcherian' parts. Fletcher, moreover, unlike the early dramatists invoked in connexion with the *Henry VI* plays, is a writer with a great mass of undisputed and well-preserved work to his credit for purposes of comparison, and with very marked stylistic idiosyncrasies, which make his work elsewhere stand out from that of his known collaborators.[2] It would be too manifestly having it both ways to cite their disagreement as an

---

[1] Peter Alexander writes that much is made of Hickson's reaching the same results as Spedding, but that once the test proposed was accepted it was merely a matter of counting syllables (*Essays and Studies of the English Association*, XVI (1930), p. 103 n. 3). This is to ignore Spedding's claim that it was the total impression that weighed most with him.

[2] See the series of articles by Cyrus Hoy in *Studies in Bibliography*, starting with vol. VIII (1956).

argument against disintegrators of the *Henry VI* plays,
and then to attribute their agreement (as far as Fletcher
is concerned) about *Henry VIII* to slavish following of
Spedding.[1] Moreover, though opinions may differ as
to the absolute value of the 'Fletcherian' scenes, there
is at least no question of invoking a less illustrious name
to relieve Shakespeare of the responsibility for manifestly inferior or careless work. On the contrary, all the
great set-pieces of the play, except the trial of Katharine,
are attributed to Fletcher: I have already (p. xiii)
quoted Johnson's eulogy of the final Katharine scene.

It may, however, be thought so unlikely that the
Folio editors would have included any substantial body
of non-Shakespearian work that the case for Fletcher is
very strongly handicapped from the start. Let us consider this for a little. The clearest statement of it is to
be found in Peter Alexander's 'Conjectural History, or
Shakespeare's *Henry VIII*' (*Essays and Studies of the
English Association* (1930), XVI, 85–120). Alexander
there argues that the acceptance of Fletcher as author of
more than half the play is not compatible with belief in
the honesty of Heminge and Condell.[2] The rejoinder
to this, it seems to me, is simple. What does Alexander
think that Heminge and Condell would have done if
Spedding's analysis of the play were correct? Omitted
it altogether? But it must have been well known, it
contained a substantial body of Shakespearian work, and
it rounds off one of the three sections of the Folio.[3] But,
it might be argued, they would have said that it *was* a

[1] There is more than a hint of this in Foakes's remark,
New Arden edition (1957), p. xxii: 'when once a lead had
been given, as it was by Spedding, his successors found it
comparatively easy to see the same peculiarities'.

[2] Pp. 118–19.

[3] This last characteristic distinguishes it from *The Two
Noble Kinsmen*.

collaborative work. Here, I think, the only tenable position is a completely agnostic one. If Shakespeare was responsible for some collaborative works, there is no way of telling *a priori* what, if anything, Heminge and Condell were likely to say about them. It is true that they did not collect every scrap in which a case can be made out for Shakespeare's hand—they left out *Pericles* and *The Two Noble Kinsmen*, as well as *Sir Thomas More* (in which his share was a relatively small one) and *Edward III*. They also deserve full credit for ignoring the apocryphal plays later published in the Third Folio, one of which, *The First Part of Sir John Oldcastle*, had been attributed to Shakespeare in his lifetime, while three others, *The Puritan*, *Thomas Lord Cromwell* and *Locrine* had appeared with 'W.S.' on the title-page. By the standards of their time, then, they were markedly responsible in their attributions. But I cannot believe that any unprepossessed person, if told that Fletcher wrote more than half of *Henry VIII*, and then asked to read Heminge and Condell's 'To the great variety of readers', would think that a charge of deception could fairly be brought against them for failure to mention this fact. Shakespeare was not a writer much given to collaboration, so the question would not inevitably arise. And if it did not arise, I can see no reason why it should have been thrust into an address assuring the reader that he was being offered a complete Shakespeare with a good text. No doubt ideally conscientious and scholarly editors would have mentioned it, but then ideally conscientious and scholarly editors would have produced an edition very different from the First Folio. If Heminge and Condell had no greater editorial sins on their conscience than failure to mention Fletcher's share in *Henry VIII*, I do not think there are many of us who would hold that very seriously against them. If this is the only *a priori* argument against Fletcher's participation,[1] I think we can with no initial prejudice consider Spedding's argument in detail.

Since those who reject the claims for Fletcher some-times[2] write as if the case rested primarily on the sort of statistical evidence that is now regarded with more caution than it used to be, it is worth pointing out at the start that Spedding laid most stress on 'the general effect produced on the mind, the ear, and the feelings by a free and broad perusal',[3] and his comments on the different impression made by the first two scenes of Act I and the last two is still as good a statement of the case as we have. In the first scene he sees 'the full stamp of Shakspere, in his latest manner: the same close-packed expression; the same life, and reality, and freshness; the same rapid and abrupt turnings of thought, so quick that language can hardly follow fast enough, the same im-patient activity of intellect and fancy, which having once disclosed an idea cannot wait to work it orderly out; the same daring confidence in the resources of language, which plunges headlong into a sentence without knowing how it is to come forth; the same careless metre which disdains to produce its harmonious effects by the ordinary devices, yet is evidently subject to a master of harmony; the same entire freedom from book language and commonplace; all the qualities, in short, which

[1] I can see nothing of moment in Alexander's later argu-ments, as far as they can be judged from the summary of his unpublished 1948 paper given by A. C. Partridge, *The Problem of 'Henry VIII' Reopened* (1949), pp. 9–10.

[2] Not always; R. A. Foakes, New Arden edition (1957), p. xviii, recognizes that 'Spedding's main argument was from his feeling that two very different styles representing two writers could explain what he saw as an incoherence of design'.

[3] *Transactions of the New Shakspere Society*, I, I (1874), Appendix, p. 7*.

distinguish the magical hand which has never yet been successfully imitated'.[1] In scene 3, on the other hand, 'I felt as if I had passed suddenly out of the language of nature into the language of the stage, or of some conventional modes of conversation. The structure of the verse was quite different and full of mannerism. The expression became suddenly diffuse and languid. The wit wanted mirth and character.'[2] So in the second Act he contrasted 'the languid and measured cadences of [Buckingham's] farewell speech' with his 'eager, impetuous, and fiery language...in the first Act'.[3] It was the force of these impressions that led him to seek confirmation from the sort of evidence that lends itself to quantitative assessment.

This evidence, in fact, proves to be quite remarkably consistent with that derived from Spedding's sense of style. Spedding himself did not pursue this type of investigation very far, but he found the Shakespearian scenes to have about the same proportion of 'redundant syllables' (feminine endings) as Shakespeare's last plays, and the Fletcherian scenes appreciably, and consistently, more. On the negative side, it is worth stressing that Spedding made no use of the much decried, and certainly hazardous, method of citing parallel passages as evidence for authorship.

Metrical analysis is all right as far as it goes, and, as will be noted later, more recent refinements of it have given some further support to Spedding's view; but it is open to sceptics to object that wide variations in the frequency of feminine endings may, and do, occur in works of single authorship, and are liable to be tied up with deliberate artistic effects. A much more satisfactory

[1] *Transactions of the New Shakspere Society*, I, 1 (1874), Appendix, p. 7*.
[2] *Ibid*. pp. 7*–8*.   [3] *Ibid*. p. 8*.

type of evidence is that afforded by trivial habits of syntax and accidence which a writer is not likely to be aware of, or to vary deliberately (or even unconsciously) in different parts of work of about the same period. It is in this field that twentieth-century investigation has confirmed Spedding's findings in several mutually independent ways; I find it quite impossible to regard the convergence of these results as fortuitous.

In 1901 A. H. Thorndike, in *The Influence of Beaumont and Fletcher on Shakespeare*, investigated the relative frequency of the pronominal forms *them* and *'em* in late plays by Shakespeare, in plays by Fletcher of about the same date as *Henry VIII*, and in *Henry VIII* itself. The figures[1] are striking. The *them/'em* ratio in Shakespeare is 64:3 in *Cymbeline*, 37:8 in *The Winter's Tale* and 38:13 in *The Tempest*. In Fletcher, it is 4:60 in *Woman's Prize*, 6:83 in *Bonduca* and 1:15 in the last two of *Four Plays in One*. In the Shakespearian part of *Henry VIII* it is 23:5 and in the Fletcherian 7:59. Results are comparable for *has/hath*, the first being Shakespeare's preference and the second Fletcher's.[2] Cumulatively, these and some other less striking examples[3] seem to me to establish the case for Fletcher beyond any reasonable doubt; especially in conjunction with the greater frequency of such contractions as *'t* and *th'* in Shakespeare.[4]

I observed earlier that metrical evidence was in itself less satisfactory than the type of linguistic evidence just examined, but it is, fortunately, not necessary to remain content with the unanalysed category of 'feminine endings'. One particular type of line that is very fre-

---

[1] Reproduced on p. 21, n. 1, of A. C. Partridge, *The Problem of 'Henry VIII' Reopened*; tabulation on p. 22.

[2] *Ibid.* p. 20.   [3] *Ibid.* pp. 20–3.

[4] *Ibid.* pp. 24–5; see also Postscript, p. xxxvii.

quent in Fletcher and that attracts the attention from time to time in *Henry VIII* is that in which the feminine ending consists of a monosyllable, often of rather a heavy kind, as in 1. 4. 57, 'Go, give 'em welcome; you can speak the French tongue'. The purely qualitative aspect of this—amounting to a clash of metre with speech stress—does not lend itself to exact analysis, though it is one of the things that contribute most to the Fletcherian feeling; but the ratio of final monosyllables to the total of feminine endings can be worked out. Ants Oras[1] has done this, and the figures, to the nearest whole number, are 14 per cent for the Shakespearian scenes and 29 per cent for the Fletcherian ones. The figures for other late plays of Shakespeare are: *Cymbeline*, 18 per cent, *Winter's Tale*, 20 per cent, *Tempest*, 23 per cent; and for plays by Fletcher of about the same date: *Valentinian*, 32 per cent, *Bonduca*, 30 per cent and *Monsieur Thomas*, 42 per cent. Absolutely, the figures are a little surprising; the upward curve in Shakespeare's other plays is reversed, and the figure for the whole play, 24 per cent, is perhaps closer to what one would have predicted for a Shakespeare play of 1613. On the other hand, as Oras points out, *The Tempest* is the one play in which this device is specially associated with one character, and seems to have a particular dramatic purpose. Without Caliban, the figure for *The Tempest* would sink to 21 per cent, and 'the slightly retarding effect of the monosyllables on the rhythm agree well with the halting sub-humanity of the fish monster's mind'.[2] At any rate, here we have again a completely new test applied to a division of the play originally

---

[1] '"Extra Monosyllables" in *Henry VIII* and the Problem of Authorship' (*Journal of English and Germanic Philology*, LII (1953), 198–213).

[2] *Ibid*. p. 202.

arrived at on other lines, and giving a wide divergence, in the right direction, between the figures for the putative authors. (The figures for *The Two Noble Kinsmen*, by the way, are 'Shakespeare', 19 per cent; 'Fletcher', 36 per cent.) Oras's analysis is also valuable on the qualitative side: I would call attention especially to his Fletcher quotations for relatively heavy final monosyllables such as past participles (cf. *Henry VIII*, 4. 2. 83, 'Spirits of peace, where are ye? are ye all gone?'), '(once) more' (1. 4. 62), '(loved) most' (2. 1. 122), '(find) none' (5. 3. 136).[1] There may be those to whom such citations are perilously close to the discredited type of 'parallel passage' argument: it is evidently a question of how idiosyncratically Fletcherian we judge such lines to be; that they are at any rate frequent in Fletcher is a matter of fact and not of opinion.

For those already convinced, the argument has probably become tedious some time ago, and I shall add only one further observation. Though the original impetus for Spedding's theory, and the consideration that has maintained it in favour, is the overwhelming impression of stylistic affinity with Fletcher's work conveyed by the scenes in *Henry VIII* attributed to him, yet such quantitative tests as can be applied are highly specific. By contrast, the respects in which these scenes are claimed to be unlike Fletcher are extremely vague, and are presented with no evidence that the characteristics lacking in *Henry VIII* either are or might be expected

---

[1] Oras, though the most thorough, is not of course the only scholar to collect Fletcherisms of this sort. The frequency of final 'one(s)' and 'else' was noted by S. Hickson (*Notes & Queries*, III (1851), 33–4), and C. K. Pooler in the Arden edition (1915) collected (pp. xxiv–xxv) many examples of the pattern, 'a supper and a great one' (1. 3. 52).

to be anything like uniformly present in Fletcher's work. Thus Baldwin Maxwell notes the infrequency of verbal repetition and the relative frequency of sententiae and parentheses in *Henry VIII* as unFletcherian,[1] and almost all critics have recognized that Fletcher seems to have toned down some of his mannerisms in this play. This is not at all surprising if he was, as Chambers suggests, 'working under the influence of Shakespeare',[2] and, indeed, the notion that collaboration with Shakespeare might be expected to have no effect on him would be a curious kind of tribute to either dramatist.

I have just used the word 'collaboration', and that leads up to a much more conjectural part of the discussion. Those who accept dual authorship of *Henry VIII* are not at all in agreement about the way in which the play came into existence in its present form. Dissatisfaction with its structure has had something to do with the theory of dual authorship from the start, and this has extended to unwillingness to believe that Shakespeare could even share responsibility for the play in its present form. Spedding, noting that 'it is by Shakspere that all the principal matters and characters are *introduced*', conjectured 'that he had conceived the idea of a great historical drama on the subject of Henry VIII, which would have included the divorce of Katharine, the fall of Wolsey, the rise of Cranmer, the coronation of Anne Bullen, and the final separation of the English from the Romish Church, which being the one great historical event of the reign, would naturally be chosen as the focus of poetic interest'; but that, after he had reached perhaps the third Act, corresponding to the beginning of the existing Act 5, a new play was wanted,

[1] *Studies in Beaumont, Fletcher, and Massinger* (1939), pp. 59–62.
[2] *William Shakespeare* (1930), I, 497.

in a hurry, for the marriage of Princess Elizabeth, and Shakespeare then handed the half-finished work to his company for rapid completion by Fletcher 'who finding the original design not very suitable to the occasion and utterly beyond his capacity, expanded the three acts into five, by interspersing scenes of show and magnificence, and passages of description, and long poetical conversations, in which his strength lay...and so turned out a splendid "historical masque, or shew-play", which was no doubt very popular then, as it has been ever since'.[1]

It is a pity that Spedding ever launched this 'bold conjecture', as it has cast some unwarranted doubt on what is sound in his analysis.[2] It is one thing to point to discrepancies in the handling of individual characters (Buckingham, Katharine and Wolsey) between the two parts of the play, and quite another to see in those parts undoubtedly by Shakespeare the promise of a radically different kind of play, and 'the final separation of the English from the Romish Church' would have been a kind of subject quite different from anything Shakespeare had ever treated in any of his other works. This objection does not apply so strongly to the view of Miss M. H. Nicolson that Shakespeare's conclusion was to have balanced the picture of Wolsey by tracing the rise and fall of Cranmer and the fate of Anne;[3] but again, such a conjecture would only be admissible if the

[1] *Transactions of the New Shakspere Society*, I, I (1874), Appendix, pp. 16*–17*.

[2] This emerges clearly from Delius's attack in *Jahrbuch der Deutschen Shakespere-Gesellschaft*, XIV (1879), in which a very pertinent attack on the 'bold conjecture' precedes any consideration of his stylistic arguments, and the later analysis of the play treats arguments against that conjecture as if they were arguments against any form of collaboration.

[3] *P.M.L.A.* XXXVII (1922), 484–502, esp. 498–500.

existing play were shown to be quite inconceivable as a version acceptable to Shakespeare. Still less plausible is the view of H. Conrad, in a posthumous article which is still valuable for some of its detailed parallels between the Shakespearian scenes and other places in Shakespeare, that Shakespeare took over a play originally by Fletcher in order to make it theatrically effective (bühnenwirksam) by a number of additions[1]—this at a time when most of the Beaumont and Fletcher collaborations were already before the public, and such independent works as *Bonduca, Monsieur Thomas* and *Valentinian* had appeared or were soon to appear!

That Shakespeare was living mainly in retirement at this time, that there was no such close everyday collaboration as we may suppose between Beaumont and Fletcher—this is very probable, and may account for some lack of cohesion in the play as a whole. But I think it would take very strong evidence to overthrow the presumption that, if by two hands, *Henry VIII* is a work of collaboration in the ordinary sense of the term.

The sources are closely followed by both dramatists, in a way not otherwise characteristic of Fletcher, as Baldwin Maxwell has pointed out.[2] Foakes goes so far as to write, in support of Shakespeare's unaided authorship, 'Passages many pages away from those of immediate relevance to the text are used, and throughout there is a constant re-shaping of the material and compression of chronology. In addition, widely scattered extracts from the sources are brought together into one scene in the play. Such an extensive and detailed study of source-material as is shown here is not easily fitted into a theory of collaborative writing: it would have to

[1] *Englische Studien*, LII (1918), 210.
[2] *Studies in Beaumont, Fletcher, and Massinger* (1939), pp. 58–9.

be assumed that each author read independently not merely the sections in the histories relevant to the scenes he wrote, but all the material on the reign of Henry'.[1] This is an overstatement, even on Foakes's own assessment of the sources, as far as the Fletcher scenes are concerned. There is, indeed, the borrowing of 5. 3. 10–15 from a passage in Hall, either directly or through Foxe, which is remote from any other passage used from either chronicler, and it would be interesting to know how this came to the dramatist's attention. But I am not convinced that Speed's *History of Great Britain* was used at all;[2] and the one clear instance of transference of a plot-element—the blunder of Ruthall attributed to Wolsey (3. 2. 120 ff.)—is in a Shakespearian passage. Granted that Shakespeare was the first planner of the play, that it was of its very nature to be a history play sticking fairly faithfully to the facts, and that there was some discussion between the two authors, I do not see that Fletcher displays any very surprising degree of intimacy with the sources as a whole, apart from the specific passages he uses.[3]

II. Sources

The last part of the discussion has brought us to the question of sources in its own right. The only important narrative sources are Holinshed's *Chronicles* (2nd edition, 1587), for the main body of the play, and Foxe's *Acts and Monuments* (first published in 1563)[4]

[1] New Arden edition (1957), p. xxiii.

[2] See below, p. xxix.

[3] For the absence from the Fletcher scenes of the transforming effect of dramatic imagination that the best of the Shakespeare scenes display, see R. A. Law, *Studies in Philology*, LVI (1959), 481–7.

[4] It assumed virtually its final form in 1570.

for the Cranmer part of Act 5. The most interesting indirect contributor to the tradition is George Cavendish in his *Life of Wolsey*,[1] which was drawn upon by various Elizabethan chroniclers including Holinshed—first by John Stow in his *Chronicles*[2] *of England* (1580). The handling of these principal sources will be discussed presently, and is analysed for individual scenes in introductory notes in the commentary; here I only raise the question of possible ancillary sources. Some use of Samuel Rowley's *When You See Me You Know Me* (1605) is probable, but of little importance.[3] Some scholars have also seen evidence for the occasional use of other chronicles. The extent to which Shakespeare at any time supplemented Holinshed by the older chronicle of Hall remains a matter of controversy.[4] The most suggestive unique agreement[5] with Hall in *Henry VIII* is 'silenced' at 1. 1. 97 ('commaunded to kepe his house in silence'). But the other parallels cited by Foakes (on 2. 4. 87, 135; 3. 2. 56–60) are very slender,[6] and I am inclined to think even the first one may be a coincidence. Foakes also cites Speed's *History of Great Britain* (1611) for 3. 2. 222–7 and 358–64, but the points of resemblance seem to me to be commonplaces.

---

[1] Now for the first time available in a reliable edition by R. S. Sylvester (*Early English Text Society*, 1959 for 1957).

[2] In later editions, *Annals*.

[3] See notes on Prol. 13–17; 1. 1. 197; 1. 2. 186; 2. 2. 1–8; 5. 1. 174; 5. 2. 22; 5. 3. 30, 81, 99.

[4] For a recent sceptical view in relation to *Richard II*, see Peter Ure's New Arden edition (1956), pp. xlix–l.

[5] Noted by W. G. Boswell-Stone, *Shakspere's Holinshed* (1896), p. 427.

[6] The references to Wolsey as a 'butcher's cur' (1. 1. 120: Hall 'Bochers dogge') may well come from oral tradition. On 5. 3. 10–15, see note *ad loc.*

Turning to the use of the chronicle material, we find
Henry VIII one of the least complex of Shakespeare's
history plays. It covers little more than a quarter of a
long reign, and begins and ends with firm landmarks:
the Field of Cloth of Gold (1520) and the christening of
Princess Elizabeth (1533). The material consists mainly
of three blocks from Holinshed: the fall of Buckingham
(1521), the divorce, followed by the fall of Wolsey
(1528–30), with which the coronation of Anne Boleyn
(1533) is introduced, and the birth and christening of
Elizabeth (1533). Before this last, there is added from
Foxe an episode illustrating Henry's trust in Cranmer
(undated in Foxe, but actually, it appears, 1544).[1] Very
little that belongs outside the period 1520–33 is introduced. The death of Katharine in 1536 is imminent in
Act 4, scene 2, and the interview with Capuchius
belongs to that year. The episode at 3. 2. 120 ff. is not
an anachronism, but a transfer to Wolsey of a story told
of the Bishop of Durham under 1508. Within the
central thirteen years, there is little more than such
interference with chronology as is necessary to bind the
sections more closely together. As Buckingham goes to
the scaffold (1521), there is already 'A buzzing of a
separation | Between the king and Katharine' (2. 1.
148–9), and Campeius has arrived in England (2. 1.
160), an event actually belonging to 1528. Similarly,
the marriage with Anne Boleyn and probably[2] her
coronation (1532–3 in Holinshed) precede the death of
Wolsey (1530). Some of the scenes that are less closely
tied up with public events defy exact historical placing
(see introductory notes on Act 1, scene 4). But none of

---

[1] See W. G. Boswell-Stone, *Shakspere's Holinshed* (1896),
p. 494.
[2] At 4. 1. 96 we hear of Wolsey's fall, but his death is
clearly announced only in 4. 2.

these minor liberties with chronology result in anything
absurdly unhistorical, and *Henry VIII* is a masterpiece
of accuracy compared with Rowley's *When You See Me
You Know Me*, which cheerfully introduces Wolsey and
Prince Edward on the stage together. The choice of a
terminal point is eminently tactful; the bastardizing of
Elizabeth and the execution of her mother (1536) lie
safely in the future.

III. The Play

In principle, it ought to be possible to criticize *Henry
VIII* in abstraction from the question of authorship.
There is nothing to prevent a collaborative play from
being good—*Eastward Ho!*, if not equal to Jonson's
greatest plays, is probably better than any single comedy
of Chapman or Marston—and equally there is nothing
to prevent a play of Shakespeare's unaided authorship
from being bad. I hope that my belief in Fletcher's
part-authorship is based on a fair evaluation of the
evidence, but I must also confess to finding *Henry VIII*
one of the least interesting plays in the canon; and this
by no means entirely in virtue of what I believe to be
its Fletcherian constituents. The history of *Henry VIII*
on the stage shows that it has many qualities which make
for popular success, but true dramatic life seems to me
almost completely lacking in it. Here, if anywhere in
the First Folio, is the 'bored' Shakespeare whom Lytton
Strachey found throughout the 'last plays'.[1] Shakespeare does, indeed, set two of the main themes—those
of Buckingham and of Wolsey—in motion with con-
siderable verve in the first two scenes;[2] though even

---

[1] *Literary Essays* (1946), p. 12.
[2] See above, pp. xx–xxi for Spedding's comments on
the first scene.

there, especially in the opening description of the Field of Cloth of Gold, one is more conscious of the mannerisms of late-Shakespearian verse than of anything of much moment being said in it. But one feels that Shakespeare's dramatic imagination at anything like full pressure would simply have shattered the mild elegiac Fletcherisms of the final scenes of Buckingham, Wolsey and Katharine. Such cohesion as the play has is in some measure the result of the fact that, as Chambers noted, if it is 'not very characteristic Fletcher', it is 'not very characteristic Shakespeare either'.[1] Fletcher, in fact, achieves a high degree of success in the scenes mentioned, and their popularity as set-pieces, however much it may owe to their appearance in the Folio, is not undeserved. It is in the connecting scenes that his inferiority is chiefly apparent. Compare, for instance, the lively handling of the complaints against Wolsey (1. 2), and the way he turns them to his ultimate advantage (1. 2. 102–6), or the preparation for Anne's advancement (2. 3), with the wooden purveying of information by the two gentlemen in 2. 1, and again in 4. 1, or with the sedately opposed pros and cons in the judgement on Wolsey in 4. 2, accomplished though the verse is in which each account is couched.[2]

There is a curious lack of momentousness about the events as they pass before us on the stage. This is not just because most of the really explosive Reformation themes have been tactfully omitted. For enough that is given prominence in the play is intrinsically weighty: the divorce, and the power and the fall of Wolsey, even if the fate of Buckingham is to be judged of secondary

---

[1] *William Shakespeare* (1930), I, 497.

[2] Perhaps the best account of the contrasting qualities of Shakespeare and Fletcher as seen in this play is that of R. A. Law, *Studies in Philology*, LVI (1959), 471–88.

importance. Yet when we look at the result, the out-spoken judgement of Mark Van Doren can hardly be found too severe:

the successive dramas in which Buckingham, Katherine, Wolsey, and Cranmer submit their wills to Henry's are not dramas of reconciliation. The theme has been watered down; resignation is now the word, and its repetition through a series of unmotivated surrenders suggests machinery. Either Shakespeare has lost the impulse which gave his final stories their mellow power, or some other poet has never felt it. Three proud persons break suddenly and bow before a dummy king who represents England, and a fourth who has never been 'unsound', Arch-bishop Cranmer, basks weeping in the sun of his accepted monarch.[1]

When a play has true dramatic life, there is something artificial in the question, 'What is it about?'; with *Henry VIII*, it is not surprising that one of the not very many critical essays it has provoked has precisely that title.[2] We are all the more prompted to ask it because

[1] *Shakespeare* (1939), pp. 332–3.
[2] Frank Kermode, 'What is Shakespeare's *Henry VIII* About?' (*Durham University Journal*, n.s. IX (1947–8), 48–55). I do not quarrel with Kermode's conclusion: 'the play may be regarded as a late morality, showing the state from which great ones may fall; the manner of their falling,...and the part played in their falls for good or ill by a King who, though human, is *ex officio* the deputy of God, and the agent of divine punishment and mercy' (p. 54). But neither do I find it very illuminating; in particular, the notion that such a description saves the play from the usual label 'episodic' does not seem to me well founded. Another recent article which fails to give any very interesting or convincing answer to the question con-tained in its title is E. M. W. Tillyard's 'Why did Shake-speare write "Henry VIII"?' (*Critical Quarterly*, III (1961), 22–7).

the Prologue and Epilogue claim to give some sort of
answers, and they are curiously unsatisfactory ones. The
Prologue warns us in some detail what not to expect—
perhaps, as has often been suggested, with a dig at
Samuel Rowley's *When You See Me You Know Me*. But
on the positive side it does little more than make a
generalized claim to the possession of seriousness, pathos
and truth to history. It is evidently the *exempla* of the
fall from greatness that we are being asked specially to
attend to—'How soon this mightiness meets misery'
(l. 30). And in the Epilogue, the only specific reference
is to the character of Katharine. It sounds as if the
author was tacitly admitting that the closing spectacle
of the christening of Elizabeth, with the prophecy of
Cranmer, is more perfunctory, or at least less climactic,
than some later admirers want to make it.

Most unsatisfactory of all, perhaps, is the presentation
of Henry himself. Even when all allowance is made for
the dangers of a more candid treatment—and by 1613
these would not be overwhelming[1]—there is a curious
half-heartedness and inconclusiveness about the way in
which the divorce is handled. In the trial scene itself,
keeping fairly close to the chronicle source, Shakespeare
gives us a moving presentation of Katharine and of a
Henry who at least puts up a good show of genuine
unwillingness to repudiate her, and pays a tribute in
which real warmth of affection seems to breathe at
2. 4. 133–43. But there are no convincing or even
interesting links backwards or forwards. There is a
sceptical reference in passing, on the part of Suffolk, to
the king's 'conscience' (2. 2. 16–17), followed by
Norfolk's speech which puts all the blame on Wolsey.
At l. 72, Wolsey is hailed by Henry as 'The quiet of

[1] See, for example, the Preface to Raleigh's *History of
the World*.

my wounded conscience', and at the end of the scene
he exclaims:

> But conscience, conscience!
> O, 'tis a tender place, and I must leave her.

Later, at 4. 1. 47, the Second Gentleman sardonically,
if sympathetically, comments 'I cannot blame his conscience'. As far as I can see, these different allusions
are simply laid side by side, without either a clear
resolution of conflicting points of view or an interesting
tension between them. (There is a good discussion of
the 'confused tone' by A. A. Parker in his essay,
'Henry VIII in Shakespeare and Calderón',[1] though
I think he goes too far in writing that the more mocking
references to 'conscience' show that 'it cannot have
been intended that Henry's plea of conscience should
be taken seriously'. On the 'fundamental moral ambiguity in Henry's motives and in the attitudes towards
the divorce', see also Madeleine Doran in her review of
Foakes's edition.)[2] The king's exclamation at the end
of 2. 2 is certainly not as Pecksniffian as it tends to seem
to a modern reader;[3] and it may also be doubted whether
an editor at the end of the nineteenth century was right
in finding the king's words at the end of the trial scene,
2. 4. 235–41, an 'impatient aside [which] brings out
with fine dramatic effect Henry's hypocrisy in protesting
his willingness to "wear his mortal state to come" with
Katharine, and in praising her as the "queen of earthly
queens" [etc.]'.[4] The phrase 'fine dramatic effect' is

---

[1] *Modern Language Review*, XLIII (1948), 331–2.
[2] *Journal of English and Germanic Philology*, LIX (1960),
291.
[3] On this, if on little else about the play, I agree with G.
Wilson Knight, *The Crown of Life* (1947), p. 309.
[4] D. Nichol Smith, Warwick edition [1899] *ad loc.*

significant. It is precisely because the effect is blurred that an editor, wishing to do his best for his author, is impelled to distort it. Nothing of real interest emerges from the combat between what Henry here says and what he has said earlier in the trial scene, and thereafter the treatment of Katharine as well as of Henry begins to falter. The scene between Katharine and the two cardinals is based on Holinshed, but it adds a degree of petulance and unfair attack on the cardinals (3. 1. 102–124) that jars with her claim to 'a great patience' (l. 137). I do not think it helps much to see in this the attributing of a human (or feminine) inconsistency to Katharine. No unified impression, not even a complex one, emerges from the scene. It reads rather as if the cardinals were being used, not just by an understandably outraged Katharine but also by the dramatist, to divert possible obloquy from Henry. Even the account, invented by the dramatist, which Katharine gives of her conduct as a wife (ll. 125–37) cannot entirely be dramatically justified on the ground that it is something it would be natural for Katharine to dwell on. All this ground has already been covered in the trial scene, and in the less tense atmosphere of this later scene we are more at leisure to reflect that the conduct of Katharine as a wife has no bearing on the question whether she was validly married or not. It is as if everything that could be said for or by Katharine must be got into this scene, in order that we should not have to revert to the question of the king's conscience, but should be prepared to go on to the next marriage and the other themes of the second half of the play without looking back (though the two principal victims, Katharine and Wolsey, are to be linked once more in death in 4. 2).

Similar comment could be made on the absence of any real incisiveness or purposefulness in the frankly episodic scenes devoted to Cranmer, well though they

are handled in detail.¹ But this unsympathetic treatment of a play which still, when all is said and done,
stands head and shoulders above all but a few English
history plays outside Shakespeare, is an ungrateful business. Yet it can at least be claimed that the case for
Henry VIII has not gone by default in recent years,²
and that the less enthusiastic estimate formed by many—
probably most—critics of the last hundred years may
still have a good deal to be said for it.

April 1961   J. C. M.

¹ The 'cyclic' method of handling—a rather kinder way
of describing it—is interestingly linked with characteristics
of the other 'last plays' by Clifford Leech, *Shakespeare
Survey*, 11 (1958), 27–9.

² See, in addition to G. Wilson Knight's account in
The Crown of Life (1947), R. A. Foakes's Introduction to
the revised Arden edition (1957), pp. xxxvii–lxii.

POSTSCRIPT. On Spedding's side, see also Marco Mincoff,
'*Henry VIII* and Fletcher', *Shakespeare Quarterly*, XII
(1961), 239–60, MacD. P. Jackson, *Notes & Queries*, CCVII
(1962), 372–4, showing that the 'Shakespearian' scenes
agree with Shakespeare's preference for *ay* over *yes*, and the
'Fletcherian' with Fletcher's for *yes* over *ay*; and D. J. Lake,
forthcoming in *Notes & Queries*, CCXIV (April, 1969),
showing the same, though less decisively, for *More/Mo* (the
latter absent both from Fletcher and the 'Fletcherian' part
of *Henry VIII*).

Cyrus Hoy, *Studies in Bibliography*, XV (1962), 76–85,
differs from Spedding in regarding 2. 1–2, 3. 2. 203*b*–end,
and 4. 1–2, as basically Shakespeare touched up and added
to by Fletcher. This is partly because the Fletcherian *ye*
tends to occur in little clusters. I find this unconvincing:
you speeches such as 2. 1. 55–78 are just as Fletcherian in
style as the supposed *ye* insertions. Except for 4. 1, the
scene for which Hoy's theory seems to me most plausible,
the 'extra monosyllables' in these scenes are on a Fletcherian
scale (Oras, cited p. xxiii, n. 1, above). [1968.]

THE STAGE-HISTORY OF
HENRY VIII

This has been a very popular play, to judge from its frequent revivals; though, curtailed in most of them, more as fine spectacle than as great drama. But disaster accompanied, or followed not long after, its introduction to the stage. The fire which destroyed the Globe Theatre, on 29 June 1613, was caused by the discharge of small pieces of ordnance; the thatch caught fire, wrote one Thomas Lorkin on the 30th, and Sir Henry Wotton on 2 July, when 'King Henry' was 'making a masque at the Cardinal Wolsey's house', and the whole building was burnt to the ground in 'less than an hour'. Though Wotton calls the play *All is True*, other letters name it *Henry VIII*, and Lorkin's and Wotton's allusions to 'Chambers discharged' at 1. 4. 38 S.D., are unmistakable. Wotton's title was probably an alternative one (cf. Prol. 9, 18, 21).[1] Ben Jonson a few years later vividly recalls the fire in a poem.[2] The only other notice of a pre-Restoration performance is of one at the rebuilt Globe on 29 July 1628, 'bespoken' by the Duke of Buckingham, who, however, left after his stage counterpart had gone out to execution (2. 1).[3]

Pepys on 10 December 1663 mentions 'a rare play

[1] For the records and dating of the first production, see R. A. Foakes's New Arden ed. (1957), pp. xxvi, xxxiii, 179–83; E. K. Chambers, *The Elizabethan Stage* (1923), II, 419–23; *William Shakespeare: Facts and Problems* (1930), II, 343–4.

[2] *Execration upon Vulcan* (c. 1623), ll. 132–8, published in *Underwood*, 1640 (see *Works*, ed. C. H. Herford and Percy and Evelyn Simpson (1925–52), VIII, 202 ff.; XI, 73).

[3] See Chambers, *William Shakespeare*, II, 347–8.

to be acted this week…the story of Henry the Eighth';
he went to see it ('much cried-up') on 1 January, but
except for 'shows and processions' found in it 'nothing
in the world good or well done'. In December he had
thought it to be by Davenant, and to bring in *all* the
king's wives; but an adaptation with so much additional
matter, yet including all the pageantry Pepys specially
praises, seems unlikely. Downes's mention twice over
of new clothes and 'new Scenes' probably stresses merely
the splendour of the costumes and the décor. Betterton
as the king, he tells us, was instructed in the part by
Davenant from what he had heard from 'old Mr
Lowen, that has his *Instructions* from Mr *Shakespear*
himself'—an invaluable testimony to the continuity of
the acting tradition. Lowen (or Lowin), 1576–1659,
an actor in Shakespeare's company, and later a manager
of the King's players, 1623–42, must have had a share
in any pre-Restoration production.[1] Of Betterton
Downes declares that as Henry 'no one can or will come
near him'. He praises also the Wolsey of Harris.
William Smith was Buckingham, Mrs Betterton
Katharine; Nokes, Lilliston and Underhill acted Norfolk, Suffolk and Gardiner, and Medbourne doubled
Campeius and Cranmer. The play ran for fifteen days,
winning general applause.[2] On 30 December 1668
Pepys saw the play again, and was now 'mightily pleased
with the history and shows of it'. Betterton retained his
part till 1709 (he died the next year). Revivals are
recorded at Lincoln's Inn Fields in November 1700[3],

[1] On Lowin, see *Elizabethan Stage*, II, 328–9; G. E.
Bentley, *The Jacobean and Caroline Stage* (1941), pp. 499–
506; and the *Dictionary of National Biography*.

[2] See John Downes, *Roscius Anglicanus* (1708), p. 24.

[3] See E. L. Avery and A. K. Scouten in *P.M.L.A.* LXIII
(1948), 116–17. Full records of the productions from 1700

at the Queen's theatre early in 1707, and at Drury Lane in 1708 and 1709. The *Daily Courant* announced a performance for 3 May 1705 but it is doubtful whether any came off.[1] Wolsey was played by Verbruggen in 1707, and by Keene, previously the Surveyor, in 1709. In both years Barton Booth took Buckingham, John Mills Norfolk and Mrs Bradshaw Anne Bullen; Colley Cibber was first Surrey, and then Cranmer; Mrs Barry and Mrs Knight acted Katharine in succession.

No further revivals are known to us till late in 1716. From then on London saw the play staged each year except two till 1749.[2] In the second half of the century it was shown in thirty-three different years, with a gap in 1762–71. Most of the revivals till then were at Drury Lane, but Lincoln's Inn Fields also put it on each year, 1725–7, and Covent Garden, 1744–9, and in 1751. After 1761 the Lane's next *Henry VIII* was late in 1788.[3] In the first period the Kings were Booth till he retired in 1727, and Quin, first at Lincoln's Inn Fields and then successively at the two patent theatres. Boheme played Wolsey at Lincoln's Inn Fields in 1726 and 1727, but Cibber had the longest run—at the Lane from 1721 to 1733; he was followed in the next three years by John Mills (Cranmer the preceding eleven). On the death of Mills in 1736, Milward acted the Cardinal till 1741, dying the next year. W. Mills, who then took the part, had been Buckingham since 1734

to 1729 are to be found in *The London Stage 1660–1830*, Part 2, ed. E. L. Avery (Carbondale, 1960).

[1] See Avery and Scouten, *op. cit.* p. 171, and C. B. Hogan, *Shakespeare in the Theatre, 1701–1800*; vol. I: *London, 1751–1800* (1952), p. 204.

[2] See C. B. Hogan, *op. cit.* pp. 205–17.

[3] See C. B. Hogan, *op. cit.* vol. II; *London, 1751–1800* (1957), pp. 295–312.

and was again in the next Lane revival, 1745. Wilks and
Bridgwater at Drury Lane, and Ryan at Lincoln's Inn
Fields had been previously the Duke, and Delane suc-
ceeded them in the final production of this period, 1749.
(It was the only time he acted in a *Henry VIII*, Theo-
philus Cibber, the Lane's Surrey in the thirties, playing
Gardiner.) Mrs Porter, Mrs Horton, and Mrs Prit-
chard were the most frequent Katharines; the last,
starting at the Garden, continued to 'queen' it at the
Lane till 1761. Other well-known actresses seen in the
part were Mrs Thurmond in 1734 and 1736, Mrs
Giffard in the 1745–6 Drury Lane season, and Peg
Woffington in 1749 and 1751 at the Garden. In
1740–1 Mrs Pritchard had been Anne Bullen at the
Lane, and Miss Bellamy personated her at Covent
Garden in April 1745 and 1749.[1] Thomas Davies,
who had been the Garden's Norfolk in 1749, records
a story he had heard in stage circles of a performance
'about 1717' at Hampton Court—that all the courtiers
laughed loudly at Wolsey's cunningly filching credit for
the king's pardon at 1. 2. 103 ff.; George I joined in
heartily after the point had been explained to him. One
hopes this is a true tradition, not an invention to stig-
matize the alien monarch's ignorance of English.[2] The
Lane's production in October and November, 1727,
was marked by a spectacular coronation of Anne Bullen
in honour of George II's coronation, which was so
popular that for many years other revivals imitated this.[3]

Till Kemble produced the play in 1788 the fewer

---

[1] On some of the above actors see T. Davies, *Dramatic
Miscellanies* (1784), I, 366–7, 385, 407; Genest, *Some
Account of the English Stage, 1660–1830* (1832), III, 197–9.

[2] Davies, *op. cit.* I, 365.

[3] See G. C. D. Odell, *Shakespeare from Betterton to
Irving* (1921), I, 307.

productions of the second half-century showed also less
players of note. Mossop was the Lane's Wolsey to
Mrs Pritchard's Katharine in the fifties, and Bensley
the Garden's in 1772–4.[1] Garrick never acted in his
own productions at Drury Lane; in the autumn of 1761
Mrs Pritchard had Mrs Yates with her as Anne Bullen.
After Garrick's retirement, 1776, Digges and Henderson were creditable Wolseys at the Haymarket and
Covent Garden, and John Palmer took Buckingham at
the former house. Miss Younge (the future Mrs Pope)
first appeared as Queen Katharine at the Garden in
1778, and acted the part till 1799, Henderson being
with her as Wolsey in 1785, with Mrs Inchbald as Anne
Bullen. Two years later Pope, his wife and Mrs Inchbald were the trio at Covent Garden with Hull as
Cranmer and Macready senior as Surrey.

After the prolonged gap at Drury Lane, J. P. Kemble
as director under Sheridan revived the play there on
25 November 1788, showing it twelve times till
29 April. The mounting was much less ornate than later
because of financial stringency. To Palmer was assigned
King Henry, with Bensley as Wolsey; Mrs Siddons
played Katharine (her part already several times in the
provinces, 1778–80). Kemble himself had a minor part
as Cromwell, though on the last night, Bensley being
ill, he took over Wolsey. This first casting mainly held
for the four subsequent Lane productions up to 1796,
the company using the Haymarket in 1792 and 1793
while Drury Lane was being rebuilt. In the latter year
a Garden revival almost coincided, the Popes, Hull and
Macready in it once more. But from May 1794 J. P.

---

[1] For an extremely unfavourable account of the Covent
Garden production of 6 November 1772 see *The Macaroni
and Theatrical Magazine* (1772), pp. 77–8. I owe this
reference to Mr J. C. Maxwell.

Kemble handed over Cromwell to his brother, Charles, whose future wife, Miss de Camp, played Anne Bullen in October. J. P. Kemble himself took Wolsey during his managership of Covent Garden, where he staged nine revivals from 1806 to 1817; in 1810 G. F. Cooke was the Henry. The 1811 productions put in the shade his earlier ones with their lavish splendour of scenery and costumes, which aimed also at historical fidelity.[1] The many changes of sets thus involved were possibly responsible for the worst feature of his acting version, the omission of the fine scene of Katharine's interview with the two cardinals (3. 1).[2] Kemble's final Wolsey was on 17 June 1817; his sister's last Katharine had been the year before on 29 June, when C. M. Young first appeared as the Cardinal. It was one of her best impersonations; Boaden could hardly 'think the Lady Macbeth a greater effort'; 'more perfect' he was sure 'it was not'.[3] In 1819 another famous actress, Miss O'Neill, was in the part at the Garden.[4]

The two revivals at the Lane in 1822 and 1830, in which alone Edmund Kean was seen in London as Wolsey, were no great successes, and the first was only given four times at a financial loss. His earliest biographer many years later praised his rendering of the proud Cardinal in his fall,[5] but at any rate the supporting cast was not a strong one; Mrs Siddons and Miss O'Neill had now retired, and there was no one

[1] See Odell's description, *op. cit.* II, 102.

[2] For a detailed account of Kemble's version, see Genest, VIII, 4–15.

[3] James Boaden, *Memoirs of Mrs Siddons* (1827), II, 266.

[4] On 'The Kemble tradition' and on Kean's divergence from it, see W. M. Merchant, *Shakespeare and the Artist* (1959), pp. 200–3 and Plates 72–4.

[5] See F. W. Hawkins, *Life of Edmund Kean* (1869), II, 189–91.

adequately filling their place. Meanwhile the greater
Macready had appeared as Wolsey—at Covent Garden,
with Charles Kemble as Cromwell and Maria Foote as
Anne Bullen, on 15 January 1823; and at Drury Lane
in June the next year when Pope rendered the King
once more. According to Archer, Wolsey was 'reckoned
among his best performances';[1] but during his years of
managership he staged only two productions of the play.
These were both at Covent Garden—one night in May
1837 when he was partnered by Helen Faucit and John
Vandenhoff (who took Henry), and again for two nights
the following May, with Bartley now in Vandenhoff's
place. But he was seen twelve times, October–
December 1847 at the Princess's Theatre, when Cooper
was the King, and Charlotte and Susan Cushman acted
Katharine and Anne Bullen. The next year he played
his final Wolseys in three different theatres—at the
Princess's with Cooper (King Henry), and Fanny
Kemble, now Mrs Butler (Katharine), on two February
nights; at Theatre Royal, Marylebone, on 1 May, under
Mrs Warner, late of Sadler's Wells; and finally on
10 July in acts 1–3 (Charlotte Cushman now having
Samuel Phelps as the King), as part of a 'command'
performance at Drury Lane, with Queen Victoria and
Prince Albert present.[2]

Phelps had already ended his first season at Sadler's
Wells, and opened his second with the play (10 April
and 12 May 1845), acting Wolsey to Mrs Warner's
Katharine, four nights in all. After his appearance
before royalty, he repeated his production at the Wells
on 13 December 1848 with Miss Glyn in Mrs Warner's

[1] W. Archer, *William Charles Macready* (1890), p. 61.
[2] On the 1847–8 productions, see *op. cit.* pp. 161, 168,
190; J. C. Trewin, *Mr Macready: a Nineteenth Century
Tragedian and his Theatre* (1955), pp. 213–15.

place. From now on he added Act 4 to the previous productions, which had ended with the fall of Wolsey. On 16 January 1850 the four acts formed part of a performance in aid of the funds for the Great Exhibition of 1851, and the next March he presented them again. He revived the play four times, 1854–62, during his last eight seasons, though with no distinguished Katharine to support him. His productions were now overlapped by Charles Kean's at the Princess's Theatre in 1855 and 1859, with himself and his wife (Ellen Tree) as the leads. The first ran for nearly a hundred nights from 16 May, a record till then. Its outstanding feature was the prodigal splendour of the settings, the most elaborate yet attempted. Kean restored 3. 1, but to allow time for the many processions and tableaux, which included an actual coronation, Acts 4 and 5 contained little else.[1] Three young people, a youth of twenty-three, and two boys barely in their teens, found themselves in wonderland. To C. L. Dodgson the play was 'the greatest theatrical treat I ever had or ever expect to have'; and to William and Henry James the 'spectacle' was so 'prodigious' that for weeks they did nothing but try to reproduce a scene with their paint-brushes, or rehearse speeches. As the younger brother recalled a scenic effect in his seventieth year, however, it seemed to him 'comparatively garish and violent'.[2] In Katharine's vision, which thus fascinated the two brothers, Ellen Terry was the top angel.[3] Such openings as

[1] For the staging and acting version, see J. W. Cole, *Life and Theatrical Times of Charles Kean* (1869), II, 143–9; Odell, *op. cit.* II, 290, 332–9.

[2] See S. D. Collingwood, *Life and Letters of 'Lewis Carroll'* (1898), p. 60; Henry James, *A Small Boy and Others* (1913), pp. 330–1.

[3] Ellen Terry, *The Story of my Life* (2nd ed. 1928), p. 21; but perhaps this was the 1859 revival.

remained for dramatic action were used to good purpose by the Keans, who were well suited for their roles.[1] In 1859 the play was the last performance of the season, 29 August, and Kean's adieu to the London stage; Phelps, after giving up managership, reappeared as Wolsey in two later revivals—at Drury Lane at the beginning of 1865, and at the Royal Aquarium at the end of February 1878. This last ('The Fall of Wolsey') alternated for eleven days with Bulwer Lytton's *Richelieu*, in which also he.played as Cardinal. On 1 March, though manifestly unwell, he acted the part of Wolsey till he all but collapsed at the close of his final speeches (3. 2. 350–459), and Cromwell (Norman Forbes-Robertson) had to assist him off the stage as the curtain fell.[2]

So we come to Henry Irving. Though as a novice under R. K. Wyndham in Edinburgh he had acted Surrey to Vandenhoff's Wolsey in 1857, he had not appeared in the play again when he mounted his only *Henry VIII* at the Lyceum in 1892. At great expense he made it approach Kean's in grandeur and sumptuousness of display, aiming also like Kean at antiquarian accuracy; and he doubled Kean's number of performances, two hundred and three between 5 January

---

[1] Cole makes more extravagant claims; *op. cit.* II, 149–52; but cf. Ellen Terry, *op. cit.* pp. 9 and 21, and *Charles Kean* in *Dict. of Nat. Biogr.* (by Joseph Knight).

[2] Cf. the remarkably close parallel of Edmund Kean's final appearance (see *Othello* in this edition, p. lxiii). With curious symbolic fitness, the last speech of each began 'Farewell'. For the details above, see John Coleman, *Memoirs of Samuel Phelps* (1886), pp. 325–8; W. May Phelps and John Forbes-Robertson, *Life and Life-Work of Samuel Phelps* (1886), pp. 307–9; and on Phelps as Wolsey, 25 February 1865, Henry Morley, *Diary of a London Playgoer* (1866), pp. 360–2.

and the end of October. His cast was a strong one, with himself as Wolsey, William Terriss as the King, and Forbes-Robertson as Buckingham; while Ellen Terry and Violet Vanbrugh played Katharine and Anne Bullen. Laurence Irving thinks that Wolsey was his grandfather's best character, and 'dominated the play'. Irving's version gave the first three acts almost uncut, but mere fragments of Act 4, and Cranmer's speech and the christening only of Act 5.[1] Sir Herbert Tree at His Majesty's Theatre, 1910, 1911, and 1912, dealt as cavalierly as Irving with the dialogue, for the sake of spectacular effects, more gorgeous than ever; but he did his best for the acting, giving to Irving's Anne Bullen (now Mrs Bourchier) Katharine, to Arthur Bourchier Henry, and acting Wolsey himself. His brother indeed thought his Wolsey far finer than Irving's, and he said that Violet Vanbrugh's Katharine 'touched the highest point of her art'.[2] On 5 July 1915 a performance was given in Tree's theatre in aid of King George's Actors' Pension Fund in the presence of Their Majesties, the same principals being aided by many other stage celebrities in minor parts.

Benson meanwhile had given the first of Stratford's five revivals to date as the Birthday play of 1902, when Ellen Terry again enacted Queen Katharine. The Bensons played Wolsey and Anne Bullen, and Frank Rodney Buckingham; in the cast were also Matheson Lang (Suffolk), Harcourt Williams (Surrey), H. O.

---

[1] For Irving's production, see L. Irving, *Henry Irving* (1951), pp. 529, 541–50; Odell, *op. cit.* II, 387, 403–4, 444–6; and the Catalogue (by Miss M. St C. Byrne), no. 80, of the Arts Council Exhibition in 1947 (*A History of Shakespearean Production*, p. 20).

[2] Max Beerbohm, *Herbert Beerbohm Tree: Some Memories of him and his Art* (1920), p. 149.

Nicholson (Griffith), and Hutin Britton (Mrs Lang) was Patience. In the tercentenary year the Old Vic company was seen at Stratford on 16 and 26 August with Ben Greet producing; first Lilian Braithwaite and then Beatrice Wilson was Katharine, N. V. Norman was Henry. Previously on 5 May Ben Greet had secured Ellen Terry one last time for one scene (3. 1) in a special matinée of scenes from different plays, and had then acted Campeius. In September he produced the play in London, now also acting Wolsey with Norman and Miss Wilson as before. Two more Old Vic revivals followed in 1918 and 1924; the first (Ben Greet again producer and Norman as Henry) saw Russell and Sybil Thorndike as Cardinal and Queen; in the second Robert Atkins (producer) and Florence Saunders had these parts, with Wilfrid Walter as the King. At the end of the next year Sybil Thorndike and Norman reappeared at the Empire Theatre with E. Lyall Swete as Wolsey, Lewis Casson producing. In 1929 the Norwich Players gave the play at their Maddermarket Theatre, and the Old Vic once more in London, Percy Walsh (the King), Rayner Barton and Esmé Church the principals, and Andrew Leigh the producer. Several productions followed in the thirties. A curtailed version, ending, after Wolsey's downfall, with the procession to the coronation, was seen in the Stone Court at Knole (Cranmer's gift to King Henry, and according to local tradition the base for his courtship of Anne Bullen) on 1 July 1931; from 7 November 1933, Tyrone Guthrie produced it at Sadler's Wells (Charles Laughton as King Hal, Flora Robson as Katharine); in the Regent's Park Open-air Theatre it was staged in June 1936 (the very first performance there), when Baliol Holloway and Phyllis Neilson-Terry were the Cardinal and the Queen; and it was again the Birthday play at Stratford in 1938, when Miss Neilson-Terry confronted James Dale and Gyles

Isham as the King and Wolsey, with Valerie Tudor as Anne Bullen. Of this last Iden Payne was the producer. Robert Atkins produced at Stratford in 1945, Antony Eustrel as Henry, George Skillan as Wolsey, and Viola Lyel as Katharine. The next year at Oxford ˙on 4 November, to celebrate the 400th anniversary of the foundation of Christ Church as a college and cathedral by Henry VIII, the undergraduates acted the play.in their hall (Wolsey's hall); in the final procession through the centre of the audience to the stage for Elizabeth's baptism the cathedral choir took part, singing Tudor music by Byrd. The Arts Theatre in Cambridge staged the play in 1949. The same year Tyrone Guthrie produced it at Stratford (Anthony Quayle, Harry Andrews and Leon Quartermaine as King, Cardinal and Buckingham, Diana Wynyard as Queen); and again the next year (with the King and Queen present the first night, 20 April, when John Gielgud spoke the Prologue).[1] Guthrie produced it once more in London for the Old Vic in 1953, the new Queen and the Duke of Edinburgh gracing the first night, 6 May, with their presence. Wolsey and Katharine were personated by Alexander Knox and Gwen Ffrangçon-Davies, and the King by Paul Rogers. A single setting by Tanya Moiseiwitch in both Guthrie's productions resulted in most effective continuous action.[2] An Old Vic production by Michael Benthall, with Harry Andrews as the King, Edith

[1] King George, present at one performance, went to the dressing-room, congratulated Quayle on his performance, and showed him 'how the Garter should be correctly worn' (see J. W. Wheeler-Bennett, *King George VI* (1958), p. 759).

[2] See the detailed critical description of the Stratford 1949 revival by Miss M. St C. Byrne in *Shakespeare Survey*, 3 (1950), pp. 120–9, and a briefer one by T. C. Kemp of the 1953 revival in *Shakespeare Survey*, 7 (1954), pp. 236–7.

Evans as Katharine, and John Gielgud as Wolsey, opened on 13 May 1958 and subsequently toured the continent, appearing at the Théâtre des Nations in Paris on 7–10 July.

America has seen much fewer revivals, and still fewer home-bred great actors in them. It was first staged in New York on 11 May 1799 (Lewis Hallam and wife as Henry and Anne Bullen; L. G. Barrett and wife as Wolsey and Katharine). Charlotte Cushman was America's outstanding Katharine—in seven different years from 1850 to 1874, her last that year with the English George Vandenhoff as Wolsey. (In 1878 Geneviève Ward, originally of the New World, was the Queen with him.) Earlier, E. L. Davenport (1858) and Edwin Booth (1863, 1878) had been excellent Cardinals. Through the years Wolseys of fame came across from Britain, from Edmund Kean, Macready, Charles Kemble, and John Vandenhoff (1826–41), to Charles Kean, Irving and Tree (1865, 1893, 1916). The Pole, Helena Modjeska, was a successful Katharine in 1891 in spite of her poor English. In California the Pasadena Playhouse presented the play in August 1935. It was the first production of the American Repertory Theatre in New York on 6 November 1946, with Walter Hampden (Wolsey), Victor Jory (the King), June Duprez (Anne Bullen), Eva Le Gallienne (Katharine); Margaret Webster (producer) also acted the Old Lady.[1]

C. B. YOUNG

1960

[1] Information received from Mr C. B. Hogan of Yale.

TO THE READER

A bracket at the beginning of a speech signifies an 'aside'.

Stage-directions taken verbatim from the First Folio are enclosed in single inverted commas.

The reference number for the first line is given at the head of each page. Numerals in square brackets are placed at the beginning of the traditional acts and scenes.

KING HENRY THE EIGHTH

The scene: London, Westminster, Kimbolton

CHARACTERS IN THE PLAY

KING HENRY *the Eighth*
CARDINAL WOLSEY
CARDINAL CAMPEIUS
CAPUCIUS, *Ambassador from the Emperor Charles V*
CRANMER, *Archbishop of Canterbury*
DUKE OF NORFOLK
DUKE OF BUCKINGHAM
DUKE OF SUFFOLK
EARL OF SURREY
Lord Chamberlain
Lord Chancellor
GARDINER, *Bishop of Winchester*
Bishop of Lincoln
LORD ABERGAVENNY
LORD SANDS
SIR HENRY GUILDFORD
SIR THOMAS LOVELL
SIR ANTHONY DENNY
SIR NICHOLAS VAUX
Secretaries to Wolsey
CROMWELL, *Servant to Wolsey*
GRIFFITH, *Gentleman-usher to Queen Katharine*
Three Gentlemen.
DOCTOR BUTTS, *Physician to the King*
Garter King-at-Arms
Surveyor to the Duke of Buckingham
BRANDON, *and a Sergeant-at-Arms*
Door-keeper of the Council-chamber
Page to Gardiner. A Crier
Porter and his Man at the gate of the Palace
QUEEN KATHARINE, *wife to King Henry, afterwards divorced*
ANNE BULLEN, *her Maid of Honour, afterwards Queen*
An old Lady, friend to Anne Bullen
PATIENCE, *woman to Queen Katharine*

Several Lords and Ladies in the Dumb Shows, Women attending upon the Queen, Scribes, Officers, Guards, and other Attendants, Spirits

THE FAMOUS HISTORY OF
THE LIFE OF
KING HENRY THE EIGHTH

The Prologue

I come no more to make you laugh; things now
That bear a weighty and a serious brow,
Sad, high, and working, full of state and woe,
Such noble scenes as draw the eye to flow,
We now present. Those that can pity, here
May, if they think it well, let fall a tear:
The subject will deserve it. Such as give
Their money out of hope they may believe
May here find truth too. Those that come to see
Only a show or two, and so agree   10
The play may pass, if they be still and willing,
I'll undertake may see away their shilling
Richly in two short hours. Only they
That come to hear a merry bawdy play,
A noise of targets, or to see a fellow
In a long motley coat guarded with yellow,
Will be deceived; for, gentle hearers, know,
To rank our chosen truth with such a show
As fool and fight is, beside forfeiting
Our own brains and the opinion that we bring   20
To make that only true we now intend,
Will leave us never an understanding friend.
Therefore, for goodness' sake, and as you are known

The first and happiest hearers of the town,
Be sad, as we would make ye. Think ye see
The very persons of our noble story
As they were living; think you see them great,
And followed with the general throng and sweat
Of thousand friends; then, in a moment, see
30 How soon this mightiness meets misery.
And if you can be merry then, I'll say
A man may weep upon his wedding-day.

[I. I.] *London. An ante-chamber in the palace*

'*Enter the* DUKE OF NORFOLK *at one door; at the other
the* DUKE OF BUCKINGHAM *and the* LORD ABERGA-
VENNY*'*

Buckingham. Good morrow, and well met. How
have ye done
Since last we saw in France?
Norfolk.   I thank your grace,
Healthful, and ever since a fresh admirer
Of what I saw there.
Buckingham.   An untimely ague
Stayed me a prisoner in my chamber when
Those suns of glory, those two lights of men,
Met in the vale of Andren.
Norfolk.   'Twixt Guynes and Arde;
I was then present, saw them salute on horseback;
Beheld them, when they lighted, how they clung
10 In their embracement, as they grew together;
Which had they, what four throned ones could
have weighed
Such a compounded one?
Buckingham.   All the whole time
I was my chamber's prisoner.

Norfolk.   Then you lost
The view of earthly glory; men might say,
Till this time pomp was single, but now married
To one above itself. Each following day
Became the next day's master, till the last
Made former wonders its. To-day the French,
All clinquant, all in gold, like heathen gods,
Shone down the English; and to-morrow they   20
Made Britain India: every man that stood
Showed like a mine. Their dwarfish pages were
As cherubins, all gilt; the madams too,
Not used to toil, did almost sweat to bear
The pride upon them, that their very labour
Was to them as a painting. Now this masque
Was cried incomparable; and th'ensuing night
Made it a fool and beggar. The two kings,
Equal in lustre, were now best, now worst,
As presence did present them: him in eye   30
Still him in praise; and being present both,
'Twas said they saw but one, and no discerner
Durst wag his tongue in censure. When these suns—
For so they phrase 'em—by their heralds challenged
The noble spirits to arms, they did perform
Beyond thought's compass, that former fabulous story,
Being now seen possible enough, got credit,
That Bevis was believed.
  Buckingham.   O, you go far.
  Norfolk. As I belong to worship, and affect
In honour honesty, the tract of every thing   40
Would by a good discourser lose some life
Which action's self was tongue to. All was royal;
To the disposing of it nought rebell'd;
Order gave each thing view; the office did
Distinctly his full function.

Buckingham.   Who did guide,
I mean, who set the body and the limbs
Of this great sport together, as you guess?
Norfolk. One, certes, that promises no element
In such a business.
Buckingham.   I pray you, who, my lord?
50 *Norfolk.* All this was ord'red by the good discretion
Of the right reverend Cardinal of York.
Buckingham. The devil speed him! no man's pie
    is freed
From his ambitious finger. What had he
To do in these fierce vanities? I wonder
That such a keech can with his very bulk
Take up the rays o'th'beneficial sun,
And keep it from the earth.
Norfolk.   Surely, sir,
There's in him stuff that puts him to these ends;
For, being not propped by ancestry, whose grace
60 Chalks successors their way, nor called upon
For high feats done to th'crown, neither allied
To eminent assistants, but spider-like,
Out of his self-drawing web, 'a gives us note,
The force of his own merit makes his way—
A gift that heaven gives for him, which buys
A place next to the king.
Abergavenny.   I cannot tell
What heaven hath given him; let some graver eye
Pierce into that; but I can see his pride
Peep through each part of him. Whence has
    he that?
70 If not from hell, the devil is a niggard,
Or has given all before, and he begins
A new hell in himself.
Buckingham.   Why the devil,

Upon this French going out, took he upon him,
Without the privity o'th'king, t'appoint
Who should attend on him? He makes up the file
Of all the gentry; for the most part such
To whom as great a charge as little honour
He meant to lay upon; and his own letter,
The honourable board of council out,
Must fetch him in he papers.
 Abergavenny.   I do know   80
Kinsmen of mine, three at the least, that have
By this so sickened their estates that never
They shall abound as formerly.
 Buckingham.   O, many
Have broke their backs with laying manors on 'em
For this great journey. What did this vanity
But minister communication of
A most poor issue?
 Norfolk.   Grievingly I think,
The peace between the French and us not values
The cost that did conclude it.
 Buckingham.   Every man,
After the hideous storm that followed, was   90
A thing inspired, and, not consulting, broke
Into a general prophecy: that this tempest,
Dashing the garment of this peace, aboded
The sudden breach on't.
 Norfolk.   Which is budded out;
For France hath flawed the league, and hath attached
Our merchants' goods at Bordeaux.
 Abergavenny.   Is it therefore
Th'ambassador is silenced?
 Norfolk.   Marry, is't.
 Abergavenny. A proper title of a peace, and purchased
At a superfluous rate!

Buckingham.　　　　　Why, all this business
100　Our reverend cardinal carried.
　　Norfolk.　　　　　　　　Like it your grace,
The state takes notice of the private difference
Betwixt you and the cardinal. I advise you—
And take it from a heart that wishes towards you
Honour and plenteous safety—that you read
The cardinal's malice and his potency
Together; to consider further that
What his high hatred would effect wants not
A minister in his power. You know his nature,
That he's revengeful, and I know his sword
110　Hath a sharp edge; it's long and 't may be said
It reaches far, and where 'twill not extend,
Thither he darts it. Bosom up my counsel;
You'll find it wholesome. Lo, where comes that rock
That I advise your shunning.

'*Enter* CARDINAL WOLSEY, *the purse borne before him,
certain of the Guard, and two Secretaries with papers.
The* CARDINAL *in his passage fixeth his eye on* BUCKING-
HAM, *and* BUCKINGHAM *on him, both full of disdain*'

　　Wolsey. The Duke of Buckingham's surveyor, ha?
Where's his examination?
　　First Secretary.　　　　　Here, so please you.
　　Wolsey. Is he in person ready?
　　First Secretary.　　　　　　　Ay, please your grace.
　　Wolsey. Well, we shall then know more;
　　　　and Buckingham
Shall lessen this big look.　　[*Wolsey* '*and his Train*' *go*
120　*Buckingham.* This butcher's cur is venomed-mouthed,
　　　　and I
Have not the power to muzzle him; therefore best
Not wake him in his slumber. A beggar's book

Outworths a noble's blood.

Norfolk.   What, are you chafed?
Ask God for temperance; that's th'appliance only
Which your disease requires.

Buckingham.   I read in's looks
Matter against me, and his eye reviled
Me as his abject object. At this instant
He bores me with some trick. He's gone to th'king;
I'll follow and outstare him.

Norfolk.   Stay, my lord,
And let your reason with your choler question   130
What 'tis you go about. To climb steep hills
Requires slow pace at first. Anger is like
A full hot horse, who being allowed his way,
Self-mettle tires him. Not a man in England
Can advise me like you; be to yourself
As you would to your friend.

Buckingham.   I'll to the king,
And from a mouth of honour quite cry down
This Ipswich fellow's insolence, or proclaim
There's difference in no persons.

Norfolk.   Be advised;
Heat not a furnace for your foe so hot   140
That it do singe yourself. We may outrun
By violent swiftness that which we run at,
And lose by over-running. Know you not
The fire that mounts the liquor till't run o'er
In seeming to augment it wastes it? Be advised.
I say again there is no English soul
More stronger to direct you than yourself,
If with the sap of reason you would quench,
Or but allay, the fire of passion.

Buckingham.   Sir,
I am thankful to you, and I'll go along   150

H. VIII–4

By your prescription; but this top-proud fellow—
Whom from the flow of gall I name not, but
From sincere motions—by intelligence
And proofs as clear as founts in July when
We see each grain of gravel, I do know
To be corrupt and treasonous.

  Norfolk.   Say not 'treasonous'.

  Buckingham. To th'king I'll say 't; and make my
    vouch as strong
As shore of rock. Attend. This holy fox,
Or wolf, or both—for he is equal ravenous
160 As he is subtle, and as prone to mischief
As able to perform't, his mind and place
Infecting one another, yea, reciprocally—
Only to show his pomp as well in France
As here at home, suggests the king our master
To this last costly treaty, th'interview,
That swallowed so much treasure, and like a glass
Did break i'th'wrenching.

  Norfolk.   Faith, and so it did.

  Buckingham. Pray give me favour, sir. This
    cunning cardinal
The articles o'th'combination drew
170 As himself pleased; and they were ratified
As he cried 'Thus let be', to as much end
As give a crutch to th'dead. But our count-cardinal
Has done this, and 'tis well; for worthy Wolsey,
Who cannot err, he did it. Now this follows—
Which, as I take it, is a kind of puppy
To th'old dam, treason—Charles the emperor,
Under pretence to see the queen his aunt—
For 'twas indeed his colour, but he came
To whisper Wolsey—here makes visitation;
180 His fears were that the interview betwixt

England and France might through their amity
Breed him some prejudice; for from this league
Peeped harms that menaced him: he privily
Deals with our cardinal; and, as I trow—
Which I do well, for I am sure the emperor
Paid ere he promised; whereby his suit
     was granted
Ere it was asked—but when the way was made
And paved with gold, the emperor thus desired,
That he would please to alter the king's course
And break the foresaid peace. Let the king know,   190
As soon he shall by me, that thus the cardinal
Does buy and sell his honour as he pleases,
And for his own advantage.
  Norfolk.   I am sorry
To hear this of him, and could wish he were
Something mistaken in't.
  Buckingham.   No, not a syllable:
I do pronounce him in that very shape
He shall appear in proof.

    '*Enter* BRANDON, *a Sergeant at arms before him,*
        and two or three of the Guard'

  Brandon. Your office, sergeant: execute it.
  Sergeant.   Sir,
My lord the Duke of Buckingham, and Earl
Of Hereford, Stafford, and Northampton, I   200
Arrest thee of high treason, in the name
Of our most sovereign king.
  Buckingham.   Lo you, my lord,
The net has fall'n upon me! I shall perish
Under device and practice.
  Brandon.   I am sorry
To see you ta'en from liberty, to look on

The business present; 'tis his highness' pleasure
You shall to the Tower.

   Buckingham.   It will help me nothing
To plead mine innocence; for that dye is on me
Which makes my whit'st part black. The will
   of heaven
210 Be done in this and all things! I obey.
O my Lord Aberga'ny, fare you well!

   Brandon. Nay, he must bear you company.

   [*To Abergavenny*] The king
Is pleased you shall to th'Tower, till you know
How he determines further.

   Abergavenny.   As the duke said,
The will of heaven be done, and the king's pleasure
By me obeyed!

   Brandon.   Here is a warrant from
The king t'attach Lord Montacute, and the bodies
Of the duke's confessor, John de la Car,
One Gilbert Parke, his chancellor—

   Buckingham.   So, so;
220 These are the limbs o'th'plot; no more, I hope.

   Brandon. A monk o'th'Chartreux.

   Buckingham.   O, Nicholas Hopkins?

   Brandon.   He.

   Buckingham. My surveyor is false; the
   o'er-great cardinal
Hath showed him gold; my life is spanned already.
I am the shadow of poor Buckingham,
Whose figure even this instant cloud puts on,
By darkening my clear sun. My lord, farewell.

                        [they go

[1. 2.]   *The same. The council-chamber, with*
a chair of State

'*Cornets. Enter* KING HENRY, *leaning on the* CARDINAL'S
shoulder; the Nobles, and SIR THOMAS LOVELL: *the*
CARDINAL *places himself under the* KING'S *feet on his*
right side'

King. My life itself, and the best heart of it,
Thanks you for this great care; I stood i'th'level
Of a full-charged confederacy, and give thanks
To you that choked it. Let be called before us
That gentleman of Buckingham's; in person
I'll hear him his confessions justify;
And point by point the treasons of his master
He shall again relate.

'*A noise within, crying* "Room for the Queen!"' *Enter*
QUEEN KATHARINE, '*ushered by the* DUKE OF
NORFOLK', *and the* DUKE OF SUFFOLK: '*she kneels.*'
The 'KING *riseth from his state, takes her up, kisses and*
placeth her by him'

Q. Katharine. Nay, we must longer kneel: I am
    a suitor.

King. Arise, and take place by us. Half your suit   10
Never name to us: you have half our power.
The other moiety ere you ask is given;
Repeat your will and take it.

Q. Katharine.   Thank your majesty.
That you would love yourself, and in that love
Not unconsideréd leave your honour nor
The dignity of your office, is the point
Of my petition.

King.   Lady mine, proceed.

Q. Katharine. I am solicited, not by a few,

And those of true condition, that your subjects
20 Are in great grievance: there have been commissions
Sent down among 'em, which hath flawed the heart
Of all their loyalties; wherein although,
My good lord cardinal, they vent reproaches
Most bitterly on you as putter-on
Of these exactions, yet the king our master—
Whose honour heaven shield from soil!—even he
     escapes not
Language unmannerly; yea, such which breaks
The sides of loyalty, and almost appears
In loud rebellion.
    Norfolk.   Not almost appears—
30 It doth appear; for, upon these taxations,
The clothiers all, not able to maintain
The many to them 'longing, have put off
The spinsters, carders, fullers, weavers, who,
Unfit for other life, compelled by hunger
And lack of other means, in desperate manner
Daring th'event to th'teeth, are all in uproar,
And danger serves among them.
    King.   Taxation?
Wherein? and what taxation? My lord cardinal,
You that are blamed for it alike with us,
40 Know you of this taxation?
    Wolsey.   Please you, sir,
I know but of a single part in aught
Pertains to th'state, and front but in that file
Where others tell steps with me.
    Q. Katharine.   No, my lord?
You know no more than others? But you frame
Things that are known alike, which are not wholesome
To those which would not know them, and yet must
Perforce be their acquaintance. These exactions,

Whereof my sovereign would have note, they are
Most pestilent to th'hearing; and to bear 'em
The back is sacrifice to th'load. They say　　　　50
They are devised by you, or else you suffer
Too hard an exclamation.

　　King.　　　　　　　　Still exaction!
The nature of it? in what kind, let's know,
Is this exaction?

　　Q. Katharine.　　　I am much too venturous
In tempting of your patience, but am bold'ned
Under your promised pardon. The subject's grief
Comes through commissions, which compels from each
The sixth part of his substance, to be levied
Without delay; and the pretence for this
Is named your wars in France. This makes
　　　bold mouths;　　　　　　　　　　　　　60
Tongues spit their duties out, and cold hearts freeze
Allegiance in them; their curses now
Live where their prayers did; and it's come to pass,
This tractable obedience is a slave
To each incensèd will. I would your highness
Would give it quick consideration, for
There is no primer business.

　　King.　　　　　　　　By my life,
This is against our pleasure.

　　Wolsey.　　　　　　　And for me,
I have no further gone in this than by
A single voice, and that not passed me but　　　70
By learned approbation of the judges. If I am
Traduced by ignorant tongues, which neither know
My faculties nor person, yet will be
The chronicles of my doing, let me say
'Tis but the fate of place, and the rough brake
That virtue must go through. We must not stint

Our necessary actions in the fear
To cope malicious censurers, which ever,
As ravenous fishes, do a vessel follow
80 That is new-trimmed, but benefit no further
Than vainly longing. What we oft do best,
By sick interpreters, once weak ones, is
Not ours or not allowed; what worst, as oft,
Hitting a grosser quality, is cried up
For our best act. If we shall stand still,
In fear our motion will be mocked or carped at,
We should take root here where we sit,
Or sit state-statues only.

   King.   Things done well,
And with a care, exempt themselves from fear;
90 Things done without example, in their issue
Are to be feared. Have you a precedent
Of this commission? I believe, not any.
We must not rend our subjects from our laws,
And stick them in our will. Sixth part of each?
A trembling contribution! Why, we take
From every tree lop, bark, and part o'th'timber,
And though we leave it with a root, thus hacked,
The air will drink the sap. To every county
Where this is questioned send our letters with
100 Free pardon to each man that has denied
The force of this commission. Pray look to't;
I put it to your care.

   Wolsey.   [*To the Secretary*] A word with you.
Let there be letters writ to every shire
Of the king's grace and pardon. The grievéd commons
Hardly conceive of me—let it be noised
That through our intercession this revokement
And pardon comes. I shall anon advise you
Further in the proceeding.   [*Secretary goes*

'Enter Surveyor'

Q. Katharine. I am sorry that the Duke
    of Buckingham
Is run in your displeasure.

  King.   It grieves many.   110
The gentleman is learned and a most rare speaker;
To nature none more bound; his training such
That he may furnish and instruct great teachers,
And never seek for aid out of himself. Yet see,
When these so noble benefits shall prove
Not well disposed, the mind growing once corrupt,
They turn to vicious forms, ten times more ugly
Than ever they were fair. This man so complete,
Who was enrolled 'mongst wonders, and when we,
Almost with ravished listening, could not find   120
His hour of speech a minute—he, my lady,
Hath into monstrous habits put the graces
That once were his, and is become as black
As if besmeared in hell. Sit by us; you shall hear—
This was his gentleman in trust—of him
Things to strike honour sad. Bid him recount
The fore-recited practices, whereof
We cannot feel too little, hear too much.

  Wolsey. Stand forth, and with bold spirit relate
    what you,
Most like a careful subject, have collected   130
Out of the Duke of Buckingham.

  King.   Speak freely.

  Surveyor. First, it was usual with him—every day
It would infect his speech—that if the king
Should without issue die, he'll carry it so
To make the sceptre his. These very words
I've heard him utter to his son-in-law,

Lord Aberga'ny, to whom by oath he menaced
Revenge upon the cardinal.
   Wolsey.   Please your highness, note
His dangerous conception in this point.
140 Not friended by his wish, to your high person
His will is most malignant, and it stretches
Beyond you to your friends.
   Q. Katharine.   My learned lord cardinal,
Deliver all with charity.
   King.   Speak on.
How grounded he his title to the crown
Upon our fail? to this point hast thou heard him
At any time speak aught?
   Surveyor.   He was brought to this
By a vain prophecy of Nicholas Henton.
   King. What was that Henton?
   Surveyor.   Sir, a Chartreux friar,
His confessor, who fed him every minute
150 With words of sovereignty.
   King.   How know'st thou this?
   Surveyor. Not long before your highness sped
      to France,
The duke being at the Rose, within the parish
Saint Lawrence Poultney, did of me demand
What was the speech among the Londoners
Concerning the French journey. I replied
Men feared the French would prove perfidious,
To the king's danger. Presently the duke
Said 'twas the fear indeed and that he doubted
'Twould prove the verity of certain words
160 Spoke by a holy monk 'that oft', says he,
'Hath sent to me, wishing me to permit
John de la Car, my chaplain, a choice hour
To hear from him a matter of some moment

Whom after under the confession's seal
He solemnly had sworn that what he spoke
My chaplain to no creature living but
To me should utter, with demure confidence
This pausingly ensued: 'Neither the king nor's heirs,
Tell you the duke, shall prosper; bid him strive
To win the love o'th'commonalty; the duke   170
Shall govern England'.
  Q. Katharine.   If I know you well,
You were the duke's surveyor, and lost your office
On the complaint o'th'tenants; take good heed
You charge not in your spleen a noble person
And spoil your nobler soul; I say, take heed;
Yes, heartily beseech you.
  King.   Let him on.
Go forward.
  Surveyor.   On my soul, I'll speak but truth.
I told my lord the duke, by th'devil's illusions
The monk might be deceived, and that
        'twas dangerous
To ruminate on this so far, until   180
It forged him some design, which, being believed,
It was much like to do. He answered 'Tush,
It can do me no damage'; adding further,
That, had the king in his last sickness failed,
The cardinal's and Sir Thomas Lovell's heads
Should have gone off.
  King.   Ha! what, so rank? Ah, ha!
There's mischief in this man. Canst thou say further?
  Surveyor. I can, my liege.
  King.   Proceed.
  Surveyor.   Being at Greenwich,
After your highness had reproved the duke
About Sir William Bulmer—

190 *King.*   I remember
Of such a time: being my sworn servant,
The duke retained him his. But on; what hence?
  Surveyor. 'If' quoth he 'I for this had
          been committed,
As to the Tower I thought, I would have played
The part my father meant to act upon
The usurper Richard; who, being at Salisbury,
Made suit to come in's presence; which if granted,
As he made semblance of his duty, would
Have put his knife into him'.
  King.   A giant traitor!
200 *Wolsey.* Now, madam, may his highness live
          in freedom,
And this man out of prison?
  Q. Katharine.   God mend all!
  King. There's something more would out of thee;
          what say'st?
  Surveyor. After 'the duke his father', with
          the 'knife',
He stretched him, and with one hand on his dagger,
Another spread on's breast, mounting his eyes,
He did discharge a horrible oath, whose tenour
Was, were he evil used, he would outgo
His father by as much as a performance
Does an irresolute purpose.
  King.   There's his period,
210 To sheathe his knife in us. He is attached;
Call him to present trial. If he may
Find mercy in the law, 'tis his; if none,
Let him not seek't of us. By day and night!
He's traitor to th'height.   [*they go*

[1. 3.]   *An antechamber in the palace*

'*Enter* Lord Chamberlain *and*
Lord Sands'

Chamberlain. Is't possible the spells of France
      should juggle
Men into such strange mysteries?
  Sands.   New customs,
Though they be never so ridiculous,
Nay, let 'em be unmanly, yet are followed.
  Chamberlain. As far as I see, all the good
      our English
Have got by the late voyage is but merely
A fit or two o'th'face; but they are shrewd ones;
For when they hold 'em, you would swear directly
Their very noses had been counsellors
To Pepin or Clotharius, they keep state so.   10
  Sands. They have all new legs, and lame ones;
      one would take it,
That never saw 'em pace before, the spavin
Or springhalt reigned among 'em
  Chamberlain.   Death! my lord,
Their clothes are after such a pagan cut to't,
That, sure, they've worn out Christendom.

'*Enter* Sir Thomas Lovell'

                                    How now?
What news, Sir Thomas Lovell?
  Lovell.   Faith, my lord,
I hear of none but the new proclamation
That's clapped upon the court gate.
  Chamberlain.   What is't for?
  Lovell. The reformation of our travelled gallants
That fill the court with quarrels, talk, and tailors.   20

Chamberlain. I'm glad 'tis there; now I would pray
　　our monsieurs
To think an English courtier may be wise,
And never see the Louvre.

Lovell.　　　　　　　　　They must either,
For so run the conditions, leave those remnants
Of fool and feather that they got in France,
With all their honourable points of ignorance
Pertaining thereunto, as fights and fireworks,
Abusing better men than they can be
Out of a foreign wisdom, renouncing clean
30　The faith they have in tennis and tall stockings,
Short blist'red breeches, and those types of travel,
And understand again like honest men,
Or pack to their old playfellows; there, I take it,
They may, cum privilegio, 'oui' away
The lag-end of their lewdness, and be laughed at.

Sands. 'Tis time to give 'em physic, their diseases
Are grown so catching.

Chamberlain.　　　　　What a loss our ladies
Will have of these trim vanities!

Lovell.　　　　　　　　　　Ay, marry,
There will be woe indeed, lords: the sly whoresons
40　Have got a speeding trick to lay down ladies.
A French song and a fiddle has no fellow.

Sands. The devil fiddle 'em! I am glad they
　　are going,
For, sure, there's no converting of 'em. Now
An honest country lord, as I am, beaten
A long time out of play, may bring his plain-song,
And have an hour of hearing; and, by'r lady,
Held current music too.

Chamberlain.　　　　　Well said, Lord Sands;
Your colt's tooth is not cast yet?

Sands.   No, my lord;
Nor shall not, while I have a stump.
　Chamberlain.   Sir Thomas,
Whither were you a-going?
　Lovell.   To the cardinal's;   50
Your lordship is a guest too.
　Chamberlain.   O, 'tis true;
This night he makes a supper, and a great one,
To many lords and ladies; there will be
The beauty of this kingdom, I'll assure you.
　Lovell. That churchman bears a bounteous
　　mind indeed,
A hand as fruitful as the land that feeds us;
His dews fall everywhere.
　Chamberlain.   No doubt he's noble;
He had a black mouth that said other of him.
　Sands. He may, my lord; has wherewithal. In him
Sparing would show a worse sin than ill doctrine: 60
Men of his way should be most liberal,
They are set here for examples.
　Chamberlain.   True, they are so;
But few now give so great ones. My barge stays;
Your lordship shall along. Come, good Sir Thomas,
We shall be late else; which I would not be,
For I was spoke to, with Sir Henry Guildford
This night to be comptrollers.
　Sands.   I am your lordship's. [*they go*

[1. 4.]   *A Hall in York Place*

'*Hautboys. A small table under a state for the* CARDINAL,
a longer table for the guests. Then enter ANNE BULLEN
*and divers other Ladies and Gentlemen as guests, at one
door; at another door, enter* SIR HENRY GUILDFORD.'

Guildford. Ladies, a general welcome from his grace
Salutes ye all; this night he dedicates
To fair content and you. None here, he hopes,
In all this noble bevy, has brought with her
One care abroad; he would have all as merry
As, first, good company, good wine, good welcome,
Can make good people.

'*Enter* LORD CHAMBERLAIN, LORD SANDS, *and*'
SIR THOMAS '*LOVELL*'

　　　　　　　　　　　O, my lord, you're tardy;
The very thought of this fair company
Clapped wings to me.
　　Chamberlain. You are young, Sir Harry Guildford.
10　*Sands.* Sir Thomas Lovell, had the cardinal
But half my lay thoughts in him, some of these
Should find a running banquet, ere they rested,
I think would better please 'em; by my life,
They are a sweet society of fair ones.
　　Lovell. O, that your lordship were but
　　　　now confessor
To one or two of these!
　　Sands. 　　　　　　　I would I were;
They should find easy penance.
　　Lovell. 　　　　　　　Faith, how easy?
　　Sands. As easy as a down bed would afford it.
　　Chamberlain. Sweet ladies, will it please you sit?
　　　Sir Harry,
20 Place you that side; I'll take the charge of this.
His grace is entering. Nay, you must not freeze.
Two women placed together makes cold weather.
My Lord Sands, you are one will keep em' waking:
Pray, sit between these ladies.
　　Sands. 　　　　　　　By my faith,

And thank your lordship. By your leave, sweet ladies.
If I chance to talk a little wild, forgive me;
I had it from my father.
 Anne.   Was he mad, sir?
 Sands. O, very mad, exceeding mad, in love too;
But he would bite none; just as I do now,
He would kiss you twenty with a breath. [*kisses her*
 Chamberlain.   Well said, my lord. 30
So, now you're fairly seated. Gentlemen,
The penance lies on you, if these fair ladies
Pass away frowning.
 Sands.   For my little cure,
Let me alone.

  '*Hautboys. Enter* CARDINAL WOLSEY, *and takes*
     his state'

 Wolsey. You're welcome, my fair guests. That
   noble lady
Or gentleman that is not freely merry,
Is not my friend. This, to confirm my welcome;
And to you all, good health.   [*drinks*
 Sands.   Your grace is noble;
Let me have such a bowl may hold my thanks,
And save me so much talking.
 Wolsey.   My Lord Sands, 40
I am beholding to you; cheer your neighbours.
Ladies, you are not merry; gentlemen,
Whose fault is this?
 Sands.   The red wine first must rise
In their fair cheeks, my lord; then we shall have 'em
Talk us to silence.
 Anne.   You are a merry gamester,
My Lord Sands.
 Sands. Yes, if I make my play.

Here's to your ladyship; and pledge it, madam,
For 'tis to such a thing—
    Anne.   You cannot show me.
    Sands. I told your grace they would talk anon.
             [*'Drum and trumpet: chambers discharged'*
    Wolsey.   What's that?
50 *Chamberlain.* Look out there, some of ye.
    Wolsey.   What warlike voice,
And to what end, is this? Nay, ladies, fear not;
By all the laws of war you're privileged.

        'Enter a Servant'

    Chamberlain. How now, what is't?
    Servant.   A noble troop of strangers,
For so they seem. They've left their barge,
    and landed;
And hither make, as great ambassadors
From foreign princes.
    Wolsey.   Good lord chamberlain,
Go, give 'em welcome: you can speak the
    French tongue;
And pray receive 'em nobly and conduct 'em
Into our presence, where this heaven of beauty
60 Shall shine at full upon them. Some attend him.
          [*Chamberlain goes out, attended. 'All rise,
                   and tables removed'*
You have now a broken banquet, but we'll mend it.
A good digestion to you all; and once more
I shower a welcome on ye: welcome all.

*'Hautboys. Enter KING and others, as masquers, habited
like shepherds, ushered by the LORD CHAMBERLAIN. They
pass directly before the CARDINAL, and gracefully :alute
him'*

A noble company! what are their pleasures?
  Chamberlain. Because they speak no English,
      thus they prayed
To tell your grace, that, having heard by fame
Of this so noble and so fair assembly
This night to meet here, they could do no less,
Out of the great respect they bear to beauty,
But leave their flocks, and, under your fair conduct,   70
Crave leave to view these ladies and entreat
An hour of revels with 'em.
  Wolsey.   Say, lord chamberlain,
They have done my poor house grace; for which
      I pay 'em
A thousand thanks and pray 'em take their pleasures.
      [*They 'choose'. The King chooses Anne Bullen*
King. The fairest hand I ever touched!
      O beauty,
Till now I never knew thee!   [*'Music. Dance'*
  Wolsey. My lord!
  Chamberlain.   Your grace?
  Wolsey.   Pray, tell 'em thus much from me:
There should be one amongst 'em by his person,
More worthy this place than myself; to whom,
If I but knew him, with my love and duty   80
I would surrender it.
  Chamberlain.   I will, my lord.
                            [*whispers the Masquers*
  Wolsey. What say they?
  Chamberlain.   Such a one, they all confess,
There is indeed; which they would have your grace
Find out, and he will take it.
  Wolsey.   Let me see then.
By all your good leaves, gentlemen; here I'll make
My royal choice.

King. [*unmasking*]. Ye have found him, cardinal.
You hold a fair assembly; you do well, lord.
You are a churchman, or, I'll tell you, cardinal,
I should judge now unhappily.
　　Wolsey.　　　　　　　　　I am glad
90 Your grace is grown so pleasant.
　　King.　　　　　　　　My lord chamberlain,
Prithee come hither: what fair lady's that?
　　Chamberlain. An't please your grace, Sir Thomas
　　　　Bullen's daughter,
The Viscount Rochford, one of her highness' women.
　　King. By heaven, she is a dainty one. Sweetheart,
I were unmannerly to take you out
And not to kiss you. A health, gentlemen!
Let it go round.
　　Wolsey. Sir Thomas Lovell, is the banquet ready
I'th'privy chamber?
　　Lovell.　　　　　　Yes, my lord.
　　Wolsey.　　　　　　　　　Your grace,
100 I fear, with dancing is a little heated.
　　King. I fear, too much.
　　Wolsey.　　　　　　There's fresher air, my lord,
In the next chamber.
　　King. Lead in your ladies, every one.
　　　　Sweet partner,
I must not yet forsake you. Let's be merry,
Good my lord cardinal: I have half a dozen healths
To drink to these fair ladies, and a measure
To lead 'em once again; and then let's dream
Who's best in favour. Let the music knock it.
　　　　　　　[*they go, to the sound of 'trumpets'*

[2. 1.]   *Westminster. A street*

'*Enter two Gentlemen*', *meeting*

1 *Gentleman*. Whither away so fast?

2 *Gentleman*.   O, God save ye!
Even to the Hall, to hear what shall become
Of the great Duke of Buckingham.

1 *Gentleman*.   I'll save you
That labour, sir. All's now done but the ceremony
Of bringing back the prisoner.

2 *Gentleman*.   Were you there?

1 *Gentleman*. Yes, indeed was I.

2 *Gentleman*.   Pray speak what has happened.

1 *Gentleman*. You may guess quickly what.

2 *Gentleman*.   Is he found guilty?

1 *Gentleman*. Yes, truly is he, and condemned upon't.

2 *Gentleman*. I am sorry for't.

1 *Gentleman*.   So are a number more.

2 *Gentleman*. But, pray, how passed it?   10

1 *Gentleman*. I'll tell you in a little. The great duke
Came to the bar; where to his accusations
He pleaded still not guilty, and allegéd
Many sharp reasons to defeat the law.
The king's attorney on the contrary
Urged on the examinations, proofs, confessions
Of divers witnesses; which the duke desired
To him brought viva voce to his face;
At which appeared against him his surveyor,
Sir Gilbert Parke his chancellor, and John Car,   20
Confessor to him, with that devil monk,
Hopkins, that made this mischief.

2 *Gentleman*.   That was he
That fed him with his prophecies?

1 *Gentleman*.   The same.

H. VIII – 5

All these accused him strongly, which he fain
Would have flung from him; but indeed he
  could not;
And so his peers upon this evidence
Have found him guilty of high treason. Much
He spoke, and learnedly, for life; but all
Was either pitied in him or forgotten.

30 2 *Gentleman.* After all this, how did he bear himself?
 1 *Gentleman.* When he was brought again to
  th'bar, to hear
His knell rung out, his judgement, he was stirred
With such an agony he sweat extremely,
And something spoke in choler, ill and hasty;
But he fell to himself again, and sweetly
In all the rest showed a most noble patience.

 2 *Gentleman.* I do not think he fears death.

 1 *Gentleman.*   Sure, he does not;
He never was so womanish; the cause
He may a little grieve at.

 2 *Gentleman.*   Certainly
40 The cardinal is the end of this.

 1 *Gentleman.*   'Tis likely,
By all conjectures: first, Kildare's attainder,
Then deputy of Ireland, who removed,
Earl Surrey was sent thither, and in haste too,
Lest he should help his father.

 2 *Gentleman.*   That trick of state
Was a deep envious one.

 1 *Gentleman.*   At his return
No doubt he will requite it. This is noted,
And generally, whoever the king favours,
The cardinal instantly will find employment,
And far enough from court too.

 2 *Gentleman.*   All the commons

Hate him perniciously, and, o' my conscience,   50
Wish him ten fathom deep. This duke as much
They love and dote on; call him
     bounteous Buckingham,
The mirror of all courtesy—

'*Enter* BUCKINGHAM *from his arraignment, tipstaves
before him, the axe with the edge towards him, halberds
on each side, accompanied with* SIR THOMAS LOVELL,
SIR NICHOLAS VAUX, SIR WALTER SANDS, *and
common people,* &c.'

   1 *Gentleman.*   Stay there, sir,
And see the noble ruined man you speak of.
   2 *Gentleman.* Let's stand close, and behold him.
   Buckingham.   All good people,
You that thus far have come to pity me,
Hear what I say, and then go home and lose me.
I have this day received a traitor's judgement,
And by that name must die; yet, heaven
     bear witness,
And if I have a conscience, let it sink me   60
Even as the axe falls, if I be not faithful!
The law I bear no malice for my death:
'T has done, upon the premises, but justice.
But those that sought it I could wish
     more Christians:
Be what they will, I heartily forgive 'em;
Yet let 'em look they glory not in mischief,
Nor build their evils on the graves of great men;
For then my guiltless blood must cry against 'em.
For further life in this world I ne'er hope,
Nor will I sue, although the king have mercies   70
More than I dare make faults. You few that
     loved me

And dare be bold to weep for Buckingham,
His noble friends and fellows, whom to leave
Is only bitter to him, only dying,
Go with me like good angels to my end;
And as the long divorce of steel falls on me,
Make of your prayers one sweet sacrifice,
And lift my soul to heaven. Lead on, o' God's name.
　Lovell. I do beseech your grace, for charity,
80 If ever any malice in your heart
Were hid against me, now to forgive me frankly.
　Buckingham. Sir Thomas Lovell, I as free
　　forgive you
As I would be forgiven: I forgive all.
There cannot be those numberless offences
'Gainst me that I cannot take peace with. No
　　black envy
Shall mark my grave. Commend me to his grace;
And if he speak of Buckingham, pray tell him
You met him half in heaven: my vows and prayers
Yet are the king's, and, till my soul forsake,
90 Shall cry for blessings on him. May he live
Longer than I have time to tell his years;
Ever beloved and loving may his rule be;
And when old time shall lead him to his end,
Goodness and he fill up one monument!
　Lovell. To the water side I must conduct
　　your grace;
Then give my charge up to Sir Nicholas Vaux,
Who undertakes you to your end.
　Vaux. 　　　　　　　Prepare there;
The duke is coming; see the barge be ready,
And fit it with such furniture as suits
100 The greatness of his person.
　Buckingham. 　　　　　Nay, Sir Nicholas,

Let it alone; my state now will but mock me.
When I came hither, I was lord high constable
And Duke of Buckingham; now, poor
    Edward Bohun.
Yet I am richer than my base accusers
That never knew what truth meant; I now seal it;
And with that blood will make 'em one day
    groan for't.
My noble father, Henry of Buckingham,
Who first raised head against usurping Richard,
Flying for succour to his servant Banister,
Being distressed, was by that wretch betrayed,   110
And without trial fell; God's peace be with him!
Henry the Seventh succeeding, truly pitying
My father's loss, like a most royal prince,
Restored me to my honours, and out of ruins
Made my name once more noble. Now his son,
Henry the Eighth, life, honour, name and all
That made me happy, at one stroke has taken
For ever from the world. I had my trial,
And must needs say a noble one; which makes me
A little happier than my wretched father;   120
Yet thus far we are one in fortunes: both
Fell by our servants, by those men we loved most—
A most unnatural and faithless service!
Heaven has an end in all. Yet, you that hear me,
This from a dying man receive as certain:
Where you are liberal of your loves and counsels
Be sure you be not loose; for those you make friends
And give your hearts to, when they once perceive
The least rub in your fortunes, fall away
Like water from ye, never found again   130
But where they mean to sink ye. All good people,
Pray for me! I must now forsake ye; the last hour

Of my long weary life is come upon me.
Farewell;
And when you would say something that is sad,
Speak how I fell. I have done; and God forgive me!

[Duke and Train go

  1 *Gentleman.* O, this is full of pity! Sir, it calls,
I fear, too many curses on their heads
That were the authors.

  2 *Gentleman.*   If the duke be guiltless,
140 'Tis full of woe; yet I can give you inkling
Of an ensuing evil, if it fall,
Greater than this.

  1 *Gentleman.*   Good angels keep it from us!
What may it be? You do not doubt my faith, sir?

  2 *Gentleman.* This secret is so weighty, 'twill require
A strong faith to conceal it.

  1 *Gentleman.*   Let me have it;
I do not talk much.

  2 *Gentleman.*   I am confident;
You shall, sir. Did you not of late days hear
A buzzing of a separation
Between the king and Katharine?

  1 *Gentleman.*   Yes, but it held not;
150 For when the king once heard it, out of anger
He sent command to the lord mayor straight
To stop the rumour and allay those tongues
That durst disperse it.

  2 *Gentleman.*   But that slander, sir,
Is found a truth now; for it grows again
Fresher than e'er it was, and held for certain
The king will venture at it. Either the cardinal
Or some about him near have, out of malice
To the good queen, possessed him with a scruple
That will undo her. To confirm this too,

Cardinal Campeius is arrived, and lately; 160
As all think, for this business.

  1 *Gentleman.*   'Tis the cardinal;
And merely to revenge him on the emperor
For not bestowing on him at his asking
The archbishopric of Toledo, this is purposed.

  2 *Gentleman.* I think you have hit the mark; but
      is't not cruel
That she should feel the smart of this? The cardinal
Will have his will, and she must fall.

  1 *Gentleman.*   'Tis woeful.
We are too open here to argue this;
Let's think in private more.   *[they go*

[2. 2.] *An ante-chamber in the palace; an inner*
     chamber at the back with a curtain before it

  '*Enter* Lord Chamberlain, *reading this letter*'

Chamberlain. 'My lord, the horses your lordship sent
for, with all the care I had, I saw well chosen, ridden,
and furnished. They were young and handsome, and
of the best breed in the north. When they were ready
to set out for London, a man of my lord cardinal's, by
commission and main power, took 'em from me, with
this reason: his master would be served before a subject,
if not before the king; which stopped our mouths, sir.'

I fear he will indeed. Well, let him have them.
He will have all, I think.   10

  '*Enter to the* Lord Chamberlain, *the* Dukes of
     Norfolk *and* Suffolk'

Norfolk. Well met, my lord chamberlain.
Chamberlain. Good day to both your graces.
Suffolk. How is the king employed?

Chamberlain.   I left him private,
Full of sad thoughts and troubles.
   Norfolk.   What's the cause?
   Chamberlain. It seems the marriage with his
     brother's wife
Has crept too near his conscience.
   (*Suffolk.*   No, his conscience
Has crept too near another lady.
   Norfolk.   'Tis so;
This is the cardinal's doing; the king-cardinal,
That blind priest, like the eldest son of fortune,
20 Turns what he list. The king will know him one day.
   Suffolk. Pray God he do! he'll never know
     himself else.
   Norfolk. How holily he works in all his business,
And with what zeal! for, now he has cracked
     the league
Between us and the emperor, the queen's
     great nephew,
He dives into the king's soul, and there scatters
Dangers, doubts, wringing of the conscience,
Fears and despairs; and all these for his marriage.
And out of all these to restore the king,
He counsels a divorce, a loss of her
30 That like a jewel has hung twenty years
About his neck, yet never lost her lustre;
Of her that loves him with that excellence
That angels love good men with, even of her
That, when the greatest stroke of fortune falls,
Will bless the king; and is not this course pious?
   Chamberlain. Heaven keep me from such counsel!
     'Tis most true
These news are everywhere; every tongue speaks 'em,
And every true heart weeps for't. All that dare

Look into these affairs see this main end,
The French king's sister. Heaven will one day open   40
The king's eyes, that so long have slept upon
This bold bad man.
  Suffolk.   And free us from his slavery
  Norfolk. We had need pray,
And heartily, for our deliverance;
Or this imperious man will work us all
From princes into pages. All men's honours
Lie like one lump before him, to be fashioned
Into what pitch he please.
  Suffolk.   For me, my lords,
I love him not, nor fear him—there's my creed;
As I am made without him, so I'll stand,
If the king please; his curses and his blessings   50
Touch me alike; they're breath I not believe in.
I knew him, and I know him; so I leave him
To him that made him proud, the pope.
  Norfolk.   Let's in;
And with some other business put the king
From these sad thoughts that work too much
    upon him:
My lord, you'll bear us company?
  Chamberlain.   Excuse me,
The king has sent me otherwhere; besides,
You'll find a most unfit time to disturb him.
Health to your lordships.
  Norfolk.   Thanks, my good lord chamberlain.   60
      [*Lord Chamberlain goes; 'the King draws
      the curtain and sits reading pensively'*
Suffolk. How sad he looks; sure, he is
    much afflicted.
King. Who's there, ha?
Norfolk.   Pray God he be not angry.

King. Who's there, I say? How dare you
    thrust yourselves
Into my private meditations?
Who am I, ha?
   Norfolk. A gracious king that pardons all offences
Malice ne'er meant. Our breach of duty this way
Is business of estate, in which we come
To know your royal pleasure.
   King.   Ye are too bold.
70 Go to; I'll make ye know your times of business.
Is this an hour for temporal affairs, ha?

'*Enter WOLSEY and CAMPEIUS, with a commission*'

Who's there? my good lord cardinal? O my Wolsey,
The quiet of my wounded conscience,
Thou art a cure fit for a king. [*to Campeius*]
      You're welcome,
Most learnéd reverend sir, into our kingdom:
Use us and it. [*to Wolsey*] My good lord, have
    great care
I be not found a talker.
   Wolsey.   Sir, you cannot.
I would your grace would give us but an hour
Of private conference.
   King [*to Norfolk and Suffolk*]. We are busy; go.
80 *Norfolk* [*aside to Suffolk*]. This priest has no
    pride in him.
   Suffolk [*aside to Norfolk*].   Not to speak of.
I would not be so sick though for his place.
But this cannot continue.
   Norfolk [*aside to Suffolk*].   If it do,
I'll venture one have-at-him.
   Suffolk [*aside to Norfolk*].   I another.
                     [*Norfolk and Suffolk go*

Wolsey. Your grace has given a precedent
    of wisdom
Above all princes, in committing freely
Your scruple to the voice of Christendom.
Who can be angry now? what envy reach you?
The Spaniard, tied by blood and favour to her,
Must now confess, if they have any goodness,
The trial just and noble. All the clerks,   90
I mean the learnéd ones, in Christian kingdoms
Have their free voices. Rome, the nurse
    of judgement,
Invited by your noble self, hath sent
One general tongue unto us, this good man,
This just and learnéd priest, Cardinal Campeius,
Whom once more I present unto your highness.
  King. And once more in mine arms I bid
    him welcome,
And thank the holy conclave for their loves.
They have sent me such a man I would have
    wished for.
  Campeius. Your grace must needs deserve all
    strangers' loves,   100
You are so noble. To your highness' hand
I tender my commission; by whose virtue,
The court of Rome commanding, you, my lord
Cardinal of York, are joined with me their servant
In the unpartial judging of this business.
  King. Two equal men. The queen shall
    be acquainted
Forthwith for what you come. Where's Gardiner?
  Wolsey. I know your majesty has always loved her·
So dear in heart not to deny her that
A woman of less place might ask by law: 110
Scholars allowed freely to argue for her.

King. Ay, and the best she shall have; and my favour
To him that does best—God forbid else. Cardinal,
Prithee call Gardiner to me, my new secretary;
I find him a fit fellow.

    '*Enter* GARDINER.' *Wolsey meets him at the door*

    (*Wolsey.* Give me your hand: much joy and favour
       to you;
You are the king's now.
    (*Gardiner.*   But to be commanded
For ever by your grace, whose hand has raised me.
    King [*rising*]. Come hither, Gardiner.
       ['*Walks*' *apart* '*and whispers*' *with* Gardiner
120   *Campeius.* My Lord of York, was not one
       Doctor Pace
In this man's place before him?
    Wolsey.   Yes, he was.
    Campeius. Was he not held a learnéd man?
    Wolsey.   Yes, surely.
    Campeius. Believe me, there's an ill opinion
       spread then,
Even of yourself, lord cardinal.
    Wolsey.   How? of me?
    Campeius. They will not stick to say you envied him,
And fearing he would rise, he was so virtuous,
Kept him a foreign man still; which so grieved him
That he ran mad and died.
    Wolsey.   Heaven's peace be with him!
That's Christian care enough; for living murmurers
130 There's places of rebuke. He was a fool;
For he would needs be virtuous. That good fellow,
If I command him, follows my appointment;
I will have none so near else. Learn this, brother,
We live not to be griped by meaner persons.

King. [*returning*]. Deliver this with modesty
    to th'queen.   [*Gardiner goes*
The most convenient place that I can think of
For such receipt of learning is Blackfriars;
There ye shall meet about this weighty business.
My Wolsey, see it furnished. O, my lord,
Would it not grieve an able man to leave   140
So sweet a bedfellow? But, conscience, conscience!
O, 'tis a tender place, and I must leave her.   [*they go*

[2. 3.] *An ante-chamber of the Queen's apartments*

'*Enter* ANNE BULLEN *and an old Lady*'

Anne. Not for that neither; here's the pang
    that pinches:
His highness having lived so long with her, and she
So good a lady that no tongue could ever
Pronounce dishonour of her—by my life,
She never knew harm-doing—O, now, after
So many courses of the sun enthronéd,
Still growing in a majesty and pomp, the which
To leave a thousand-fold more bitter than
'Tis sweet at first t'acquire—after this process,
To give her the avaunt, it is a pity   10
Would move a monster.
  Old Lady.   Hearts of most hard temper
Melt and lament for her.
   Anne.   O, God's will! much better
She ne'er had known pomp; though't be temporal,
Yet, if that quarrel, fortune, do divorce
It from the bearer, 'tis a sufferance panging
As soul and body's severing.
  Old Lady.   Alas, poor lady!
She's a stranger now again.

Anne.   So much the more
Must pity drop upon her. Verily,
I swear, 'tis better to be lowly born
20 And range with humble livers in content
Than to be perked up in a glistering grief
And wear a golden sorrow.
    Old Lady.   Our content
Is our best having.
    Anne.   By my troth and maidenhead,
I would not be a queen.
    Old Lady.   Beshrew me, I would,
And venture maidenhead for't; and so would you,
For all this spice of your hypocrisy.
You that have so fair parts of woman on you,
Have too a woman's heart, which ever yet
Affected eminence, wealth, sovereignty;
30 Which, to say sooth, are blessings; and which gifts,
Saving your mincing, the capacity
Of your soft cheveril conscience would receive,
If you might please to stretch it.
    Anne.   Nay, good troth.
    Old Lady. Yes, troth and troth; you would not be
      a queen?
    Anne. No, not for all the riches under heaven.
    Old Lady. 'Tis strange: a threepence bowed would
      hire me,
Old as I am, to queen it. But, I pray you,
What think you of a duchess? have you limbs
To bear that load of title?
    Anne.   No, in truth.
40   *Old Lady.* Then you are weakly made. Pluck off
      a little;
I would not be a young count in your way,
For more than blushing comes to. If your back

Cannot vouchsafe this burden, 'tis too weak
Ever to get a boy.
  Anne.   How you do talk!
I swear again, I would not be a queen
For all the world.
  Old Lady.   In faith, for little England
You'ld venture an emballing. I myself
Would for Caernarvonshire, although there 'longed
No more to th'crown but that. Lo, who comes here?

      '*Enter* LORD CHAMBERLAIN'

  Chamberlain. Good morrow, ladies. What were't
      worth to know   50
The secret of your conference?
  Anne.   My good lord,
Not your demand; it values not your asking.
Our mistress' sorrows we were pitying.
  Chamberlain. It was a gentle business, and becoming
The action of good women; there is hope
All will be well.
  Anne.   Now, I pray God, amen!
  Chamberlain. You bear a gentle mind, and
      heavenly blessings
Follow such creatures. That you may, fair lady,
Perceive I speak sincerely, and high note's
Ta'en of your many virtues, the king's majesty   60
Commends his good opinion of you, and
Does purpose honour to you no less flowing
Than Marchioness of Pembroke; to which title
A thousand pound a year, annual support,
Out of his grace he adds.
  Anne.   I do not know
What kind of my obedience I should tender;
More than my all is nothing; nor my prayers

Are not words duly hallowed, nor my wishes
More worth than empty vanities; yet prayers
　　　and wishes
70 Are all I can return. Beseech your lordship,
Vouchsafe to speak my thanks and my obedience,
As from a blushing handmaid, to his highness;
Whose health and royalty I pray for.
　　　Chamberlain.　　　　　　　　　　Lady,
I shall not fail t'approve the fair conceit
The king hath of you. [*aside*] I have perused
　　　her well;
Beauty and honour in her are so mingled
That they have caught the king; and who knows yet
But from this lady may proceed a gem
To lighten all this isle? [*aloud*] I'll to the king,
80 And say I spoke with you.
　　　Anne.　　　　　　　　　My honoured lord.
　　　　　　　　　　　　　　　[*Lord Chamberlain goes*
　　　Old Lady. Why, this it is: see, see!
I have been begging sixteen years in court,
Am yet a courtier beggarly, nor could
Come pat betwixt too early and too late
For any suit of pounds; and you, O fate!
A very fresh fish here—fie, fie, fie upon
This compelled fortune!—have your mouth filled up
Before you open it.
　　　Anne.　　　　　　This is strange to me.
　　　Old Lady. How tastes it? is it bitter? forty pence, no.
90 There was a lady once—'tis an old story—
That would not be a queen, that would she not,
For all the mud in Egypt; have you heard it?
　　　Anne. Come, you are pleasant.
　　　Old Lady.　　　　　　　　　With your theme, I could
O'ermount the lark. The Marchioness of Pembroke?

A thousand pounds a year for pure respect?
No other obligation? By my life,
That promises moe thousands: honour's train
Is longer than his foreskirt. By this time
I know your back will bear a duchess. Say,
Are you not stronger than you were?

Anne.   Good lady,   100
Make yourself mirth with your particular fancy,
And leave me out on't. Would I had no being,
If this salute my blood a jot; it faints me,
To think what follows.
The queen is comfortless, and we forgetful
In our long absence: pray, do not deliver
What here you've heard to her.

Old Lady.   What do you think me?

                                        [*they go*

[2. 4.]   *A hall in Blackfriars*

'*Trumpets, sennet and cornets. Enter two Vergers, with
short silver wands; next them, two Scribes, in the habit of
doctors; after them, the* [ARCH]BISHOP OF CANTERBURY
alone; after him, the BISHOPS OF LINCOLN, ELY,
ROCHESTER, *and* SAINT ASAPH; *next them, with some
small distance, follows a Gentleman bearing the purse,
with the great seal, and a cardinal's hat; then two Priests,
bearing each a silver cross; then a Gentleman Usher bare-
headed, accompanied with a Sergeant at arms bearing
a silver mace; then two Gentlemen bearing two great
silver pillars; after them, side by side, the two* CARDINALS;
two Noblemen with the sword and mace. The KING *takes
place under the cloth of state; the two* CARDINALS *sit
under him as judges. The* QUEEN *takes place some distance
from the* KING. *The* BISHOPS *place themselves on each
side the court, in manner of a consistory; below them, the*

Scribes. The LORDS *sit next the* BISHOPS. *The rest of the Attendants stand in convenient order about the stage*'

Wolsey. Whilst our commission from Rome is read,
Let silence be commanded.
 King.   What's the need?
It hath already publicly been read,
And on all sides th'authority allowed;
You may then spare that time.
 Wolsey.   Be't so. Proceed.
 Scribe. Say 'Henry King of England, come into
the court'.
 Crier. Henry King of England, &c.
 King. Here.
10 *Scribe.* Say 'Katharine Queen of England, come
into the court'.
 Crier. Katharine Queen of England, &c.

 ['*The Queen makes no answer, rises out of her chair,*
    goes about the court, comes to the King,
    and kneels at his feet; then speaks'

 Q. Katharine. Sir, I desire you do me right
  and justice,
And to bestow your pity on me; for
I am a most poor woman and a stranger,
Born out of your dominions; having here
No judge indifferent, nor no more assurance
Of equal friendship and proceeding. Alas, sir,
In what have I offended you? what cause
20 Hath my behaviour given to your displeasure
That thus you should proceed to put me off
And take your good grace from me? Heaven witness,
I have been to you a true and humble wife,
At all times to your will conformable,
Ever in fear to kindle your dislike,
Yea, subject to your countenance, glad or sorry

As I saw it inclined. When was the hour
I ever contradicted your desire,
Or made it not mine too? Or which of your friends
Have I not strove to love, although I knew   30
He were mine enemy? what friend of mine
That had to him derived your anger did I
Continue in my liking? nay, gave notice
He was from thence discharged? Sir, call to mind
That I have been your wife in this obedience
Upward of twenty years, and have been blest
With many children by you. If, in the course
And process of this time, you can report,
And prove it too, against mine honour aught,
My bond to wedlock or my love and duty,   40
Against your sacred person, in God's name,
Turn me away, and let the foul'st contempt
Shut door upon me, and so give me up
To the sharp'st kind of justice. Please you, sir,
The king, your father, was reputed for
A prince most prudent, of an excellent
And unmatched wit and judgement; Ferdinand,
My father, king of Spain, was reckoned one
The wisest prince that there had reigned by many
A year before. It is not to be questioned   50
That they had gathered a wise council to them
Of every realm that did debate this business,
Who deemed our marriage lawful. Wherefore
    I humbly
Beseech you, sir, to spare me, till I may
Be by my friends in Spain advised, whose counsel
I will implore. If not, i'th'name of God,
Your pleasure be fulfilled!
  Wolsey.   You have here, lady,
And of your choice, these reverend fathers, men

Of singular integrity and learning,
60 Yea, the elect o'th'land, who are assembled
To plead your cause. It shall be therefore bootless
That longer you desire the court, as well
For your own quiet, as to rectify
What is unsettled in the king.

    Campeius.　　　　　　　　　His grace
Hath spoken well and justly; therefore, madam,
It's fit this royal session do proceed,
And that without delay their arguments
Be now produced and heard.

    Q. Katharine.　　　　　　Lord cardinal,
To you I speak.

    Wolsey.　　　　Your pleasure, madam?

    Q. Katharine.　　　　　　　　　Sir,
70 I am about to weep; but, thinking that
We are a queen, or long have dreamed so, certain
The daughter of a king, my drops of tears
I'll turn to sparks of fire.

    Wolsey.　　　　　　　Be patient yet.

    Q. Katharine. I will, when you are humble;
      nay, before,
Or God will punish me. I do believe,
Induced by potent circumstances, that
You are mine enemy, and make my challenge
You shall not be my judge; for it is you
Have blown this coal betwixt my lord and me—
80 Which God's dew quench! Therefore I say again,
I utterly abhor, yea, from my soul
Refuse you for my judge, whom, yet once more,
I hold my most malicious foe and think not
At all a friend to truth.

    Wolsey.　　　　　　　I do profess
You speak not like yourself, who ever yet

Have stood to charity and displayed the effects
Of disposition gentle and of wisdom
O'ertopping woman's power. Madam, you do
     me wrong:
I have no spleen against you, nor injustice
For you or any; how far I have proceeded,   90
Or how far further shall, is warranted
By a commission from the consistory,
Yea, the whole consistory of Rome. You
     charge me
That I have blown this coal. I do deny it;
The king is present; if it be known to him
That I gainsay my deed, how may he wound,
And worthily, my falsehood! yea, as much
As you have done my truth. If he know
That I am free of your report, he knows
I am not of your wrong. Therefore in him   100
It lies to cure me, and the cure is to
Remove these thoughts from you; the which before
His highness shall speak in, I do beseech
You, gracious madam, to unthink your speaking
And to say so no more.
   Q. Katharine.   My lord, my lord,
I am a simple woman, much too weak
T'oppose your cunning. You're meek and
     humble-mouthed;
You sign your place and calling, in full seeming,
With meekness and humility; but your heart
Is crammed with arrogancy, spleen, and pride.   110
You have, by fortune and his highness' favours,
Gone slightly o'er low steps, and now are mounted
Where powers are your retainers, and your words,
Domestics to you, serve your will as't please
Yourself pronounce their office. I must tell you,

You tender more your person's honour than
Your high profession spiritual; that again
I do refuse you for my judge, and here,
Before you all, appeal unto the pope,
120 To bring my whole cause 'fore his holiness,
And to be judged by him.

> ['*She curtsies to the King, and offers to depart*'

Campeius.   The queen is obstinate,
Stubborn to justice, apt to accuse it and
Disdainful to be tried by't; 'tis not well.
She's going away.

   King. Call her again.

   Crier. Katharine Queen of England, come into
     the court.

   Gentleman Usher. Madam, you are called back.

   Q. Katharine. What need you note it? pray you
     keep your way;
When you are called, return. Now the Lord help!
130 They vex me past my patience. Pray you pass on:
I will not tarry; no, nor ever more
Upon this business my appearance make
In any of their courts. ['*Queen and her Attendants*' go

   King.   Go thy ways, Kate;
That man i'th'world who shall report he has
A better wife, let him in nought be trusted,
For speaking false in that. Thou art, alone—
If thy rare qualities, sweet gentleness,
Thy meekness saint-like, wife-like government,
Obeying in commanding, and thy parts
140 Sovereign and pious else, could speak thee out—
The queen of earthly queens. She's noble born,
And like her true nobility she has
Carried herself towards me.

   Wolsey.   Most gracious sir,

In humblest manner I require your highness,
That it shall please you to declare in hearing
Of all these ears—for where I am robbed and bound,
There must I be unloosed, although not there
At once and fully satisfied—whether ever I
Did broach this business to your highness, or
Laid any scruple in your way which might   150
Induce you to the question on't, or ever
Have to you, but with thanks to God for such
A royal lady, spake one the least word that might
Be to the prejudice of her present state,
Or touch of her good person?
　King.   My lord cardinal,
I do excuse you; yea, upon mine honour,
I free you from't. You are not to be taught
That you have many enemies that know not
Why they are so, but, like to village curs,
Bark when their fellows do. By some of these   160
The queen is put in anger. You're excused.
But will you be more justified? you ever
Have wished the sleeping of this business,
　　never desired
It to be stirred, but oft have hind'red, oft,
The passages made toward it. On my honour
I speak my good lord cardinal to this point,
And thus far clear him. Now, what moved me to't,
I will be bold with time and your attention.
Then mark the inducement. Thus it came; give
　　heed to't:
My conscience first received a tenderness,   170
Scruple, and prick, on certain speeches uttered
By th'Bishop of Bayonne, then French ambassador,
Who had been hither sent on the debating
A marriage 'twixt the Duke of Orleans and

Our daughter Mary. I'th'progress of this business,
Ere a determinate resolution, he,
I mean the bishop, did require a respite,
Wherein he might the king his lord advertise
Whether our daughter were legitimate,
180 Respecting this our marriage with the dowager,
Sometimes our brother's wife. This respite shook
The bosom of my conscience, entered me,
Yea, with a spitting power, and made to tremble
The region of my breast; which forced such way
That many mazed considerings did throng
And pressed in with this caution. First, methought
I stood not in the smile of heaven, who had
Commanded nature that my lady's womb,
If it conceived a male child by me, should
190 Do no more offices of life to't than
The grave does to the dead; for her male issue
Or died where they were made, or shortly after
This world had aired them. Hence I took a thought
This was a judgement on me, that my kingdom,
Well worthy the best heir o'th'world, should not
Be gladded in't by me. Then follows that
I weighed the danger which my realms stood in
By this my issue's fail, and that gave to me
Many a groaning throe. Thus hulling in
200 The wild sea of my conscience, I did steer
Toward this remedy whereupon we are
Now present here together; that's to say,
I meant to rectify my conscience, which
I then did feel full sick, and yet not well,
By all the reverend fathers of the land
And doctors learned. First I began in private
With you, my Lord of Lincoln; you remember
How under my oppression I did reek,

When I first moved you.
 Lincoln.   Very well, my liege.
 King. I have spoke long; be pleased yourself to say　210
How far you satisfied me.
 Lincoln.   So please your highness,
The question did at first so stagger me,
Bearing a state of mighty moment in't
And consequence of dread, that I committed
The daring'st counsel which I had to doubt,
And did entreat your highness to this course
Which you are running here.
 King.   I then moved you,
My Lord of Canterbury, and got your leave
To make this present summons. Unsolicited
I left no reverend person in this court,   220
But by particular consent proceeded
Under your hands and seals; therefore, go on,
For no dislike i'th'world against the person
Of the good queen, but the sharp thorny points
Of my allegéd reasons, drives this forward:
Prove but our marriage lawful, by my life
And kingly dignity, we are contented
To wear our mortal state to come with her,.
Katharine our queen, before the primest creature
That's paragoned o'th'world.
 Campeius.   So please your highness, 230
The queen being absent, 'tis a needful fitness
That we adjourn this court till further day;
Meanwhile must be an earnest motion
Made to the queen to call back her appeal
She intends unto his holiness.
 (*King.*   I may perceive
These cardinals trifle with me. I abhor
This dilatory sloth and tricks of Rome.

My learned and well-belovéd servant, Cranmer,
Prithee return; with thy approach, I know,
240 My comfort comes along. [*aloud*] Break up the court;
I say, set on.

> [*they go out 'in manner as they entered'*]

[3. 1.]   *London. The Queen's apartments*

'*Enter* QUEEN *and her Women, as at work*'

Q. Katharine. Take thy lute, wench; my soul grows
sad with troubles;
Sing and disperse 'em, if thou canst; leave working.

Song

> Orpheus with his lute made trees,
> And the mountain tops that freeze,
>   Bow themselves when he did sing.
> To his music plants and flowers
> Ever sprung, as sun and showers
>   There had made a lasting spring.
>
> Every thing that heard him play,
10   Even the billows of the sea,
>   Hung their heads, and then lay by.
> In sweet music is such art,
> Killing care and grief of heart
>   Fall asleep, or hearing die.

'*Enter a Gentleman*'

Q. Katharine. How now?
Gentleman. An't please your grace, the two
great cardinals
Wait in the presence.
Q. Katharine.   Would they speak with me?
Gentleman. They willed me say so, madam.

Q. Katharine.   Pray their graces
To come near. What can be their business
With me, a poor weak woman, fall'n from favour?   20
I do not like their coming. Now I think on't,
They should be good men, their affairs as righteous;
But all hoods make not monks.

'*Enter the two* CARDINALS, WOLSEY *and* CAMPEIUS',
      ushered in by the Gentleman

Wolsey.   Peace to your highness!
  Q. Katharine. Your graces find me here part of
      a housewife—
I would be all—against the worst may happen.
What are your pleasures with me, reverend lords?
  Wolsey. May it please you, noble madam,
      to withdraw
Into your private chamber, we shall give you
The full cause of our coming.
  Q. Katharine.   Speak it here;
There's nothing I have done yet, o' my conscience,   30
Deserves a corner. Would all other women
Could speak this with as free a soul as I do!
My lords, I care not—so much I am happy
Above a number—if my actions
Were tried by every tongue, every eye saw 'em,
Envy and base opinion set against 'em,
I know my life so even. If your business
Seek me out, and that way I am wife in,
Out with it boldly: truth loves open dealing.
  Wolsey. Tanta est erga te mentis integritas, regina   40
serenissima—
  Q. *Katharine.* O, good my lord, no Latin;
I am not such a truant since my coming,
As not to know the language I have lived in;

A strange tongue makes my cause more
     strange, suspicious;
Pray speak in English; here are some will thank you,
If you speak truth, for their poor mistress' sake;
Believe me, she has had much wrong. Lord cardinal,
The willing'st sin I ever yet committed
50 May be absolved in English.
    Wolsey.   Noble lady,
I am sorry my integrity should breed,
And service to his majesty and you,
So deep suspicion, where all faith was meant.
We come not by the way of accusation,
To taint that honour every good tongue blesses,
Nor to betray you any way to sorrow—
You have too much, good lady—but to know
How you stand minded in the weighty difference
Between the king and you, and to deliver,
60 Like free and honest men, our just opinions
And comforts to your cause.
    Campeius.   Most honoured madam,
My Lord of York, out of his noble nature,
Zeal and obedience he still bore your grace,
Forgetting, like a good man, your late censure
Both of his truth and him, which was too far,
Offers, as I do, in a sign of peace,
His service and his counsel.
    (*Q. Katharine*.   To betray me.
[*aloud*] My lords, I thank you both for your good wills;
Ye speak like honest men—pray God ye prove so!—
70 But how to make ye suddenly an answer,
In such a point of weight, so near mine honour,
More near my life, I fear, with my weak wit,
And to such men of gravity and learning,
In truth I know not. I was set at work

Among my maids, full little, God knows, looking
Either for such men or such business.
For her sake that I have been—for I feel
The last fit of my greatness—good your graces,
Let me have time and counsel for my cause.
Alas, I am a woman, friendless, hopeless!   80
  Wolsey. Madam, you wrong the king's love with
      these fears;
Your hopes and friends are infinite.
  Q. Katharine.   In England
But little for my profit; can you think, lords,
That any Englishman dare give me counsel?
Or be a known friend, 'gainst his highness' pleasure—
Though he be grown so desperate to be honest—
And live a subject? Nay, forsooth, my friends,
They that must weigh out my afflictions,
They that my trust must grow to, live not here;
They are, as all my other comforts, far hence   90
In mine own country, lords.
  Campeius.   I would your grace
Would leave your griefs, and take my counsel.
  Q. Katharine.   How, sir?
  Campeius. Put your main cause into the
      king's protection;
He's loving and most gracious. 'Twill be much
Both for your honour better and your cause;
For if the trial of the law o'ertake ye,
You'll part away disgraced.
  Wolsey.   He tells you rightly.
  Q. Katharine. Ye tell me what ye wish for both,
      my ruin.
Is this your Christian counsel? out upon ye!
Heaven is above all yet; there sits a judge   100
That no king can corrupt.

Campeius.   Your rage mistakes us.

Q. Katharine. The more shame for ye; holy men
            I thought ye,
Upon my soul, two reverend cardinal virtues;
But cardinal sins and hollow hearts I fear ye.
Mend 'em, for shame, my lords. Is this
            your comfort?
The cordial that ye bring a wretched lady,
A woman lost among ye, laughed at, scorned?
I will not wish ye half my miseries:
I have more charity. But say I warned ye;
110 Take heed, for heaven's sake, take heed, lest at once
The burden of my sorrows fall upon ye.

Wolsey. Madam, this is a mere distraction;
You turn the good we offer into envy.

Q. Katharine. Ye turn me into nothing. Woe
            upon ye,
And all such false professors! would you have me—
If you have any justice, any pity,
If ye be any thing but churchmen's habits—
Put my sick cause into his hands that hates me?
Alas, has banished me his bed already,
120 His love, too long ago! I am old, my lords,
And all the fellowship I hold now with him
Is only my obedience. What can happen
To me above this wretchedness? all your studies
Make me a curse like this.

Campeius.   Your fears are worse.

Q. Katharine. Have I lived thus long—let me
            speak myself,
Since virtue finds no friends—a wife, a true one?
A woman, I dare say without vain-glory,
Never yet branded with suspicion?
Have I with all my full affections

Still met the king? loved him next heaven?   130
　　obeyed him?
Been, out of fondness, superstitious to him?
Almost forgot my prayers to content him?
And am I thus rewarded? 'tis not well, lords.
Bring me a constant woman to her husband,
One that ne'er dreamed a joy beyond his pleasure,
And to that woman, when she has done most,
Yet will I add an honour—a great patience.
　Wolsey. Madam, you wander from the good we
　　aim at.
　Q. Katharine. My lord, I dare not make myself
　　so guilty
To give up willingly that noble title   140
Your master wed me to; nothing but death
Shall e'er divorce my dignities.
　Wolsey.   Pray hear me.
　Q. Katharine. Would I had never trod this
　　English earth,
Or felt the flatteries that grow upon it!
Ye have angels' faces, but heaven knows your hearts.
What will become of me now, wretched lady!
I am the most unhappy woman living.
Alas, poor wenches, where are now your fortunes?
Shipwrecked upon a kingdom, where no pity,
No friends, no hope; no kindred weep for me;   150
Almost no grave allowed me. Like the lily,
That once was mistress of the field, and flourished,
I'll hang my head and perish.
　Wolsey.   If your grace
Could but be brought to know our ends
　　are honest,
You'd feel more comfort. Why should we,
　　good lady,

Upon what cause, wrong you? alas, our places,
The way of our profession is against it;
We are to cure such sorrows, not to sow 'em.
For goodness' sake, consider what you do;
160 How you may hurt yourself, ay, utterly
Grow from the king's acquaintance, by this carriage.
The hearts of princes kiss obedience,
So much they love it; but to stubborn spirits
They swell, and grow as terrible as storms.
I know you have a gentle, noble temper,
A soul as even as a calm. Pray think us
Those we profess, peace-makers, friends and servants.
  Campeius. Madam, you'll find it so. You wrong
    your virtues
With these weak women's fears. A noble spirit,
170 As yours was put into you, ever casts
Such doubts, as false coin, from it. The king
    loves you;
Beware you lose it not. For us, if you please
To trust us in your business, we are ready
To use our utmost studies in your service.
  Q. Katharine. Do what ye will, my lords; and
    pray forgive me;
If I have used myself unmannerly,
You know I am a woman, lacking wit
To make a seemly answer to such persons.
Pray do my service to his majesty;
180 He has my heart yet, and shall have my prayers
While I shall have my life. Come, reverend fathers,
Bestow your counsels on me; she now begs
That little thought, when she set footing here,
She should have bought her dignities so dear. [*they go*

[3. 2.]   *Ante-chamber to the King's apartment*

'*Enter the DUKE OF NORFOLK, DUKE OF SUFFOLK,
LORD SURREY, and LORD CHAMBERLAIN*'

Norfolk. If you will now unite in your complaints
And force them with a constancy, the cardinal
Cannot stand under them. If you omit
The offer of this time, I cannot promise
But that you shall sustain moe new disgraces,
With these you bear already.
  Surrey.   I am joyful
To meet the least occasion that may give me
Remembrance of my father-in-law, the duke,
To be revenged on him.
  Suffolk.   Which of the peers
Have uncontemned gone by him, or at least   10
Strangely neglected? when did he regard
The stamp of nobleness in any person
Out of himself?
  Chamberlain.   My lords, you speak your pleasures.
What he deserves of you and me I know;
What we can do to him, though now the time
Gives way to us, I much fear. If you cannot
Bar his access to th'king, never attempt
Any thing on him; for he hath a witchcraft
Over the king in's tongue.
  Norfolk.   O, fear him not;
His spell in that is out; the king hath found   20
Matter against him that for ever mars
The honey of his language. No, he's settled,
Not to come off, in his displeasure.
  Surrey.   Sir,
I should be glad to hear such news as this
Once every hour.

Norfolk.   Believe it, this is true.
In the divorce his contrary proceedings
Are all unfolded; wherein he appears
As I would wish mine enemy.
   Surrey.   How came
His practices to light?
   Suffolk.   Most strangely.
   Surrey.   O, how, how?
30 *Suffolk.* The cardinal's letters to the
          pope miscarried,
And came to th'eye o'th'king; wherein was read
How that the cardinal did entreat his holiness
To stay the judgement o'th'divorce; for if
It did take place, 'I do' quoth he 'perceive
My king is tangled in affection to
A creature of the queen's, Lady Anne Bullen'.
   Surrey. Has the king this?
   Suffolk.   Believe it.
   Surrey.   Will this work?
   Chamberlain. The king in this perceives him how
          he coasts
And hedges his own way. But in this point
40 All his tricks founder and he brings his physic
After his patient's death: the king already
Hath married the fair lady.
   Surrey.   Would he had!
   Suffolk. May you be happy in your wish, my lord!
For, I profess, you have it.
   Surrey.   Now, all my joy
Trace the conjunction!
   Suffolk.   My amen to't!
   Norfolk.   All men's!
   Suffolk. There's order given for her coronation;
Marry, this is yet but young, and may be left

To some ears unrecounted. But my lords,
She is a gallant creature and complete
In mind and feature. I persuade me, from her   50
Will fall some blessing to this land, which shall
In it be memorized.
  Surrey.   But will the king
Digest this letter of the cardinal's?
The Lord forbid!
  Norfolk.   Marry, amen!
  Suffolk.   No, no;
There be moe wasps that buzz about his nose
Will make this sting the sooner. Cardinal Campeius
Is stol'n away to Rome; hath ta'en no leave;
Has left the cause o'th'king unhandled, and
Is posted as the agent of our cardinal
To second all his plot. I do assure you   60
The king cried 'Ha!' at this.
  Chamberlain.   Now God incense him,
And let him cry 'Ha!' louder!
  Norfolk.   But, my lord,
When returns Cranmer?
  Suffolk. He is returned in his opinions, which
Have satisfied the king for his divorce,
Together with all famous colleges
Almost in Christendom. Shortly, I believe,
His second marriage shall be published, and
Her coronation. Katharine no more
Shall be called queen, but princess dowager   70
And widow to Prince Arthur.
  Norfolk.   This same Cranmer's
A worthy fellow, and hath ta'en much pain
In the king's business.
  Suffolk.   He has; and we shall see him
For it an archbishop.

Norfolk.   So I hear.
Suffolk.   'Tis so.
The cardinal!

'*Enter WOLSEY and CROMWELL*'

Norfolk.   Observe, observe, he's moody.
Wolsey. The packet, Cromwell,
Gave't you the king?
   Cromwell.   To his own hand, in's bedchamber.
Wolsey. Looked he o'th'inside of the paper?
   Cromwell.   Presently
He did unseal them, and the first he viewed,
80 He did it with a serious mind; a heed
Was in his countenance. You he bade
Attend him here this morning.
   Wolsey.   Is he ready
To come abroad?
   Cromwell.   I think by this he is.
   Wolsey. Leave me awhile.   [*Cromwell goes*
[*aside*] It shall be to the Duchess of Alençon,
The French king's sister; he shall marry her.
Anne Bullen? No; I'll no Anne Bullens for him;
There's more in't than fair visage. Bullen?
No, we'll no Bullens. Speedily I wish
90 To hear from Rome. The Marchioness
    of Pembroke?
   Norfolk. He's discontented.
   Suffolk.   May be he hears the king
Does whet his anger to him.
   Surrey.   Sharp enough,
Lord, for thy justice!
   (*Wolsey.* The late queen's gentlewoman, a
    knight's daughter,
To be her mistress' mistress? the queen's queen?

This candle burns not clear; 'tis I must snuff it,
Then out it goes. What though I know
          her virtuous
And well deserving? yet I know her for
A spleeny Lutheran, and not wholesome to
Our cause that she should lie i'th'bosom of   100
Our hard-ruled king. Again, there is sprung up
An heretic, an arch one, Cranmer, one
Hath crawled into the favour of the king,
And is his oracle.
    Norfolk.   He is vexed at something.

'*Enter* KING, *reading of a schedule*', *and* LOVELL

    Surrey. I would 'twere something that would fret
          the string,
The master-cord on's heart!
    Suffolk.   The king, the king!
    King. What piles of wealth hath he accumulated
To his own portion! and what expense by th'hour
Seems to flow from him! How, i'th'name of thrift,
Does he rake this together? Now, my lords,   110
Saw you the cardinal?
    Norfolk.   My lord, we have
Stood here observing him. Some strange commotion
Is in his brain: he bites his lip, and starts;
Stops on a sudden, looks upon the ground,
Then lays his finger on his temple; straight
Springs out into fast gait; then stops again,
Strikes his breast hard, and anon he casts
His eye against the moon. In most strange postures
We have seen him set himself.
    King.   It may well be
There is a mutiny in's mind. This morning   120
Papers of state he sent me to peruse,

10

As I required; and wot you what I found
There, on my conscience, put unwittingly?
Forsooth, an inventory, thus importing:
The several parcels of his plate, his treasure,
Rich stuffs, and ornaments of household, which
I find at such proud rate that it outspeaks
Possession of a subject.

 Norfolk.   It's heaven's will;
Some spirit put this paper in the packet
130 To bless your eye withal.

 King.   If we did think
His contemplation were above the earth,
And fixed on spiritual object, he should still
Dwell in his musings; but I am afraid
His thinkings are below the moon, not worth
His serious considering.

         ['*King takes his seat; whispers Lovell, who
             goes to the Cardinal*'

 Wolsey.   Heaven forgive me!
Ever God bless your highness!

 King.   Good my lord,
You are full of heavenly stuff, and bear the inventory
Of your best graces in your mind; the which
You were now running o'er. You have scarce time
140 To steal from spiritual leisure a brief span
To keep your earthly audit; sure, in that
I deem you an ill husband, and am glad
To have you therein my companion.

 Wolsey.   Sir,
For holy offices I have a time; a time
To think upon the part of business which
I bear i'th'state; and Nature does require
Her times of preservation, which perforce
I, her frail son, amongst my brethren mortal,

Must give my tendance to.

  King.   You have said well.

  Wolsey. And ever may your highness yoke together, 150
As I will lend you cause, my doing well
With my well saying!

  King.   'Tis well said again;
And 'tis a kind of good deed to say well;
And yet words are no deeds. My father loved you,
He said he did, and with his deed did crown
His word upon you. Since I had my office
I have kept you next my heart; have not alone
Employed you where high profits might come home,
But pared my present havings, to bestow
My bounties upon you.

  (*Wolsey.*   What should this mean? 160

  (*Surrey.* The Lord increase this business!

  King.   Have I not made you
The prime man of the state? I pray you tell me
If what I now pronounce you have found true;
And, if you may confess it, say withal,
If you are bound to us or no. What say you?

  Wolsey. My sovereign, I confess your royal graces,
Showered on me daily, have been more than could
My studied purposes requite; which went
Beyond all man's endeavours. My endeavours
Have ever come too short of my desires, 170
Yet filed with my abilities; mine own ends
Have been mine so that evermore they pointed
To th'good of your most sacred person and
The profit of the state. For your great graces
Heaped upon me, poor undeserver, I
Can nothing render but allegiant thanks,
My prayers to heaven for you, my loyalty,
Which ever has and ever shall be growing

Till death, that winter, kill it.

King.　　　　　　　　　　　Fairly answered;
180 A loyal and obedient subject is
Therein illustrated; the honour of it
Does pay the act of it; as, i'th'contrary,
The foulness is the punishment. I presume
That, as my hand has opened bounty to you,
My heart dropped love, my power rained honour, more
On you than any, so your hand and heart,
Your brain and every function of your power,
Should, notwithstanding that your bond of duty,
As 'twere in love's particular, be more
190 To me, your friend, than any.

Wolsey.　　　　　　　　　I do profess
That for your highness' good I ever laboured
More than mine own; that am, have, and will be—
Though all the world should crack their duty to you,
And throw it from their soul; though perils did
Abound, as thick as thought could make 'em, and
Appear in forms more horrid—yet my duty,
As doth a rock against the chiding flood,
Should the approach of this wild river break,
And stand unshaken yours.

King.　　　　　　　　　　　'Tis nobly spoken.
200 Take notice, lords, he has a loyal breast,
For you have seen him open't. [*giving him papers*]
　　　　Read o'er this;
And after, this; and then to breakfast with
What appetite you have.

　　[*King departs, 'frowning upon the Cardinal: the nobles
　　　　　throng after him, smiling and whispering*'
　　Wolsey.　　　　　　　　What should this mean?
What sudden anger's this? how have I reaped it?

He parted frowning from me, as if ruin
Leaped from his eyes. So looks the chaféd lion
Upon the daring huntsman that has galled him;
Then makes him nothing. I must read this paper;
I fear, the story of his anger. 'Tis so;
This paper has undone me. 'Tis the account   210
Of all that world of wealth I have drawn together
For mine own ends; indeed, to gain the popedom,
And fee my friends in Rome. O negligence,
Fit for a fool to fall by! what cross devil
Made me put this main secret in the packet
I sent the king? Is there no way to cure this?
No new device to beat this from his brains?
I know 'twill stir him strongly; yet I know
A way, if it take right, in spite of fortune
Will bring me off again. What's this? 'To th'Pope'?   220
The letter, as I live, with all the business
I writ to's holiness. Nay then, farewell!
I have touched the highest point of all my greatness,
And, from that full meridian of my glory,
I haste now to my setting. I shall fall
Like a bright exhalation in the evening,
And no man see me more.

'*Enter to* WOLSEY *the* DUKES OF NORFOLK *and* SUFFOLK,
the EARL OF SURREY, *and the* LORD CHAMBERLAIN'

Norfolk. Hear the king's pleasure, cardinal, who
      commands you
To render up the great seal presently
Into our hands, and to confine yourself   230
To Asher house, my Lord of Winchester's,
Till you hear further from his highness.
   Wolsey.   Stay:
Where's your commission, lords? words cannot carry

Authority so weighty.

Suffolk. Who dare cross 'em,
Bearing the king's will from his mouth expressly?

Wolsey. Till I find more than will or words to
do it—
I mean your malice—know, officious lords,
I dare, and must deny it. Now I feel
Of what coarse metal ye are moulded—envy;
240 How eagerly ye follow my disgraces,
As if it fed ye; and how sleek and wanton
Ye appear in every thing may bring my ruin!
Follow your envious courses, men of malice;
You have Christian warrant for 'em, and no doubt
In time will find their fit rewards. That seal
You ask with such a violence, the king,
Mine and your master, with his own hand gave me;
Bade me enjoy it, with the place and honours,
During my life; and, to confirm his goodness,
250 Tied it by letters-patents. Now, who'll take it?

Surrey. The king, that gave it.

Wolsey. It must be himself, then.

Surrey. Thou art a proud traitor, priest.

Wolsey. Proud lord, thou liest.
Within these forty hours Surrey durst better
Have burnt that tongue than said so.

Surrey. Thy ambition,
Thou scarlet sin, robbed this bewailing land
Of noble Buckingham, my father-in-law.
The heads of all thy brother cardinals,
With thee and all thy best parts bound together,
Weighed not a hair of his. Plague of your policy!
260 You sent me deputy for Ireland;
Far from his succour, from the king, from all
That might have mercy on the fault thou gavest him;

Whilst your great goodness, out of holy pity,
Absolved him with an axe.

  Wolsey.   This, and all else
This talking lord can lay upon my credit,
I answer, is most false. The duke by law
Found his deserts. How innocent I was
From any private malice in his end,
His noble jury and foul cause can witness.
If I loved many words, lord, I should tell you   270
You have as little honesty as honour,
That in the way of loyalty and truth
Toward the king, my ever royal master,
Dare mate a sounder man than Surrey can be,
And all that love his follies.

  Surrey.   By my soul,
Your long coat, priest, protects you; thou shouldst feel
My sword i'th'life-blood of thee else. My lords,
Can ye endure to hear this arrogance?
And from this fellow? If we live thus tamely,
To be thus jaded by a piece of scarlet,   280
Farewell nobility; let his grace go forward,
And dare us with his cap like larks.

  Wolsey.   All goodness
Is poison to thy stomach.

  Surrey.   Yes, that goodness
Of gleaning all the land's wealth into one,
Into your own hands, cardinal, by extortion;
The goodness of your intercepted packets
You writ to th'pope against the king: your goodness,
Since you provoke me, shall be most notorious.
My Lord of Norfolk, as you are truly noble,
As you respect the common good, the state   290
Of our despised nobility, our issues,

Who, if he live, will scarce be gentlemen,
Produce the grand sum of his sins, the articles
Collected from his life. I'll startle you
Worse than the sacring bell, when the brown wench
Lay kissing in your arms, lord cardinal.

Wolsey. How much, methinks, I could despise
    this man,
But that I am bound in charity against it!

Norfolk. Those articles, my lord, are in the
    king's hand;
300 But, thus much, they are foul ones.

    Wolsey.   So much fairer
And spotless shall mine innocence arise,
When the king knows my truth.

    Surrey.   This cannot save you.
I thank my memory I yet remember
Some of these articles, and out they shall.
Now, if you can blush and cry 'guilty', cardinal,
You'll show a little honesty.

    Wolsey.   Speak on, sir;
I dare your worst objections; if I blush,
It is to see a nobleman want manners.

    Surrey. I had rather want those than my head.
    Have at you!
310 First that, without the king's assent or knowledge,
You wrought to be a legate; by which power
You maimed the jurisdiction of all bishops.

    Norfolk. Then that in all you writ to Rome, or else
To foreign princes, 'Ego et Rex meus'
Was still inscribed; in which you brought the king
To be your servant.

    Suffolk.   Then, that without the knowledge
Either of king or council, when you went
Ambassador to the emperor, you made bold

To carry into Flanders the great seal.

  Surrey. Item, you sent a large commission   320
To Gregory de Cassado, to conclude,
Without the king's will or the state's allowance,
A league between his highness and Ferrara.

  Suffolk. That out of mere ambition you have caused
Your holy hat to be stamped on the king's coin.

  Surrey. Then that you have sent
     innumerable substance—
By what means got, I leave to your own conscience—
To furnish Rome and to prepare the ways
You have for dignities, to the mere undoing
Of all the kingdom. Many more there are;   330
Which, since they are of you and odious,
I will not taint my mouth with.

  Chamberlain.   O my lord!
Press not a falling man too far; 'tis virtue.
His faults lie open to the laws; let them,
Not you, correct him. My heart weeps to see him
So little of his great self.

  Surrey.   I forgive him.

  Suffolk. Lord cardinal, the king's further
     pleasure is—
Because all those things you have done of late,
By your power legatine, within this kingdom,
Fall into th'compass of a præmunire—   340
That therefore such a writ be sued against you:
To forfeit all your goods, lands, tenements,
Chattels, and whatsoever, and to be
Out of the king's protection. This is my charge.

  Norfolk. And so we'll leave you to your meditations
How to live better. For your stubborn answer
About the giving back the great seal to us,
The king shall know it, and, no doubt, shall thank you.

So fare you well, my little good lord cardinal.

['*all but Wolsey*' go

350   *Wolsey*. So farewell to the little good you bear me.
Farewell! a long farewell to all my greatness!
This is the state of man: to-day he puts forth
The tender leaves of hopes; to-morrow blossoms,
And bears his blushing honours thick upon him;
The third day comes a frost, a killing frost,
And, when he thinks, good easy man, full surely
His greatness is a-ripening, nips his root,
And then he falls, as I do. I have ventured,
Like little wanton boys that swim on bladders,
360 This many summers in a sea of glory,
But far beyond my depth; my high-blown pride
At length broke under me and now has left me,
Weary and old with service, to the mercy
Of a rude stream that must for ever hide me.
Vain pomp and glory of this world, I hate ye:
I feel my heart new opened. O, how wretched
Is that poor man that hangs on princes' favours!
There is, betwixt that smile we would aspire to,
That sweet aspect of princes, and their ruin,
370 More pangs and fears than wars or women have;
And when he falls, he falls like Lucifer,
Never to hope again.

'*Enter* CROMWELL, *standing amazed*'

                    Why, how now, Cromwell?
  Cromwell. I have no power to speak, sir.
  Wolsey.   What, amazed
At my misfortunes? can thy spirit wonder
A great man should decline? Nay, an you weep,
I am fall'n indeed.
  Cromwell.   How does your grace?

Wolsey.   Why, well;
Never so truly happy, my good Cromwell.
I know myself now; and I feel within me
A peace above all earthly dignities,
A still and quiet conscience. The king has cured me,   380
I humbly thank his grace; and from these shoulders,
These ruined pillars, out of pity, taken
A load would sink a navy—too much honour.
O, 'tis a burden, Cromwell, 'tis a burden
Too heavy for a man that hopes for heaven!
  Cromwell. I am glad your grace has made that
        right use of it.
  Wolsey. I hope I have. I am able now, methinks,
Out of a fortitude of soul I feel,
To endure more miseries and greater far
Than my weak-hearted enemies dare offer.   390
What news abroad?
  Cromwell.   The heaviest and the worst
Is your displeasure with the king.
  Wolsey.   God bless him!
  Cromwell. The next is, that Sir Thomas More
        is chosen
Lord chancellor in your place.
  Wolsey.   That's somewhat sudden.
But he's a learnéd man. May he continue
Long in his highness' favour, and do justice
For truth's sake and his conscience; that his bones,
When he has run his course and sleeps in blessings,
May have a tomb of orphans' tears wept on him!
What more?
  Cromwell. That Cranmer is returned with welcome,   400
Installed lord archbishop of Canterbury.
  Wolsey. That's news indeed.
  Cromwell.   Last, that the Lady Anne,

Whom the king hath in secrecy long married,
This day was viewed in open as his queen,
Going to chapel; and the voice is now
Only about her coronation.

   Wolsey. There was the weight that pulled me
        down. O Cromwell,
The king has gone beyond me. All my glories
In that one woman I have lost for ever.
410 No sun shall ever usher forth mine honours,
Or gild again the noble troops that waited
Upon my smiles. Go get thee from me, Cromwell;
I am a poor fall'n man, unworthy now
To be thy lord and master. Seek the king—
That sun I pray may never set—I have told him
What and how true thou art; he will advance thee;
Some little memory of me will stir him—
I know his noble nature—not to let
Thy hopeful service perish too. Good Cromwell,
420 Neglect him not; make use now, and provide
For thine own future safety.

   Cromwell.　　　　　　O my lord,
Must I then leave you? must I needs forego
So good, so noble and so true a master?
Bear witness, all that have not hearts of iron,
With what a sorrow Cromwell leaves his lord.
The king shall have my service, but my prayers
For ever and for ever shall be yours.

   Wolsey. Cromwell, I did not think to shed a tear
In all my miseries; but thou hast forced me,
430 Out of thy honest truth, to play the woman.
Let's dry our eyes; and thus far hear me, Cromwell;
And when I am forgotten, as I shall be,
And sleep in dull cold marble, where no mention
Of me more must be heard of, say I taught thee,

Say, Wolsey, that once trod the ways of glory,
And sounded all the depths and shoals of honour,
Found thee a way, out of his wreck, to rise in—
A sure and safe one, though thy master missed it.
Mark but my fall and that that ruined me.
Cromwell, I charge thee, fling away ambition: 440
By that sin fell the angels; how can man then,
The image of his Maker, hope to win by it?
Love thyself last; cherish those hearts that hate thee;
Corruption wins not more than honesty.
Still in thy right hand carry gentle peace
To silence envious tongues. Be just, and fear not;
Let all the ends thou aim'st at be thy country's,
Thy God's, and truth's; then if thou fall'st,
      O Cromwell,
Thou fall'st a blessed martyr. Serve the king;
And prithee, lead me in: 450
There take an inventory of all I have
To the last penny; 'tis the king's. My robe,
And my integrity to heaven, is all
I dare now call mine own. O Cromwell, Cromwell,
Had I but served my God with half the zeal
I served my king, he would not in mine age
Have left me naked to mine enemies.
    Cromwell. Good sir, have patience.
    Wolsey.   So I have. Farewell
The hopes of court! my hopes in heaven do dwell.
                                        [*they go*

[4. 1.]   *A street in Westminster*

      '*Enter two Gentlemen, meeting one another*'

1 *Gentleman.* You're well met once again.
2 *Gentleman.*   So are you.

1 *Gentleman.* You come to take your stand here,
    and behold
The Lady Anne pass from her coronation?
    2 *Gentleman.* 'Tis all my business. At our
    last encounter
The Duke of Buckingham came from his trial.
    1 *Gentleman.* 'Tis very true. But that time
    offered sorrow;
This, general joy.
    2 *Gentleman.*   'Tis well. The citizens,
I am sure, have shown at full their royal minds—
As, let 'em have their rights, they are ever forward—
10 In celebration of this day with shows,
Pageants, and sights of honour.
    1 *Gentleman.*   Never greater,
Nor, I'll assure you, better taken, sir.
    2 *Gentleman.* May I be bold to ask what
    that contains,
That paper in your hand?
    1 *Gentleman.*   Yes, 'tis the list
Of those that claim their offices this day
By custom of the coronation.
The Duke of Suffolk is the first, and claims
To be high steward; next, the Duke of Norfolk,
He to be earl marshal; you may read the rest.
20   2 *Gentleman.* I thank you, sir; had I not known
    those customs,
I should have been beholding to your paper.
But, I beseech you, what's become of Katharine,
The princess dowager? how goes her business?
    1 *Gentleman.* That I can tell you too.
      The Archbishop
Of Canterbury, accompanied with other
Learnéd and reverend fathers of his order,

Held a late court at Dunstable, six miles off
From Ampthill, where the princess lay; to which
She was often cited by them, but appeared not;
And, to be short, for not appearance and　　　　　30
The king's late scruple, by the main assent
Of all these learnéd men she was divorced,
And the late marriage made of none effect;
Since which she was removed to Kimbolton,
Where she remains now sick.

2 *Gentleman*.　　　　　　　Alas, good lady!

[*trumpets*

The trumpets sound: stand close, the queen
　　is coming.

['*hautboys*'

'THE ORDER OF THE CORONATION

1. *A lively flourish of trumpets.*
2. *Then two judges.*
3. *LORD CHANCELLOR, with purse and mace before him.*
4. *Choristers, singing.*　　　　　　　　Music.
5. *Mayor of London, bearing the mace. Then Garter, in his coat of arms, and on his head he wore a gilt copper crown.*
6. *MARQUESS DORSET, bearing a sceptre of gold, on his head a demicoronal of gold. With him, the EARL OF SURREY, bearing the rod of silver with the dove, crowned with an earl's coronet. Collars of SS.*
7. *DUKE OF SUFFOLK, in his robe of estate, his coronet on his head, bearing a long white wand, as High Steward. With him, the DUKE OF NORFOLK, with the rod of marshalship, a coronet on his head. Collars of SS.*
8. *A canopy borne by four of the Cinque-ports; under it, the QUEEN in her robe, in her hair, richly adorned*

with pearl, crowned. On each side her, the BISHOPS
OF LONDON *and* WINCHESTER.

9. *The old* DUCHESS OF NORFOLK, *in a coronal of gold,*
    wrought with flowers, bearing the QUEEN'S *train*.

10. *Certain Ladies or Countesses, with plain circlets of*
     gold without flowers'
     As they pass 'over the stage in order and state', the
     two Gentlemen comment upon them

2 *Gentleman.* A royal train, believe me. These
    I know.
Who's that that bears the sceptre?
    1 *Gentleman.*   Marquess Dorset;
And that the Earl of Surrey, with the rod.
40   2 *Gentleman.* A bold brave gentleman. That
      should be
The Duke of Suffolk?
    1 *Gentleman.*   'Tis the same: high steward.
    2 *Gentleman.* And that my Lord of Norfolk?
    1 *Gentleman.*   Yes.
    2 *Gentleman* [*looking on the Queen*].   Heaven
      bless thee!
Thou hast the sweetest face I ever looked on..
Sir, as I have a soul, she is an angel;
Our king has all the Indies in his arms,
And more and richer, when he strains that lady;
I cannot blame his conscience.
    1 *Gentleman.*   They that bear
The cloth of honour over her, are four barons
Of the Cinque-ports.
50   2 *Gentleman.* Those men are happy; and so are all
      are near her.
I take it, she that carries up the train
Is that old noble lady, Duchess of Norfolk.

1 *Gentleman.* It is, and all the rest are countesses.

2 *Gentleman.* Their coronets say so. These are
  stars indeed.

1 *Gentleman.* And sometimes falling ones.

2 *Gentleman.*   No more of that.
  [*The last of the procession leaves; 'and then a great*
                              flourish of trumpets' sounds

        '*Enter a third Gentleman*'

1 *Gentleman.* God save you, sir! where have you
  been broiling?

3 *Gentleman.* Among the crowd i'th'abbey; where
  a finger
Could not be wedged in more: I am stifled
With the mere rankness of their joy.

  2 *Gentleman.*   You saw
The ceremony?

  3 *Gentleman.*   That I did.

  1 *Gentleman.*   How was it?   60

  3 *Gentleman.* Well worth the seeing.

  2 *Gentleman.*   Good sir, speak it to us.

  3 *Gentleman.* As well as I am able. The
  rich stream
Of lords and ladies, having brought the queen
To a prepared place in the choir, fell off
A distance from her; while her grace sat down
To rest awhile, some half an hour or so,
In a rich chair of state, opposing freely
The beauty of her person to the people.
Believe me, sir, she is the goodliest woman
That ever lay by man; which when the people   70
Had the full view of, such a noise arose
As the shrouds make at sea in a stiff tempest,
As loud and to as many tunes; hats, cloaks,—

Doublets, I think—flew up, and had their faces
Been loose, this day they had been lost. Such joy
I never saw before. Great-bellied women,
That had not half a week to go, like rams
In the old time of war, would shake the press,
And make 'em reel before 'em. No man living
80 Could say 'This is my wife' there, all were woven
So strangely in one piece.

    2 *Gentleman*.   But what followed?

    3 *Gentleman*. At length her grace rose, and with
      modest paces
Came to the altar, where she kneeled, and saintlike
Cast her fair eyes to heaven and prayed devoutly;
Then rose again and bowed her to the people;
When by the Archbishop of Canterbury
She had all the royal makings of a queen,
As holy oil, Edward Confessor's crown,
The rod, and bird of peace, and all such emblems
90 Laid nobly on her; which performed, the choir,
With all the choicest music of the kingdom,
Together sung 'Te Deum'. So she parted,
And with the same full state paced back again
To York place, where the feast is held.

    1 *Gentleman*.   Sir,
You must no more call it York place: that's past;
For since the cardinal fell that title's lost:
'Tis now the king's, and called Whitehall.

    3 *Gentleman*.   I know it;
But 'tis so lately altered that the old name
Is fresh about me.

    2 *Gentleman*.   What two reverend bishops
100 Were those that went on each side of the queen?

    3 *Gentleman*. Stokesly and Gardiner: the one
      of Winchester,

Newly preferred from the king's secretary,
The other, London.

  2 *Gentleman.*   He of Winchester
Is held no great good lover of the archbishop's,
The virtuous Cranmer.

  3 *Gentleman.*   All the land knows that:
However, yet there is no great breach; when
     it comes,
Cranmer will find a friend will not shrink from him.

  2 *Gentleman.* Who may that be, I pray you?

  3 *Gentleman.*   Thomas Cromwell,
A man in much esteem with th'king, and truly
A worthy friend. The king has made him master   110
O'th'jewel house,
And one, already, of the privy council.

  2 *Gentleman.* He will deserve more.

  3 *Gentleman.*   Yes, without all doubt.
Come, gentlemen, ye shall go my way,
Which is to th'court, and there ye shall be my guests;
Something I can command. As I walk thither,
I'll tell ye more.

  Both.   You may command us, sir.

                        [they go

[4. 2.]   *Kimbolton*

   '*Enter* KATHARINE, *Dowager, sick; led between*
      GRIFFITH, *her Gentleman Usher, and*
         PATIENCE, *her woman*'

  Griffith. How does your grace?

  Katharine.   O Griffith, sick to death.
My legs like loaden branches bow to th'earth,
Willing to leave their burden. Reach a chair.
So—now, methinks, I feel a little ease.
Didst thou not tell me, Griffith, as thou led'st me,

That the great child of honour, Cardinal Wolsey,
Was dead?
   Griffith. Yes, madam; but I think your grace,
Out of the pain you suffered, gave no ear to't.
   Katharine. Prithee, good Griffith, tell me how
        he died.
10 If well, he stepped before me happily
For my example.
   Griffith.   Well, the voice goes, madam;
For after the stout Earl Northumberland
Arrested him at York, and brought him forward,
As a man sorely tainted, to his answer,
He fell sick suddenly, and grew so ill
He could not sit his mule.
   Katharine.   Alas, poor man!
   Griffith. At last, with easy roads, he came to Leicester,
Lodged in the abbey; where the reverend abbot,
With all his covent, honourably received him;
20 To whom he gave these words, 'O father abbot,
An old man, broken with the storms of state,
Is come to lay his weary bones among ye;
Give him a little earth for charity'.
So went to bed; where eagerly his sickness
Pursued him still; and three nights after this,
About the hour of eight, which he himself
Foretold should be his last, full of repentance,
Continual meditations, tears and sorrows,
He gave his honours to the world again,
30 His blessèd part to heaven, and slept in peace.
   Katharine. So may he rest; his faults lie gently
        on him!
Yet thus far, Griffith, give me leave to speak him,
And yet with charity. He was a man
Of an unbounded stomach, ever ranking

Himself with princes; one that by suggestion
Tied all the kingdom: simony was fair play;
His own opinion was his law. I'th'presence
He would say untruths, and be ever double
Both in his words and meaning. He was never,
But where he meant to ruin, pitiful.   40
His promises were, as he then was, mighty;
But his performance, as he is now, nothing.
Of his own body he was ill, and gave
The clergy ill example.
  Griffith.   Noble madam,
Men's evil manners live in brass; their virtues
We write in water. May it please your highness
To hear me speak his good now?
  Katharine.   Yes, good Griffith;
I were malicious else.
  Griffith.   This Cardinal,
Though from an humble stock, undoubtedly
Was fashioned to much honour from his cradle.   50
He was a scholar, and a ripe and good one;
Exceeding wise, fair-spoken and persuading;
Lofty and sour to them that loved him not,
But to those men that sought him, sweet as summer.
And though he were unsatisfied in getting,
Which was a sin, yet in bestowing, madam,
He was most princely: ever witness for him
Those twins of learning that he raised in you,
Ipswich and Oxford! one of which fell with him,
Unwilling to outlive the good that did it;   60
The other, though unfinished, yet so famous,
So excellent in art, and still so rising,
That Christendom shall ever speak his virtue.
His overthrow heaped happiness upon him;
For then, and not till then, he felt himself,

H. VIII – 8

And found the blessedness of being little.
And, to add greater honours to his age
Than man could give him, he died fearing God.

   Katharine. After my death I wish no other herald,
70 No other speaker of my living actions,
To keep mine honour from corruption,
But such an honest chronicler as Griffith.
Whom I most hated living, thou hast made me,
With thy religious truth and modesty,
Now in his ashes honour: peace be with him!
Patience, be near me still, and set me lower:
I have not long to trouble thee. Good Griffith,
Cause the musicians play me that sad note
I named my knell, whilst I sit meditating
80 On that celestial harmony I go to.

                      ['*sad and solemn music*'

   Griffith. She is asleep. Good wench, let's sit
     down quiet,
For fear we wake her. Softly, gentle Patience.

             '*The vision.*

*Enter, solemnly tripping one after another, six personages,
clad in white robes, wearing on their heads garlands of
bays, and golden vizards on their faces; branches of bays
or palm in their hands. They first congee unto her, then
dance; and, at certain changes, the first two hold a spare
garland over her head; at which the other four make
reverent curtsies; then the two that held the garland
deliver the same to the other next two, who observe the
same order in their changes, and holding the garland over
her head; which done, they deliver the same garland to the
last two, who likewise observe the same order; at which, as
it were by inspiration, she makes in her sleep signs of
rejoicing, and holdeth up her hands to heaven; and so in*

their dancing vanish, carrying the garland with them.
The music continues'

  Katharine. Spirits of peace, where are ye? are ye
      all gone,
And leave me here in wretchedness behind ye?
  Griffith. Madam, we are here.
  Katharine.   It is not you I call for
Saw ye none enter since I slept?
  Griffith.   None, madam.
  Katharine. No? Saw you not even now a
      blesséd troop
Invite me to a banquet, whose bright faces
Cast thousand beams upon me, like the sun?
They promised me eternal happiness,   90
And brought me garlands, Griffith, which I feel
I am not worthy yet to wear: I shall, assuredly.
  Griffith. I am most joyful, madam, such good dreams
Possess your fancy.
  Katharine.   Bid the music leave;
They are harsh and heavy to me.   ['*music ceases.*'
  Patience.   Do you note
How much her grace is altered on the sudden?
How long her face is drawn? how pale she looks,
And of an earthy cold? Mark her eyes.
  Griffith. She is going, wench. Pray, pray.
  Patience.   Heaven comfort her!

      '*Enter a Messenger*'

  Messenger. An't like your grace—
  Katharine.   You are a saucy fellow; 100
Deserve we no more reverence?
  Griffith.   You are to blame,
Knowing she will not lose her wonted greatness,

To use so rude behaviour. Go to, kneel.
  Messenger. I humbly do entreat your highness' pardon:
My haste made me unmannerly. There is staying
A gentleman, sent from the king, to see you.
  Katharine. Admit him entrance, Griffith: but
    this fellow
Let me ne'er see again.   [*Messenger goes*

GRIFFITH ushers in CAPUCIUS

             If my sight fail not,
You should be lord ambassador from the emperor,
110 My royal nephew, and your name Capucius.
  Capucius. Madam, the same. Your servant.
  Katharine.   O, my lord,
The times and titles now are altered strangely
With me since first you knew me. But I pray you,
What is your pleasure with me?
  Capucius.   Noble lady,
First, mine own service to your grace; the next,
The king's request that I would visit you,
Who grieves much for your weakness, and by me
Sends you his princely commendations,
And heartily entreats you take good comfort.
120   *Katharine.* O my good lord, that comfort comes
    too late;
'Tis like a pardon after execution.
That gentle physic, given in time, had cured me;
But now I am past all comforts here but prayers.
How does his highness?
  Capucius.   Madam, in good health.
  Katharine. So may he ever do! and ever flourish,
When I shall dwell with worms, and my poor name
Banished the kingdom! Patience, is that letter
I caused you write yet sent away?

Patience.   No, madam.

                              [*giving it to Katharine*

Katharine. Sir, I most humbly pray you to deliver
This to my lord the king.

Capucius.   Most willing, madam.   130

Katharine. In which I have commended to
      his goodness
The model of our chaste loves, his young daughter—
The dews of heaven fall thick in blessings on her!—
Beseeching him to give her virtuous breeding—
She is young, and of a noble modest nature;
I hope she will deserve well—and a little
To love her for her mother's sake that loved him
Heaven knows how dearly. My next poor petition
Is that his noble grace would have some pity
Upon my wretched women that so long   140
Have followed both my fortunes faithfully;
Of which there is not one, I dare avow—
And now I should not lie—but will deserve,
For virtue and true beauty of the soul,
For honesty and decent carriage,
A right good husband, let him be a noble;
And, sure, those men are happy that shall have 'em.
The last is, for my men; they are the poorest,
But poverty could never draw 'em from me;
That they may have their wages duly paid 'em,   150
And something over to remember me by.
If heaven had pleased to have given me longer life
And able means, we had not parted thus.
These are the whole contents; and, good my lord,
By that you love the dearest in this world,
As you wish Christian peace to souls departed,
Stand these poor people's friend, and urge the king
To do me this last right.

Capucius.   By heaven, I will,
Or let me lose the fashion of a man!
160   *Katharine.* I thank you, honest lord. Remember me
In all humility unto his highness;
Say his long trouble now is passing
Out of this world. Tell him in death I blessed him,
For so I will. Mine eyes grow dim. Farewell,
My lord. Griffith, farewell. Nay, Patience,
You must not leave me yet. I must to bed;
Call in more women. When I am dead, good wench,
Let me be used with honour; strew me over
With maiden flowers, that all the world may know
170 I was a chaste wife to my grave. Embalm me,
Then lay me forth; although unqueened, yet like
A queen and daughter to a king, inter me.
I can no more.   [*They go out, 'leading Katharine'*

[5. 1.]   *London. A gallery in the palace*

'*Enter* GARDINER, *Bishop of Winchester, a Page with
a torch before him, met by* SIR THOMAS LOVELL'

Gardiner. It's one o'clock, boy, is't not?
Boy.   It hath struck.
Gardiner. These should be hours for necessities,
Not for delights; times to repair our nature
With comforting repose, and not for us
To waste these times. Good hour of night,
     Sir Thomas!
Whither so late?
   Lovell.   Came you from the king, my lord?
   Gardiner. I did, Sir Thomas, and left him
     at primero
With the Duke of Suffolk.
   Lovell.   I must to him too,

Before he go to bed. I'll take my leave.

 Gardiner. Not yet, Sir Thomas Lovell. What's 10
  the matter?
It seems you are in haste; an if there be
No great offence belongs to't, give your friend
Some touch of your late business. Affairs that walk,
As they say spirits do, at midnight, have
In them a wilder nature than the business
That seeks dispatch by day.

 Lovell.   My lord, I love you;
And durst commend a secret to your ear
Much weightier than this work. The queen's
  in labour,
They say, in great extremity, and feared
She'll with the labour end.

 Gardiner.   The fruit she goes with 20
I pray for heartily, that it may find
Good time, and live; but for the stock, Sir Thomas,
I wish it grubbed up now.

 Lovell.   Methinks I could
Cry the amen; and yet my conscience says
She's a good creature, and, sweet lady, does
Deserve our better wishes.

 Gardiner.   But, sir, sir,
Hear me, Sir Thomas, you're a gentleman
Of mine own way; I know you wise, religious;
And, let me tell you, it will ne'er be well,
'Twill not, Sir Thomas Lovell, take't of me, 30
Till Cranmer, Cromwell, her two hands, and she,
Sleep in their graves.

 Lovell.   Now, sir, you speak of two
The most remarked i'th'kingdom. As for Cromwell,
Beside that of the jewel house, is made master
O'th'rolls, and the king's secretary; further, sir,

Stands in the gap and trade of moe preferments,
With which the time will load him. Th'archbishop
Is the king's hand and tongue, and who dare speak
One syllable against him?
   Gardiner.   Yes, yes, Sir Thomas,
40 There are that dare; and I myself have ventured
To speak my mind of him; and indeed this day,
Sir, I may tell it you, I think I have
Insensed the lords o'th'council that he is—
For, so I know he is, they know he is—
A most arch heretic, a pestilence
That does infect the land; with which they moved
Have broken with the king, who hath so far
Given ear to our complaint, of his great grace
And princely care foreseeing those fell mischiefs
50 Our reasons laid before him, hath commanded
To-morrow morning to the council board
He be convented. He's a rank weed, Sir Thomas,
And we must root him out. From your affairs
I hinder you too long. Good night, Sir Thomas.
                          ['*Gardiner and Page*' go
  Lovell. Many good nights, my lord; I rest
    your servant.

'*Enter* KING *and* SUFFOLK'

  King. Charles, I will play no more to-night;
My mind's not on't; you are too hard for me.
  Suffolk. Sir, I did never win of you before.
  King. But little, Charles,
60 Nor shall not, when my fancy's on my play.
Now, Lovell, from the queen what is the news?
  Lovell. I could not personally deliver to her
What you commanded me, but by her woman
I sent your message; who returned her thanks

In the great'st humbleness, and desired your highness
Most heartily to pray for her.
  King.   What say'st thou, ha?
To pray for her? what, is she crying out?
  Lovell. So said her woman, and that her
     sufferance made
Almost each pang a death.
  King.   Alas, good lady!
  Suffolk. God safely quit her of her burden, and   70
With gentle travail, to the gladding of
Your highness with an heir!
  King.   'Tis midnight, Charles;
Prithee, to bed; and in thy prayers remember
Th'estate of my poor queen. Leave me alone;
For I must think of that which company
Would not be friendly to.
  Suffolk.   I wish your highness
A quiet night, and my good mistress will
Remember in my prayers.
  King.   Charles, good night. [*Suffolk goes*

     '*Enter* Sir Anthony Denny'

Well, sir, what follows?
  Denny. Sir, I have brought my lord the archbishop, 80
As you commanded me.
  King.   Ha? Canterbury?
  Denny. Ay, my good lord.
  King.   'Tis true: where is he, Denny?
  Denny. He attends your highness' pleasure.
  King.   Bring him to us.
                     [*Denny goes*
(*Lovell.* This is about that which the bishop spake;
I am happily come hither.

'Enter CRANMER and DENNY'

King. Avoid the gallery. [*'Lovell seems to stay'*] Ha?
        I have said. Be gone.
What!   [*'Lovell and Denny' go*
(*Cranmer.* I am fearful. Wherefore frowns he thus?
'Tis his aspect of terror. All's not well.
        King. How now, my lord? you·do desire to know
90 Wherefore I sent for you.
        Cranmer [*kneeling*].   It is my duty
T'attend your highness' pleasure.
        King.   Pray you, arise,
My good and gracious Lord of Canterbury.
Come, you and I must walk a turn together;
I have news to tell you; come, come, give me
        your hand.
Ah, my good lord, I grieve at what I speak,
And am right sorry to repeat what follows.
I have, and most unwillingly, of late
Heard many grievous, I do say, my lord,
Grievous complaints of you; which, being considered,
100 Have moved us and our council, that you shall
This morning come before us; where I know
You cannot with such freedom purge yourself
But that, till further trial in those charges
Which will require your answer, you must take
Your patience to you and be well contented
To make your house our Tower; you a brother of us,
It fits we thus proceed, or else no witness
Would come against you.
        Cranmer [*kneeling*].   I humbly thank your highness,
And am right glad to catch this good occasion
110 Most throughly to be winnowéd, where my chaff
And corn shall fly asunder; for I know

There's none stands under more calumnious tongues
Than I myself, poor man.
   King.   Stand up, good Canterbury;
Thy truth and thy integrity is rooted
In us, thy friend. Give me thy hand, stand up;
Prithee, let's walk. Now, by my holidame,
What manner of man are you? My lord, I looked
You would have given me your petition, that
I should have ta'en some pains to bring together
Yourself and your accusers, and to have heard you,   120
Without indurance further.
   Cranmer.   Most dread liege,
The good I stand on is my truth and honesty;
If they shall fail, I with mine enemies
Will triumph o'er my person; which I weigh not,
Being of those virtues vacant. I fear nothing
What can be said against me.
   King.   Know you not
How your state stands i'th'world, with the
       whole world?
Your enemies are many, and not small; their practices
Must bear the same proportion; and not ever
The justice and the truth o'th'question carries   130
The due o'th'verdict with it; at what ease
Might corrupt minds procure knaves as corrupt
To swear against you? Such things have been done.
You are potently opposed, and with a malice
Of as great size. Ween you of better luck,
I mean, in perjured witness, than your master,
Whose minister you are, whiles here he lived
Upon this naughty earth? Go to, go to;
You take a precipice for no leap of danger,
And woo your own destruction.
   Cranmer.   God and your majesty 140

Protect mine innocence, or I fall into
The trap is laid for me!
  King.   Be of good cheer;
They shall no more prevail than we give way to.
Keep comfort to you, and this morning see
You do appear before them. If they shall chance,
In charging you with matters, to commit you,
The best persuasions to the contrary
Fail not to use, and with what vehemency
The occasion shall instruct you. If entreaties
150 Will render you no remedy, this ring
Deliver them, and your appeal to us
There make before them. Look, the good man weeps!
He's honest, on mine honour. God's blest mother,
I swear he is true-hearted, and a soul
None better in my kingdom. Get you gone,
And do as I have bid you. [*Cranmer goes*] He
       has strangled
His language in his tears.

    '*Enter Old Lady*'; LOVELL *following*

  Gentleman ['*within*'].   Come back: what mean you?
  Old Lady. I'll not come back; the tidings that I bring
Will make my boldness manners. Now, good angels
160 Fly o'er thy royal head, and shade thy person
Under their blessed wings!
  King.   Now by thy looks
I guess thy message. Is the queen delivered?
Say 'ay', and of a boy.
  Old Lady.   Ay, ay, my liege,
And of a lovely boy: the God of heaven
Both now and ever bless her! 'tis a girl
Promises boys hereafter. Sir, your queen
Desires your visitation, and to be

Acquainted with this stranger; 'tis as like you
As cherry is to cherry.
  King.   Lovell!
  Lovell.   Sir?
  King. Give her an hundred marks. I'll to   170
    the queen.   [*goes*
  Old Lady. An hundred marks? By this light, I'll
    ha' more.
An ordinary groom is for such payment.
I will have more, or scold it out of him.
Said I for this, the girl was like to him? I'll
Have more, or else unsay't; and now, while 'tis hot,
I'll put it to the issue.   [*they go*

[5. 2.] *Before the door of the council-chamber*

'*Enter* CRANMER, *Archbishop of Canterbury*'

  Cranmer. I hope I am not too late; and yet
    the gentleman
That was sent to me from the council prayed me
To make great haste. All fast? what means this? Ho!
Who waits there? [*The* '*keeper*' *comes forth*] Sure,
    you know me?
  Keeper.   Yes, my lord;
But yet I cannot help you.
  Cranmer. Why?
  Keeper. Your grace must wait till you be called for.

'*Enter* DOCTOR BUTTS'

  Cranmer.   So.
  (*Butts.* This is a piece of malice. I am glad
I came this way so happily. The king
Shall understand it presently.   [*goes*
  (*Cranmer.*   'Tis Butts,   10

The king's physician; as he passed along,
How earnestly he cast his eyes upon me!
Pray heaven he sound not my disgrace! For certain,
This is of purpose laid by some that hate me—
God turn their hearts! I never sought their malice—
To quench mine honour; they would shame to
    make me
Wait else at door, a fellow-councillor,
'Mong boys, grooms and lackeys. But their pleasures
Must be fulfilled, and I attend with patience.

'Enter the KING and BUTTS at a window above'

20 *Butts.* I'll show your grace the strangest sight—
    King.   What's that, Butts?
    Butts. I think your highness saw this many a day.
    King. Body o' me, where is it?
    Butts.   There, my lord:
The high promotion of his grace of Canterbury,
Who holds his state at door 'mongst pursuivants,
Pages and footboys.
    King.   Ha? 'tis he, indeed.
Is this the honour they do one another?
'Tis well there's one above 'em yet; I had thought
They had parted so much honesty among 'em,
At least good manners, as not thus to suffer
30 A man of his place and so near our favour
To dance attendance on their lordships' pleasures,
And at the door too, like a post with packets.
By holy Mary, Butts, there's knavery.
Let 'em alone, and draw the curtain close;
We shall hear more anon.
                      [they withdraw behind the curtain;
                          Cranmer waits without

[5. 3.]   *The Council-chamber, with a chair of*
state and beneath it a table with
chairs and stools

'*Enter* LORD CHANCELLOR, *places himself at the upper*
end of the table on the left hand; a seat being left void
above him, as for CANTERBURY'S *seat;* DUKE OF SUFFOLK,
DUKE OF NORFOLK, SURREY, LORD CHAMBERLAIN,
GARDINER, *seat themselves in order on each side.* CROM-
WELL *at lower end, as secretary.*' *Keeper at the door*

Chancellor. Speak to the business, master secretary;
Why are we met in council?
Cromwell.   Please your honours,
The chief cause concerns his grace of Canterbury.
Gardiner. Has he had knowledge of it?
Cromwell.   Yes.
Norfolk.   Who waits there?
Keeper. Without, my noble lords?
Gardiner.   Yes.
Keeper.   My lord archbishop;
And has done half an hour, to know your pleasures.
Chancellor. Let him come in.
Keeper.   Your grace may enter now.
    ['*Cranmer*' *enters and* '*approaches the council-table*']
Chancellor. My good lord archbishop, I'm
        very sorry
To sit here at this present and behold
That chair stand empty; but we are all men,   10
In our own natures frail and capable
Of our flesh; few are angels; out of which frailty
And want of wisdom, you, that best should
        teach us,
Have misdemeaned yourself, and not a little,
Toward the king first, then his laws, in filling

The whole realm, by your teaching and
    your chaplains'—
For so we are informed—with new opinions,
Divers and dangerous; which are heresies,
And, not reformed, may prove pernicious.

20   *Gardiner.* Which reformation must be sudden too,
My noble lords; for those that tame wild horses
Pace 'em not in their hands to make 'em gentle,
But stop their mouths with stubborn bits and
    spur 'em
Till they obey the manage. If we suffer,
Out of our easiness and childish pity
To one man's honour, this contagious sickness,
Farewell all physic; and what follows then?
Commotions, uproars, with a general taint
Of the whole state; as of late days our neighbours,
30 The upper Germany, can dearly witness,
Yet freshly pitied in our memories.
  Cranmer. My good lords, hitherto, in all the progress
Both of my life and office, I have laboured,
And with no little study, that my teaching
And the strong course of my authority
Might go one way, and safely; and the end
Was ever to do well; nor is there living,
I speak it with a single heart, my lords,
A man that more detests, more stirs against,
40 Both in his private conscience and his place,
Defacers of a public peace, than I do.
Pray heaven, the king may never find a heart
With less allegiance in it! Men that make
Envy and crookéd malice nourishment
Dare bite the best. I do beseech your lordships,
That, in this case of justice, my accusers,
Be what they will, may stand forth face to face,

And freely urge against me.

  Suffolk.　　　　　　　　　　Nay, my lord,
That cannot be; you are a councillor,
And, by that virtue, no man dare accuse you.　　　50

  Gardiner. My lord, because we have business of
　　more moment,
We will be short with you. 'Tis his
　　highness' pleasure,
And our consent, for better trial of you,
From hence you be committed to the Tower;
Where, being but a private man again,
You shall know many dare accuse you boldly,
More than, I fear, you are provided for.

  Cranmer. Ah, my good Lord of Winchester, I
　　thank you;
You are always my good friend; if your will pass,
I shall both find your lordship judge and juror,　　60
You are so merciful. I see your end;
'Tis my undoing. Love and meekness, lord,
Become a churchman better than ambition;
Win straying souls with modesty again,
Cast none away. That I shall clear myself,
Lay all the weight ye can upon my patience,
I make as little doubt as you do conscience
In doing daily wrongs. I could say more,
But reverence to your calling makes me modest.

  Gardiner. My lord, my lord, you are a sectary,　　70
That's the plain truth; your painted gloss discovers,
To men that understand you, words and weakness.

  Cromwell. My Lord of Winchester, you are a little,
By your good favour, too sharp; men so noble,
However faulty, yet should find respect
For what they have been; 'tis a cruelty
To load a falling man.

    H. VIII – 9

Gardiner.   Good master secretary,
I cry your honour mercy; you may, worst
Of all this table, say so.

Cromwell.   Why, my lord?

80   *Gardiner.* Do not I know you for a favourer
Of this new sect? ye are not sound.

Cromwell.   Not sound?

Gardiner. Not sound, I say.

Cromwell.   Would you were half so honest!
Men's prayers then would seek you, not their fears.

Gardiner. I shall remember this bold language.

Cromwell.   Do.
Remember your bold life too.

Chancellor.   This is too much;
Forbear, for shame, my lords.

Gardiner.   I have done.

Cromwell.   And I.

Chancellor. Then thus for you, my lord: it
     stands agreed,
I take it, by all voices, that forthwith
You be conveyed to th'Tower a prisoner;
90 There to remain till the king's further pleasure
Be known unto us. Are you all agreed, lords?

All. We are.

Cranmer.   Is there no other way of mercy,
But I must needs to th'Tower, my lords?

Gardiner.   What other
Would you expect? you are strangely troublesome.
Let some o'th'guard be ready there.

'*Enter the Guard*'

Cranmer.   For me?
Must I go like a traitor thither?

Gardiner.   Receive him,

And see him safe i'th'Tower.

Cranmer.   Stay, good my lords,
I have a little yet to say. Look there, my lords;
By virtue of that ring, I take my cause
Out of the gripes of cruel men, and give it   100
To a most noble judge, the king my master.

Chamberlain. This is the king's ring.

Surrey.   'Tis no counterfeit.

Suffolk. 'Tis the right ring, by heaven. I told ye all,
When we first put this dangerous stone a-rolling,
'Twould fall upon ourselves.

Norfolk.   Do you think, my lords,
The king will suffer but the little finger
Of this man to be vexed?

Chamberlain.   'Tis now too certain;
How much more is his life in value with him?
Would I were fairly out on't!

Cromwell.   My mind gave me,
In seeking tales and informations   110
Against this man, whose honesty the devil
And his disciples only envy at,
Ye blew the fire that burns ye; now have at ye!

'*Enter KING, frowning on them; takes his seat*'

Gardiner. Dread sovereign, how much are we bound
          to heaven
In daily thanks, that gave us such a prince,
Not only good and wise, but most religious;
One that in all obedience makes the church
The chief aim of his honour, and, to strengthen
That holy duty, out of dear respect,
His royal self in judgement comes to hear   120
The cause betwixt her and this great offender.

King. You were ever good at sudden commendations,

Bishop of Winchester. But know, I come not
To hear such flattery now, and in my presence
They are too thin and bare to hide offences.
To me you cannot reach you play the spaniel,
And think with wagging of your tongue to win me;
But, whatsoe'er thou takest me for, I'm sure
Thou hast a cruel nature and a bloody.

130 [*to Cranmer*] Good man, sit down. Now let me see
           the proudest,
He that dares most, but wag his finger at thee.
By all that's holy, he had better starve
Than but once think this place becomes thee not.
    Surrey. May it please your grace—
    King.   No, sir, it does not please me.
I had thought I had had men of some understanding
And wisdom of my council; but I find none.
Was it discretion, lords, to let this man,
This good man—few of you deserve that title—
This honest man, wait like a lousy footboy

140 At chamber door? and one as great as you are?
Why, what a shame was this! Did my commission
Bid ye so far forget yourselves? I gave ye
Power as he was a councillor to try him,
Not as a groom. There's some of ye, I see,
More out of malice than integrity,
Would try him to the utmost, had ye mean;
Which ye shall never have while I live.
    Chancellor.   Thus far,
My most dread sovereign, may it like your grace
To let my tongue excuse all. What was purposed

150 Concerning his imprisonment, was rather,
If there be faith in men, meant for his trial
And fair purgation to the world, than malice,
I'm sure, in me.

King.   Well, well, my lords, respect him;
Take him and use him well; he's worthy of it.
I will say thus much for him, if a prince
May be beholding to a subject, I
Am for his love and service so to him.
Make me no more ado, but all embrace him:
Be friends, for shame, my lords. My Lord
          of Canterbury,
I have a suit which you must not deny me: 160
That is, a fair young maid that yet wants baptism;
You must be godfather, and answer for her.
  Cranmer. The greatest monarch now alive may glory
In such an honour; how may I deserve it,
That am a poor and humble subject to you?
  King. Come, come, my lord, you'ld spare your
spoons. You shall have two noble partners with you:
the old Duchess of Norfolk, and Lady Marquess
Dorset. Will these please you?
Once more, my Lord of Winchester, I charge you,   170
Embrace and love this man.
  Gardiner.   With a true heart
And brother-love I do it.
  Cranmer.   And let heaven
Witness how dear I hold this confirmation.
  King. Good man, those joyful tears show thy
          true heart.
The common voice, I see, is verified
Of thee, which says thus: 'Do my Lord of Canterbury
A shrewd turn, and he is your friend for ever'.
Come, lords, we trifle time away; I long
To have this young one made a Christian.
As I have made ye one, lords, one remain;   180
So I grow stronger, you more honour gain.   [*they go*

[5. 4.]   *The palace yard; near the gate*

'*Noise and tumult*' *outside*. '*Enter Porter and
his Man*'

Porter. You'll leave your noise anon, ye rascals; do
you take the court for Parish garden? ye rude slaves,
leave your gaping.
[*A voice from without*] Good master porter, I belong
to th'larder.
Porter. Belong to th'gallows, and be hanged, ye rogue!
Is this a place to roar in? Fetch me a dozen crab-tree
staves, and strong ones: these are but switches to 'em.
I'll scratch your heads. You must be seeing christen-
10 ings? do you look for ale and cakes here, you rude
rascals?
Man. Pray, sir, be patient; 'tis as much impossible—
Unless we sweep 'em from the door with cannons—
To scatter 'em, as 'tis to make 'em sleep
On May-day morning, which will never be:
We may as well push against Paul's as stir 'em.
Porter. How got they in, and be hanged?
Man. Alas, I know not: how gets the tide in?
As much as one sound cudgel of four foot—
20 You see the poor remainder—could distribute,
I made no spare, sir.
Porter.   You did nothing, sir.
Man. I am not Samson, nor Sir Guy, nor Colbrand,
To mow 'em down before me; but if I spared any
That had a head to hit, either young or old,
He or she, cuckold or cuckold-maker,
Let me ne'er hope to see a chine again;
And that I would not for a cow, God save her!
[*Another voice from without*] Do you hear,
        master porter?

Porter. I shall be with you presently, good master puppy. Keep the door close, sirrah.   30

Man. What would you have me do?

Porter. What should you do, but knock 'em down by th'dozens? Is this Moorfields to muster in? or have we some strange Indian with the great tool come to court, the women so besiege us? Bless me, what a fry of fornication is at door! On my Christian conscience, this one christening will beget a thousand; here will be father, godfather, and all together.

Man. The spoons will be the bigger, sir. There is a fellow somewhat near the door, he should be a brazier 40 by his face, for, o' my conscience, twenty of the dog-days now reign in's nose; all that stand about him are under the line, they need no other penance; that fire-drake did I hit three times on·the head, and three times was his nose discharged against me; he stands there, like a mortarpiece, to blow us. There was a haberdasher's wife of small wit near him, that railed upon me till her pinked porringer fell off her head, for kindling such a combustion in the state. I missed the meteor once, and hit that woman, who cried out 'Clubs!' when I 50 might see from far some forty truncheoners draw to her succour, which were the hope o'th'Strand, where she was quartered. They fell on; I made good my place; at length they came to th'broomstaff with me; I defied 'em still; when suddenly a file of boys behind 'em, loose shot, delivered such a shower of pebbles, that I was fain to draw mine honour in and let 'em win the work; the devil was amongst 'em, I think, surely.

Porter. These are the youths that thunder at a play-house and fight for bitten apples; that no audience, but 60 the tribulation of Tower-hill, or the limbs of Limehouse, their dear brothers, are able to endure. I have some

of 'em in Limbo Patrum, and there they are like to
dance these three days; besides the running banquet of
two beadles that is to come.

'*Enter* LORD CHAMBERLAIN'

Chamberlain. Mercy o' me, what a multitude are here!
They grow still too; from all parts they are coming,
As if we kept a fair here. Where are these porters,
These lazy knaves? You've made a fine hand, fellows.
70 There's a trim rabble let in: are all these
Your faithful friends o'th'suburbs? We shall have
Great store of room, no doubt, left for the ladies,
When they pass back from the christening.

Porter.   An't please your honour,
We are but men; and what so many may do,
Not being torn a-pieces, we have done:
An army cannot rule 'em.

Chamberlain.   As I live,
If the king blame me for't, I'll lay ye all
By the heels, and suddenly; and on your heads
Clap round fines for neglect. You're lazy knaves;
80 And here ye lie baiting of bombards when
Ye should do service. Hark! the trumpets sound;
They're come already from the christening;
Go, break among the press, and find a way out
To let the troop pass fairly, or I'll find
A Marshalsea shall hold ye play these two months.

Porter. Make way there for the princess.

Man.   You great fellow,
Stand close up, or I'll make your head ache.

Porter. You i'th'camlet, get up o'th'rail;
I'll peck you o'er the pales else.

[*They open the gate and beat back the crowd*

[5. 5.] '*Enter Trumpets, sounding; then two Aldermen, Lord Mayor, Garter,* CRANMER, DUKE OF NORFOLK *with his marshal's staff,* DUKE OF SUFFOLK, *two Noblemen bearing great standing-bowls for the christening-gifts; then four Noblemen bearing a canopy, under which the* DUCHESS OF NORFOLK, *godmother, bearing the child richly habited in a mantle, &c., train borne by a Lady; then follows the* MARCHIONESS DORSET, *the other god-mother, and Ladies. The troop pass once about the stage, and Garter speaks*'

Garter. Heaven, from thy endless goodness, send prosperous life, long, and ever happy, to the high and mighty princess of England, Elizabeth!

'*Flourish. Enter* KING *and Guard*'

Cranmer [*kneeling*]. And to your royal grace, and the good queen.
My noble partners and myself thus pray:
All comfort, joy, in this most gracious lady
Heaven ever laid up to make parents happy
May hourly fall upon ye!
  King.   Thank you, good lord archbishop.
What is her name?
  Cranmer.   Elizabeth.
  King.   Stand up, lord.
             [*The King kisses the child*
With this kiss take my blessing: God protect thee!   10
Into whose hand I give thy life.
  Cranmer.   Amen.
  King. My noble gossips, you've been too prodigal;
I thank ye heartily; so shall this lady,
When she has so much English.
  Cranmer.   Let me speak, sir,

For heaven now bids me; and the words I utter
Let none think flattery, for they'll find 'em truth.
This royal infant—heaven still move about her!—
Though in her cradle, yet now promises
Upon this land a thousand thousand blessings,
20 Which time shall bring to ripeness. She shall be—
But few now living can behold that goodness—
A pattern to all princes living with her
And all that shall succeed. Saba was never
More covetous of wisdom and fair virtue
Than this pure soul shall be. All princely graces
That mould up such a mighty piece as this is,
With all the virtues that attend the good,
Shall still be doubled on her. Truth shall nurse her,
Holy and heavenly thoughts still counsel her;
30 She shall be loved and feared. Her own shall
　　bless her;
Her foes shake like a field of beaten corn,
And hang their heads with sorrow. Good grows
　　with her;
In her days every man shall eat in safety
Under his own vine what he plants, and sing
The merry songs of peace to all his neighbours.
God shall be truly known, and those about her
From her shall read the perfect ways of honour,
And by those claim their greatness, not by blood.
Nor shall this peace sleep with her; but as when
40 The bird of wonder dies, the maiden phoenix,
Her ashes new create another heir
As great in admiration as herself,
So shall she leave her blessedness to one—
When heaven shall call her from this cloud
　　of darkness—
Who from the sacred ashes of her honour

Shall star-like rise, as great in fame as she was,
And so stand fixed. Peace, plenty, love, truth, terror,
That were the servants to this chosen infant,
Shall then be his, and like a vine grow to him;
Wherever the bright sun of heaven shall shine,　　　50
His honour and the greatness of his name
Shall be, and make new nations; he shall flourish,
And like a mountain cedar reach his branches
To all the plains about him; our children's children
Shall see this, and bless heaven.

  King.　　　　　　　　Thou speakest wonders.

  Cranmer. She shall be, to the happiness of England,
An agéd princess; many days shall see her,
And yet no day without a deed to crown it.
Would I had known no more! but she must die—
She must, the saints must have her—yet a virgin,　　　60
A most unspotted lily shall she pass
To th'ground, and all the world shall mourn her.

  King. O lord archbishop,
Thou hast made me now a man; never before
This happy child did I get anything.
This oracle of comfort has so pleased me
That when I am in heaven I shall desire
To see what this child does, and praise my Maker.
I thank ye all. To you, my good lord mayor,
And your good brethren, I am much beholding;　　　70
I have received much honour by your presence,
And ye shall find me thankful. Lead the way, lords;
Ye must all see the queen, and she must thank ye;
She will be sick else. This day, no man think
Has business at his house; for all shall stay:
This little one shall make it holiday.　　　　　*[they go*

The Epilogue

'Tis ten to one this play can never please
All that are here. Some come to take their ease,
And sleep an act or two; but those, we fear,
We've frighted with our trumpets; so, 'tis clear,
They'll say 'tis naught; others, to hear the city
Abused extremely, and to cry 'That's witty!'
Which we have not done neither; that, I fear,
All the expected good we're like to hear
For this play at this time, is only in
10 The merciful construction of good women;
For such a one we showed 'em. If they smile,
And say 'twill do, I know, within a while
All the best men are ours; for 'tis ill hap
If they hold when their ladies bid 'em clap.

THE COPY FOR
HENRY VIII, 1623

The Folio text of *Henry VIII* is, in the main, extremely
tidy, and affords little help towards solving the problem
of authorship discussed in the Introduction. The
accepted view about it is cautiously summarized by
Sir Walter Greg: 'The copy for F was clearly a care-
fully prepared manuscript, in whose hand or hands
there is no evidence to show. It could have been used
as a prompt-book, but there is no indication that it was.'[1]
No evidence for more than one scribal hand has been
found, and, as will be seen, the case against use as a
prompt-book is perhaps stronger than Sir Walter allows.
If the evidence for divided authorship drawn from
pronominal forms and from colloquial abbreviations is
valid,[2] the scribe cannot have gone far in imposing his
own preferences, if any, on his original. On the other
hand, there are very few odd spellings or irregular
punctuations to suggest the persistence of authorial
characteristics. There are, however, a few variations in
speech-prefixes, though not of an elaborately 'functional' kind.[3] Wolsey is 'Cardinall Wolsey' in the stage-
direction for his first entry (1. 1. 114), and 'Car.' in his
three speeches in the first scene. In 1. 2 and 1. 4 he
enters as 'The Cardinall', and is then 'Card.', but in
2. 2, where confusion with Campeius must be avoided,
he is 'Wolsey' in his entry and 'Wol.' in prefixes. There

---

[1] *The Shakespeare First Folio* (1955), p. 425.
[2] See above, pp. xxii–iv.
[3] The basic discussion of this is R. B. McKerrow,
Review of English Studies, XI (1935), 459–65.

is the same need for distinction in 2. 4, but there, curiously enough, there is an ambiguity right at the start with speeches prefixed 'Car.', in ll. 1 (catchword 'Card.') and 5, although 'the two Cardinalls' have been mentioned in the initial stage-direction. Thereafter, 'Wol.' is properly distinguished from 'Camp.' in this scene. In 3. 1, there is once more irregularity. The entry at l. 23 is for 'the two Cardinalls, Wolsey & Campian [*sic*]', but after 'Wol[s].' at ll. 23 and 27, Wolsey becomes 'Card.' at ll. 40 and 51, only reverting to 'Wol.' after the intervention of 'Camp.' at l. 61. From l. 112 on, Wolsey is again 'Car.'. This last change coincides with a change of compositor (*A* to *B*),[1] but it would be rash to assume that either the irregularity on *A*'s page (V 3ᵛ = 3. 1. 1–108) or the regularity on *B*'s (V 4ʳ = 3. 1. 109–3. 2. 30) is the result of compositorial interference. At any rate, Wolsey's last scene, 3. 2, which belongs entirely to *B*, varies between a more frequent 'Car[d].' and an occasional 'Wol.'. These irregularities, especially in scenes where Campeius is on stage, make it improbable that the printer's copy had been previously used as prompt-copy.[2]

No other character has such capricious prefixes as Wolsey. Henry is 'King Henry' at his first entry (1. 2. init.), but thereafter '[the] King' in stage-directions and

---

[1] On these two compositors in general, see Alice Walker, *Textual Problems of the First Folio* (1955), pp. 8–12, and on this play, R. A. Foakes, *Studies in Bibliography*, XI (1958), 55–60.

[2] There is no correlation between irregularity and putative authorship. Three scenes attributed to Shakespeare (1. 1, 1. 2, first part of 3. 2) and two attributed to Fletcher (1. 4, 2. 2) are regular. One scene attributed to Shakespeare (2. 4) and two attributed to Fletcher (3. 1, second part of 3. 2) are irregular.

'Kin[g].' in speech-prefixes. Katharine undergoes a straightforward functional change from 'the Queene' (1. 2. 8 S.D.) and 'Queen' or 'Qu[ee].' in prefixes to 'Katherine Dowager' (4. 2. init. S.D.), with 'Kath.' in prefixes. A variant which led to some confusion was concerned with the designation of the Lord Chamberlain. In 1. 3 (init.) and at 1. 4. 7 he enters as 'L. Chamberlaine', and is prefixed 'L. Ch[am].' in 1. 3 and 'Cham.' in 1. 4. These forms continue to alternate, without confusion, in 2. 2–3 and 3. 2, but in 5. 3 the Lord Chancellor and the Lord Chamberlain are on stage together, with prefixes 'Chan.' and 'Cham.', and it is generally agreed that emendation is required at ll. 85 and 87.

The division of the play between two compositors has already been referred to. By application of the usual tests, R. A. Foakes has concluded that *A* set fifteen pages and *B* thirteen.[1] It has been customary to regard *B* as much more unreliable than *A*, but there is no evidence of that in *Henry VIII*. The number of errors that can certainly or probably be assigned to the compositors is in fact unusually small. There are a good number of places where the punctuation is misleading even by the normal practice of the day, but it is impossible to tell whether the compositor or the copyist is to blame. These errors are divided fairly evenly between *A* and *B*. Errors that seem more likely than not to go back to copy are the confusions in the assignment of speeches at 1. 1. 42–9 and 4. 1. 55 (though here, and at 4. 1. 20, the compositor ought to have noticed the impossible sequence of prefixes); and the undeleted false start at

[1] Foakes works out the distribution correctly but makes two errors in tabulating it in *Studies in Bibliography*, XI (1958), 55, where Compositor A is credited with 16 pages, and the last two of his pages, x4^r and x4^v, are omitted.

1. 2. 180 (authorial). Either a copyist or a compositor might be responsible for the wrong expansion of an abbreviation (in the first instance, misread as well), at 1. 1. 221 and 3. 1. 23 S.D. Most of the other errors, certain or probable, are very slight and fall into familiar classes. Short words are omitted at 1. 1. 183 and 1. 2. 170 (and possibly at 4. 2. 98). There is apparently an addition, caught from the next line, at 2. 3. 61, and I suspect additions also at 1. 2. 111, 2. 4. 29 and 3. 2. 325. Short words are confused at 1. 2. 139, 2. 4. 174, 3. 1. 61, 3. 2. 292 (possibly an authorial slip), 5. 3. 133, 5. 4. 54 and 5. 5. 70. A final 's' is added or dropped at 1. 1. 226, 5. 3. 174 and 5. 5. 37. This leaves a residue of errors that may be due to misreading by a copyist or a compositor, in the strict sense of mistaking one set of letters for another: 1. 1. 63, 200, 219; 1. 2. 67, 156; 1. 3. 13; 2. 1. 20, 86; 3. 2. 171, 343; 4. 2. 7; 5. 2. 8, 85 sp.-pref., 87 sp.-pref., 125 (and perhaps 2. 4. 182). In all of the above, the error is very slight: 'a:u', 'e:d', 'r:c', etc., or the omission of single letters. Not quite so straightforward are 1. 1. 219 ('Councillour' for 'Chancellour') and 1. 2. 164 ('Commissions' for 'Confessions'), where an associated meaning, rather than pure misreading, seems to have led to the mistake. At 4. 2. 36, the text is uncertain. There are a few other trifling irregularities: unmetrical abbreviations (very likely authorial) at 2. 4. 191 and 5. 3. 73, and an occasional omission (common in F as a whole) of the apostrophe in ''s' (for 'is'). As far as I can judge, there is no real textual crux in the play.

One of the misreadings is of particular interest in relation to the nature of the copy. Foakes points out that the misreading 'Pecke' for 'Perke' occurs once in the share of each putative author (1. 1. 219, Shakespeare: 2. 1. 20, Fletcher). His conclusion that 'it is safe to assume that the author(s) wrote "Perke", which the scribe misread as "Pecke"',[1] goes, however, a little too far; and indeed in the next sentence he himself allows for the possibility that the error was compositorial in origin: 'However the form arose, it must have been written in the same way at the two places where it appeared in the manuscript from which the text was set'. None the less, this twin error tells slightly against dual authorship. But of course the important question to decide is how strong the evidence on the other side is, and I have made my opinion on this clear in the Introduction.

Charlton Hinman, *The Printing and Proof-Reading of the First Folio* (1963), II, 214–7, inclines to credit the non-*B* pages of *Henry VIII* to the compositor he calls *C,* rather than to *A.* [1968.]

---

[1] *Studies in Bibliography,* XI (1958), 59; Foakes's statement in his note on 2. 1. 20 that the two lines were set by different compositors is wrong: as his own analysis shows, both were set by *A.*

NOTES

All significant departures from F are recorded, the source of the accepted reading being indicated in brackets. Square brackets about an author's name mean that he is responsible for the substance of the note that precedes; round brackets a verbatim quotation from him. Italics in F are retained for quotations from the dialogue, but not for stage-directions and speech-prefixes cited in isolation.

F stands for First Folio (1623); F2, F3, F4 for Second, Third and Fourth Folios (1632, 1663, 1685); G. for Glossary; *O.E.D.* for the *Oxford English Dictionary*; S.D. for stage-direction; Sh. for Shakespeare or Shakespearian; sp.-pref. for speech-prefix. Common words are also usually abbreviated; e.g. sp. = spelling or spelt, prob. = probable or probably, om. = omitted, etc.

The following is a list of other works cited in abridged forms:

Abbott = *A Shakespearian Grammar*, by E. A. Abbott (3rd ed. 1870).

Al. = ed. of Sh. by Peter Alexander, 1951.

Beaumont and Fletcher = Works of Francis Beaumont and John Fletcher, Variorum ed., 1904–12 [incomplete; cited by act, scene and line]; for other plays, *Works*, ed. A. Glover and A. R. Waller, 1905–12 [cited by volume and page].

B.C.P. = Book of Common Prayer.

Boswell = J. Boswell, cited from 1821 Variorum ed.

Boswell-Stone = *Sh.'s Holinshed*, by W. G. Boswell-Stone, 1896.

Camb. = *The Cambridge Sh.*, 1865, 1892.

Cap. = ed. of Sh. by Edward Capell, 1768.

Chambers, *E.S.* = *The Elizabethan Stage*, by E. K. Chambers, 1923.

Chambers, *Wm. Sh.* = *William Sh.*, by E. K. Chambers, 1930.

Clar. = ed. by W. Aldis Wright (*Clarendon Sh.*), 1891.

Clarke = ed. of Sh. by Charles and Mary Cowden Clarke [1864–8].

Collier = ed. of Sh. by J. P. Collier, 1842–4, 1858.

Conrad = 'Henry VIII Fletchers Werk, überarbeitet von Sh.' (*Englische Studien*, LII (1918), 204–64).

Craig = ed. by W. J. Craig (*Little Quarto Sh.*), 1904.

Deighton = ed. by K. Deighton, 1895.

Dekker = *Dramatic Works of Thomas Dekker*, ed. by F. Bowers, 1953–61.

Delius = ed. of Sh. by N. Delius (3rd ed. 1872).

D.N.S. = ed. by D. Nichol Smith (*Warwick Sh.*) [1899].

Douce = *Illustrations of Sh.*, by F. Douce, 1807.

Dyce = ed. of Sh. by A. Dyce, 1857, 1864–6.

Elze = ed. by K. Elze of S. Rowley's *When You See Me, You Know Me*, 1874.

Foakes = ed. by R. A. Foakes (*Arden Sh.*), 1957.

Foxe = *Acts and Monuments*, 1597.

Franz = *Die Sprache Shakespeares*, by W. Franz (4th ed. of *Shakespeare-Grammatik*), 1939.

Grant White = ed. of Sh. by R. Grant White, 1859.

Han. = ed. of Sh. by Sir Thomas Hanmer, 1743–4.

Hol. = *Chronicles of England*, by R. Holinshed, 1587.

Hunter = ed. by John Hunter, 1860.

Hunter[2] = ed. by John Hunter, 1872.

J. = ed. of Sh. by Samuel Johnson, 1765.

Jonson = *Works of Ben Jonson*, ed. by C. H. Herford and Percy and Evelyn Simpson, 1925–52.

Kökeritz = *Sh.'s Pronunciation*, by H. Kökeritz, 1953.

Mal. = ed. of Sh. by E. Malone, 1790 (notes incorporated in final form in 1821 Variorum, ed. J. Boswell).

Marlowe = *Works of Christopher Marlowe*, General Editor R. H. Case, 1930–3.

Massinger = *Plays of Philip Massinger*, ed. by W. Gifford (2nd ed. 1813).

M.L.R. = *Modern Language Review*.

M.S.R. = Malone Society Reprint.

Nashe = *Works of Thomas Nashe*, ed. by R. B. McKerrow, 1904–10.

Noble = *Sh.'s Biblical Knowledge*, by R. Noble, 1935.

N. & Q. = *Notes and Queries*.

O.D.E.P. = *Oxford Dictionary of English Proverbs*, by W. G. Smith (2nd ed. 1948).

Onions = *A Sh. Glossary*, by C. T. Onions, 1911 (last corrected impression, 1946).

Pooler = ed. by C. K. Pooler (*Arden Sh.*), 1915.

Pope = ed. of Sh. by A. Pope, 1723–5.

R.E.S. = *Review of English Studies*.

Rolfe = ed. by W. J. Rolfe (*Friendly Edition*), 1891.

Rowe = ed. of Sh. by N. Rowe, 1709–10 (2 edd.), 1714.

Schmidt = *Sh.-Lexicon*, by A. Schmidt (3rd ed. 1902).

Sh. Apocr. = *Sh. Apocrypha*, ed. by C. F. T. Brooke, 1908.

Sh. Eng. = *Shakespeare's England*, 1916.

Sisson = ed. of Sh. by C. J. Sisson [1954].

Steev. = ed. of Sh. by G. Steevens, 1773 (supplemented in later edd. up to 1803).

Sugden = *A Topographical Dictionary to the Works of Sh. and his Fellow Dramatists*, by E. H. Sugden, 1925.

Symons = ed. by A. Symons (*Henry Irving Sh.*), 1890.

Theob. = ed. of Sh. by L. Theobald, 1733.

Tilley = *A Dictionary of the Proverbs in England in the Sixteenth and Seventeenth Centuries*, by M. P. Tilley, 1950.

T.L.S. = *Times Literary Supplement*.

Var. = Variorum ed. of Sh., ed. by J. Boswell, 1821.

Vaughan = *New Readings and New Renderings of Sh.'s Tragedies*, by H. H. Vaughan, vol. III, 1886.

Warb. = ed. of Sh. by W. Warburton, 1747.

Webster = *Works of John Webster*, ed. by F. L. Lucas, 1927.

Yale = ed. by J. M. Berdan and Tucker Brooke (*Yale Sh.*), 1925.

The above list does not include a number of names occasionally cited from the Cambridge Shakespeare critical apparatus, or from the 1821 Variorum.

Prologue

Authorship. Both the prologue and the epilogue resemble those of *The Two Noble Kinsmen.* I see no reason to deny them to Fletcher.

1. *no more* The last play was prob. a comedy [Clar.]. See Chambers, *E.S.* II, 217, for the King's plays of 1612–13.

3. *sad...working* See G. *state and woe* see G. 'state (i)'. The notion that affairs of state are involved may also be conveyed as perh. at 2. 4. 213. Vaughan notes that 'state' and 'woe' occur close together in *R. II*, 3. 4. 27–8.

9. *truth* Here, and at ll. 18, 20–1, there is prob. a reference to the alternative title 'All is True' recorded by Wotton (see Chambers, *Wm. Sh.* II, 344).

12. *shilling* On the 'twelvepenny room next the stage', see Dekker, *Gull's Handbook* (ed. R. B. McKerrow (1907), p. 9), and other quotations in Chambers, *E.S.* II, 534, n. 1.

13. *two short hours* This length is often given in conventional references of this kind: see quotations in Chambers, *E.S.* II, 543, n. 2, where times up to three hours are also mentioned.

13–17. *Only...deceived* Plausibly taken by Boswell

as glancing at Samuel Rowley's *When You See Me You Know Me* (1605), in which the Fool, Will Summers, plays a prominent part. The statement of editors that it 'appears to have been revived in 1613' (Clar.) may be true, but seems to be purely conjectural, based on this reference and on the reprint of the play in 1613. W. J. Lawrence argues that the title 'All is True', and the unusual concern for accuracy in minute details (especially the S.D.'s for the Coronation in 4. 1), points to deliberate rivalry with Rowley's play (*T.L.S.* 18 Dec. 1930, p. 1085).

15. *noise of targets* Cf. *When You See Me*, sc. 5, which contains a sword and buckler fight between King Henry in disguise and a highwayman [Boswell].

16. *motley* See G.; for an unorthodox view, L. Hotson's *Sh.'s Motley* (1952); and for the most recent discussion E. W. Ives, *Sh. Survey*, 13 (1960), 98–103.

18–19. *such...is* R. Boyle, *New Sh. Soc. Trans.* I, 8–10 (1880–6), 451, compared Fletcher, *Women Pleas'd*, Act 5 (VII, 301): 'To what end do I walk? for men to wonder at, | And fight, and fool?'

19–20. *forfeiting...brains* 'abandoning all claims to intelligence' (Deighton). Pooler cites Fletcher, *Bonduca*, 3. 2. 2 (VI, 113), 'It forfeits all our understandings'.

20–1. *opinion...intend* 'reputation we bring with us of making the representation which we have in view simply in accordance with truth' (Clar.).

22. *understanding* Perh. (Foakes) with the common word-play on the spectators who 'stood under' the stage: cf. Chambers, *E.S.* II, 527 n. 6; though such references are normally ironical and this is, at most, condescending. For another possible pun on the word, see 1. 3. 32.

23. *for goodness' sake* 'out of your good nature' (Deighton); again at 3. 1. 159.

24. *happiest* See G. There may also be a suggestion of 'felicitous [in judgment]' (*O.E.D.* 5).

25. *sad* See G.

25–6. *see...story* For this type of rhyme, cf. Epil. 9–10. Mason (*ap.* Var.) called attention to it in both places and Boswell discussed it in his Essay on Sh.'s Versification (Var. 1, 577). For more recent discussions see G. C. Moore Smith, *M.L.R.* xv (1920), 300–3 and P. Simpson, *M.L.R.* xxxviii (1943), 127–9. Paul Maas (*M.L.R.* xxxix (1944), 179) comments that Sh. uses the device only in the play of Pyramus and Thisbe (*M.N.D.* 5. 1. 158–9), but it is also the most natural way to read the rhyme 'woodbine | eglantine' in *M.N.D.* 2. 1. 251–2, and unavoidable in *L.L.L.* 5. 2. 462–3, 'comedy | zany'; cf. also *R. II*, 2. 1. 22–3, 'nation [two syllables] | imitation [five syllables]'.

27. *As...living* Either 'as if they were alive' or (less prob.) 'as they were when alive'.

29. *thousand* Without article also at 4. 2. 89, *Per.* 1. 2. 97 [Foakes]. Hickson (*N. & Q.* III (1851), 33) cited the usage as Fletcherian; in Sh., it occurs in *Tit.* 3. 1. 196, *Cor.* 2. 2. 77 (without a noun); also 'thousandfold' (adv.) in *Troil.* 1. 2. 285.

1. 1

Authorship. Shakespeare.

Material. There is slight compression of time. The meeting of the Field of Cloth of Gold (June 1520) is still recent, but Buck.'s arrest belongs to April 1521.

Hol. (p. 858) describes the meeting: 'The daie of the meeting was appointed to be on the thursdaie the seauenth of Iune, vpon which daie the two kings met in the vale of Andren, accompanied with such a number of the nobilitie of both realmes, so richlie appointed in apparell, and costlie iewels,...that a woonder it was to behold and view them in their order and roomes, which euerie man kept according to his appointment [ll. 42–5].

'The two kings meeting in the field, either saluted other in most louing wise, first on horssebacke, and after alighting on foot eftsoones imbraced with courteous words', and then adjourned for banquetting to a 'rich tent of cloath of gold', after which they 'departed for that night, the one [Henry] to Guisnes, the other to Ard'.

On p. 860 he tells how on Saturday 17 June 'the lord cardinall...conducted forward the French king, and in their way they incountered and met the king of England and his companie right in the vallie of Anderne, apparelled in their masking apparell' [l. 26].

The account of Wolsey's arbitrary behaviour, and of Buck.'s hatred for Wolsey, draws on Hol. p. 855: 'The peeres of the realme...seemed to grudge, that such a costlie iournie should be taken in hand to their importunate charges and expenses, without consent of the whole boord of the councell [ll. 75–80]', and 'namelie [especially] the duke of Buckingham, being a man of a loftie courage, but not most liberall, sore repined that he should be at so great charges for his furniture foorth at this time, saieng; that he knew not for what cause so much monie should be spent about the sight of a vaine talke to be had, and communication to be ministred of things of no importance [ll. 85–7]'. There are also marginal notes on p. 853, 'Note the ambitious humor of the cardinal of yorke', and 'The whole maner of the interview cōmitted to the cardinall' [ll. 45–53].

The storm of ll. 89–94 is ominous in Hol., pp. 860–1, 'on mondaie, the eighteenth of Iune, was such an hideous storme of wind and weather, that manie coniectured it did prognosticate trouble and hatred shortlie after to follow betweene princes', but is not directly connected with the measures against the merchants, p. 872, 'the French king commanded all Englishmens goods, being in Burdeaux, to be attached and put vnder arrest', in retaliation for which the French ambassador was 'commanded to keepe his house' (p. 873).

The further insistence on Wolsey's predominance in ll. 168–93 draws on Hol., p. 858, 'the king...had giuen

vnto the said cardinall full authoritie...to affirme and confirme...whatsoeuer should be in question betweene him and
the French king'; but the idea that the Emperor's main
purpose in his visit [Whitsuntide, 1520] was 'to whisper
Wolsey' [l. 179] is Sh.'s own: Hol., p. 856 writes that
'speciallie to see the queene of England his aunt was the
emperour his intent [in going to Canterbury]', and treats
the political aim, to prevent the meeting with the French
king, as being forwarded by direct conversation with
Henry himself.

The arrest of Buck. is from Hol., p. 863, where Buck.
'was sent for vp to London, & at his comming thither, was
streightwaies attached, and brought to the Tower by
sir Henrie Marneie, capteine of the gard, the sixteenth of
April [1521]. There was also attached the foresaid Chartreux monke [Nicholas Hopkins], maister Iohn de la Car
alias de la Court, the dukes confessor, and Sir Gilbert
Perke, priest, the dukes chancellor'. The grounds for the
arrest, given on the same page, are reserved for sc. 2.

Loc. (Theob.). Clar. (after Mal. on **1. 3.** 63) suggests the palace of Bridewell as a setting for **1. 1–3**;
Yale, noting that Bridewell was not yet built (which
Sh. may not have known), suggests Greenwich. This
would have the advantage of agreeing with the
(historical) setting of the final scene. *Entry* (F).

2. *saw* See G. 'see'.

3. *fresh admirer* 'an admirer still feeling the impression as if it were hourly renewed' (J.).

6. *suns* Perh. with quibble on 'sons' (which F 3 reads).

7. *Guynes and Arde* Guynes was in English hands,
Arde (so Hol. for mod. 'Ardres') in French.

10. *grew together* See G., and cf. *M.N.D.* **3. 2.** 208
[Steev.]; *Ven*. 540 [Mal.]; *Two Noble Kinsmen*, **5. 3.**
97–9, 'Were they metamorphisd | Both into one! oh
why? there were no woman | Worth so composd a
Man' [Symons]; Spenser, *F.Q.* (1590 ed.), iii. xii. 46;
and various Fletcher quotations *ap*. Pooler.

12–13. *All...prisoner* In fact, Buckingham was present at the Field of Cloth of Gold (Hol. p. 860), and Norfolk was in England.

14. *The view* 'the view *par excellence*' (Deighton, citing Abbott, § 92).

15. *single*. Besides the sense 'unmarried' which the metaphor demands, this prob. carries a suggestion of 'small' and 'insignificant' [Vaughan], or 'comparatively simple or plain' (Clarke); cf. *Mac.* 1. 6. 16, 'poor and single business', where the context is rather like that here.

16–17. *Each...master* Hunter[2] notes as proverbial, and cites J. Wheeler, *A Treatise of Commerce* (1601, p. 24), 'one day still being a Schoole-master vnto the other'; from Publilius Syrus (Loeb ed.), 146, 'Discipulus est prioris posterior dies'.

18. *Made...its* 'united in itself all the wonders of the preceding days' (Clar.). *its* Infrequent in Sh.; usu. 'his'.

21. *India* As 'mine' in l. 22 shows, the 'India' of the New World is meant; cf. 4. 1. 45; *1 H. IV*, 3. 1. 167 [Conrad]; *Tw. N.* 2. 5. 15; Donne, *The Sunne Rising*, l. 17, 'both the'India's of spice and Myne'.

26. *Was...painting* 'heightened their colour, so as to make the use of cosmetics unnecessary' (Clar., after Warb.)

32–3. *no...censure* no one dared to single out either as superior to the other; it is not clear whether 'dis-cerner' has a strong sense of 'person of judgment' (On.), or more neutrally 'judge', i.e. one who gives judgment; the choice of word was no doubt influenced by the fact that the subject is the impossibility of *discriminating* (or even, in the preceding clause, distinguishing) between the two kings.

33. *censure*. (Rowe) F 'cenfure,'.

36. *former fabulous story* 'the stories of old times hitherto thought fabulous' (Clar.); 'former' having a double function, as adj. and as adv. with 'fabulous' as Vaughan notes.

38. *Bevis* See G. *go far* go a long way in praise; not necessarily, as edd. say, quite as much as 'exaggerate'; cf. *Cym.* 1. 1. 24 [Hunter²], and below, 4. 2. 32.

39–40. *affect...honesty* have an honourable regard for truth. Sh. brings the two words together in *Oth.* 5. 2. 248, 'But why should honour outlive honesty?'. See also 3. 2. 271 (Fletcher) below.

40–2. *The...to* 'The course of these triumphs and pleasures, however well related, must lose in the description part of that spirit and energy which were expressed in the real action' (J.).

42. *to* (F2) F 'too', as frequently when postpositive.

42–9. *All...business* (as Theob.) F '*Buc.* All... together? *Nor.* As you gueſſe:...buſineſſe'. Some edd. retain the assignment of 'As you guess' to Norfolk, treating it as a recognition that Buckingham really knew the answer to his own question; but l. 49 shows Buckingham genuinely ignorant.

44. *office* See G.

45. *Distinctly* See G.

48. *no element* Prob. plays on different senses of the word. Schmidt paraphrases, 'it could not be expected that he would find his proper sphere in such a business' (cf. 'in (out of) one's element': Tilley, E 107, 108); this is rather forced. Clar. (after Delius), 'no component part'.

52–3. *no...finger* Cf. Tilley, F 228.

54. *fierce* 'wild, extravagant' (Clar., citing *Cym.* 5. 5. 382, on which see note in this ed.).

55. *keech* See G. (not pre-Sh. in *O.E.D.*, but

H. Hulme, *R.E.S.* n.s. x (1959), 22, cites examples in Stratford records from 1595 on); 'here used in reference to Wolsey's supposed origin, as the son of a butcher' (Clar., after Steev.). 'Sh. perh. thought of Wolsey as a fat man' (Foakes).

56. *Take up* See G.

59. *grace* Has a wide range of meanings, relating to favour and the qualities that win favour; here almost 'prestige'.

60. *successors* For the stress 'súccessors', cf. *Meas.* 2. 2. 99, 'súccessive'.

60–1. *called...feats* summoned to public service because of past exploits; 'feats' suggests primarily military exploits [J.D.W.].

61. *allied* See G.; a reference to blood-relationship (Pooler, tentatively) is not required.

62. *assistants* For the sense 'public functionary' (Schmidt *ad loc.*), cf. *Ham.* 2. 2. 166, and note on Polonius in this ed., p. 141.

63. *web, 'a* (Cap. conj., reading 'web, he') F 'Web. O'. An exclamation seems pointless here, and 'O' is more readily explained as arising from 'a' than from 'he'.

64. *makes his way* wins advancement for him. *way—* (Al.) F 'way'.

65. *gives for him* merit is 'the gift which God gives on Wolsey's behalf, and in Wolsey's place' (Vaughan).

69. *Peep...him* Cf. *Troil.* 4. 5. 56–7, 'her wanton spirits look out | At every joint and motive of her body' [Steev.].

69–70. *that?...hell,* (Warb., *ap.* Theob.) F 'that, ...Hell?'.

77–8. *To...upon* The repetition of a preposition is common (Abbott, § 407); the variation of it less so, but there is no need to emend.

79. *The...out* As Mal. noted, the general sense is given by Hol., 'without consent of the whole boord of the councell'; 'out' must mean 'not concerned in the matter', whether we take the exact force to be 'without the concurrence of the council' (Pope) or 'council not then sitting' (J.). *council out,* (Pope, substantially) F 'Councell, out'.

80. *him...papers* him whom he sets down in his list; cf. *O.E.D.* 'paper' (v.) 1, citing from 1594 'ech ones name is papered'.

84. *broke...'em* The idea is common; for examples in addition to those in Tilley, L 452, see Var. and Pooler on this passage; also *Revenger's Tragedy*, 2. 1. 238; *2 H. VI*, 1. 3. 78 (cited by Munro, *London Sh.*, 1958), with n. in this ed.; W. D. Briggs on Marlowe's *Edward II* (1914), l. 700; Foakes refers also to Tilley, W 61, 'All his wardrobe is on his back'.

86. *minister...issue* Directly from Hol., 'communication to be ministred of things of no importance'. In both, the sense of 'minister communication' would appear to be 'provide occasion for talking about'; by 'issue' Sh. lays more stress on the lack of outcome of the talk (perh. corresponding to the immediately preceding 'vaine talke' in Hol.).

87. *issue?* (Pope) F 'iffue.'. *Grievingly* Foakes notes that this, like 'pausingly' (1. 2. 168) seems to be a coinage; cf. also *All's*, 1. 1. 30, 'admiringly ånd mourningly' (the latter once recorded earlier).

91. *not consulting* 'independently of each other' (Rolfe).

97. *silenced* In Hall, 'commaunded to kepe his house in silence' (Boswell-Stone, p. 427). As Hol. drops 'in silence', this suggests that Hall was consulted.

98. *A...peace* 'a fine thing to call a peace!' (Clar., after J.).

99. *superfluous* See G.

100. *carried* See G.   *Like it* if it please;
'a polite way of introducing an unpleasant subject'
(Deighton).

101–2. *difference...cardinal* This 'difference' is not
prominent in Hol. till 1521, but cf. p. 855 (1520),
with marginal note, 'Great hatred betweene the
cardinall, and the Duke of Buckingham'.

104. *plenteous safety* Perh. 'safety combined with
the enjoyment of plenty' rather than simply 'ample
safety'.

104–6. *that...to* Cf. Abbott, § 415, for the shift of
construction, which is found as early as Chaucer,
Kn. T. I (A), 1133–5.

110. *'t may be said* Prob., as Vaughan holds, this
governs not only 'It reaches far' but also 'and...
darts it'.

111. *It reaches far* Cf. *2 H. VI*, 4. 7. 76, and
Tilley, K 87, 'Kings have long arms'.

114. *advise* (F2) F 'aduice'; a sp. found also in
Lr. 3. 7. 9 (F; same compositor).   S.D. (F).

115. *surveyor* Charles Knyvet, Buckingham's
cousin.

119. S.D. F 'Exeunt Cardinall, and his Traine'.

120. *butcher's cur* Cf. Tilley, B 764, 'as surly as a
butcher's dog' [Foakes].   *venomed-mouthed* F
'venom'd-mouth'd' Pope 'venom-mouth'd' (after
Rowe, 'venome mouth'd'). The F text could be the
result of an *e/d* corruption, but it is a perfectly acceptable form. A number of edd. (Grant White, Clar.,
Rolfe) concede that it might be correct, and Schmidt,
O.E.D., On. and Yale all accept it. Cf. *The Fair Maid
of the Inn* (Beaumont and Fletcher, ed. Waller, IX,
155; Webster, ed. Lucas, 1. 2. 18), 'oyl'd tongu'd'
[F2 'oy'ld', attempting to correct F1 'old'].

121–2. *best...slumber* That it is ill to waken a

sleeping dog (Tilley, W 7) has long been proverbial: see Chaucer, *Troil.* III. 764, with F. N. Robinson's note.

122. *A beggar's book* 'The literary qualifications of a bookish beggar' (J.). Lettsom *ap.* Dyce (2nd ed.) cites *2 H. VI*, 4. 7. 68, 'My book preferred me to the king'.

123. *What,* (F 3) F 'What'.

124. *appliance* See G.

127. *abject object* For this jingle, Foakes cites Jonson, *Poetaster*, 1. 3. 58, Marston, *Histriomastix* (ed. H. H. Wood, III, 293); cf. also *R. III*, 1. 1. 106, for play on 'abjects' with a glance at 'subjects'.

128. *bores* See G.; Pooler cites also 'bore one's nose' = cheat (Tilley, N 229).

133–4. *A...him* Cf. Tilley, H 642, 'A free horse will soon tire' [Foakes].   *who...him* As Clar. notes, the same construction as at *M.V.* 4. 1. 134–5, 'a Wolf, who hanged for human slaughter, | Even from the gallows did his fell soul fleet'. It is artificial to treat this as a 'participle used with a nominative absolute' (Abbott, § 376, citing the *M.V.* passage).

134. *Self-mettle* 'his own ardour' (D.N.S.). For 'self-' = 'one's own', see On. 'self-', 1.   *Self-mettle...him* Cf. *Lucr.* 707, 'Till, like a jade, Self-will himself doth tire' [Mal.].

137. *from a mouth of honour* 'with such outspoken language as befits a man of rank' (Deighton).

139. *difference...persons* no respect for differences of rank.   *Be advised* See G.

140–1. *Heat...yourself* Norfolk's wisdom here and throughout this speech is of a proverbial cast, as Foakes notes, but does not come very close to specific recorded proverbs.

148. *sap of reason* Cf. *Wint.* 4. 4. 562, 'There is some sap in this'.

150–1. *go along | By* 'guide my steps by' (Deighton). Conflation of 'go along with' (fig. in *Ham.* 1. 2. 15–16) and 'go by' (*R. III*, 2. 2. 153).

152–3. *Whom…motions* whom I so describe not out of personal malice, but from sincere motives. The language is that of the old physiology; see G. 'gall', 'motion' [J.D.W. after Foakes].

154. *July* (F2) F '*Inly*', the italics showing that '*Iuly*' was intended.

155. *each…gravel* In a rather similar passage, Sh. less explicitly links 'grain' with penetrating to the bottom of water: 'The providence that's in a watchful state | Knows almost every grain of Pluto's gold, | Finds bottom in th'uncomprehensive deeps' (*Troil.* 3. 3. 196–8). The 'clear | muddy' contrast is a favourite with Sh.: *Tit.* 5. 2. 171, with n. in this ed.

158–9. *fox…wolf* The traditional characters of both are invoked; cf. Tilley, F 629, 'as wily as a fox', W 601, 'as hungry as a wolf' [Foakes].

161–2. *his…reciprocally* It is his mind that makes him 'prone to mischief', his place that makes him 'able to perform it'; and each plays into the hands of the other. As Delius puts it, 'the minister in Wol. corrupts the man, as the man the minister'.

164. *suggests* See G.

167. *wrenching* This word raises a problem of modernization; it is a pun (now obsolete except in dialect) on 'rinsing' (which Pope read), but it is difficult to believe that it was merely fortuitous that Sh. chose the homophone (and, unless his spelling has been altered, the homograph) of a word he uses elsewhere with reference to violence, literal and figurative. Foakes (while wrongly denying that the meaning is 'rinsing') points to Buckingham's next speech as concerned with 'wrenching' = 'distortion of meaning'. We have to choose between imperfect modernization and

sacrificing some contextual suggestions of the original form.

168. *give...favour* 'do me the kindness to hear me out' (Deighton).

172. *count-cardinal* Foakes accepts Pope's 'court-cardinal', comparing 'king-cardinal' at 2. 2. 18, but the force of the latter expression is clear, whereas 'court-cardinal' could not easily mean more than 'a cardinal who is much about the court'. What is here required is an expression for a cardinal who takes upon him what does not belong to a cardinal as such. It is true that 'count-cardinal' is an odd choice, and Foakes is justified in pointing out that there is no other reference to Wolsey's status as Count-Palatine because of holding the see of Durham *in commendam* [Cap.]. But the word does at least suggest the secular nature of his activities. The statement in *O.E.D.* 'count', 3, that Wol. 'as Archbishop of York, was Count of Hexhamshire', is baseless.

178. *colour* See G.

183. *he* (F2); om. F. The second of two short pronouns could readily have been dropped, and as F is odd grammatically as well as metrically, it seems safer to emend.

184. *as I trow* The principal clause that should follow is lost in parentheses.

192. *buy and sell* See G., 'buy', and cf. Tilley, B 787, 'To be bought and sold' = 'to be tricked', and earlier instances in *O.D.E.P.* p. 58.

195. *mistaken* See G.

197. *appear in proof* For omission of a second 'in', cf. Abbott, § 394.   *proof* See G.   S.D. (F). *Brandon* Identity doubtful: in Hol., the arrest is performed by 'sir Henrie Marneie, capteine of the gard'. Foakes's suggestion that he is Charles Brandon, earl of Suffolk, is not very probable. It is true that Sh. knows

Suffolk's christian name at 5. 1. 56 (Foakes, p. 3), but this could well be drawn from Rowley's *When You See Me* (l. 139); and it would be odd so to introduce here a character who figures as 'Suffolk' in the rest of the play. It looks as if he chose a fairly prominent surname more or less arbitrarily, and without any specific holder in mind.

200. *Hereford* (Cap.) F '*Hertford*'. The name is regularly disyllabic in *R. II*, where 'Herford' is the normal Q, F spelling.

204. *practice* See G.

205. *to look on* Generally taken to mean 'and to witness', perh. rightly. But the asyndeton is odd, and I am inclined to take 'ta'en...present' as meaning 'taken from liberty to witness [euphemistic for 'undergo'] what is now happening'; cf. *O.E.D.* 'see', 10, for such phrases as 'see the day'. So Hunter, glossing 'look on' by 'attend to'.

208. *dye* The choice of word is prob. influenced by the thought of the vb. 'taint' (see *O.E.D.*), in which two words, = 'tinge' and 'accuse' (attaint) have come together. *O.E.D.*'s first fig. example of the sb. is from 1601 and the first in connexion with crime from 1665.

212. S.D. (J.).

218. *confessor* 'cónfessor' also at 1. 2. 149, and elsewhere in Sh. (though *Meas.* 2. 1. 35 is equivocal); contrast 1. 4. 15, 2. 1. 21, 4. 1. 88 (Fletcher).

219. *Parke* I adopt the normal mod. sp. (used also by Steev.) for the proper name, though in fact it seems to be Hol.'s error (<Hall) for 'clerk' [Clar.]. F '*Pecke*', Foakes 'Perk' <Hol. 'Perke'. *chancellor* (Theob. *ap.* Pope, ed. 2 <Hol.) F 'councellour'.

221. *Nicholas* (Theob. *ap.* Pope, ed. 2, < Hol.) F '*Michaell*' The name is given correctly at 1. 2. 147 (though there with an incorrect surname). Mal. notes that 'In the MS *Nich.* only was probably set down,

and mistaken for *Mich.*'; the mistake could be that of scribe or compositor, or even of the author working from his rough notes.

223. *spanned* See G., and cf. *Tim.* 5. 3. 3 n. for the Biblical background.

224–6. *I...sun* A very obscure image. Sh. first thinks of Buckingham as the shadow of his former self; this then suggests the idea of a shadow cast by misfortune which obscures his glory, and the two are loosely united by the conceit of the cloud of misfortune assuming the shape of Buckingham himself (Grant White, substantially). As far as I can see, 'by' cannot mean strictly 'by means of', but must be more loosely 'in the process of'.

226. *lord* (Rowe) F 'Lords'. Foakes (on l. 197) notes that this could be retained if Brandon = Suffolk, but it is prob. a coincidental error.   S.D. F. 'Exe.'.

I. 2

Authorship. Shakespeare.

Material. Hol. is more closely followed than in sc. 1, though there is also bolder conflation: the rebellion of the weavers belongs to 1525, and Katharine's championing of them is Sh.'s invention.

The accusations against Buck. come from Hol., pp. 862–4, 'the cardinall boiling in hatred against the duke of Buckingham, & thirsting for his bloud, deuised to make Charles Kneuet, that had beene the dukes surueior, and put from him...an instrument to bring the duke to destruction. This Kneuet being had in examination before the cardinall, disclosed all the dukes life. And first he uttered, that the duke was accustomed by waie of talke, to saie, how he meant so to use the matter, that he would atteine to the crowne, if king Henrie chanced to die without issue: & that he had talke and conference of that matter on a time with George Neuill, lord of Aburgauennie, vnto whome he had giuen his daughter in marriage; and also that he threatned

to punish the cardinall for his manifold misdooings, being
without cause his mortall enimie [ll. 132–42].

'The cardinall...procured Kneuet with manie com-
fortable words and great promises, that he should with a
bold spirit and countenance [ll. 129–31] obiect and laie
these things to the dukes charge....Then Kneuet partlie
prouoked with desire to be reuenged and ˜partlie mooued
with hope of reward [cf. 1. 1. 222–3], openlie confessed,
that the duke had once fullie determined to deuise meanes
how to make the king away, being brought into a full hope
that he should be king, by a vaine prophesie which one
Nicholas Hopkins, a monke of an house of the Chartreux
order beside Bristow, called Henton, sometime his confessor, had opened vnto him [ll. 142–50].'

Wol. then reported all this to the king, as implied in
ll. 1–8 of this scene, and Buck. was arrested (cf. *Material*
for 1. 1). Knevet's accusation continues (p. 864), 'the same
duke the tenth of Maie, in the twelfe yeare of the kings
reigne [1520], at London in a place called the Rose, within
the parish of saint Laurence Poultnie in Canwike street
ward, demanded of the said Charles Kneuet, esquier, what
was the talke amongest the Londoners concerning the kings
iourneie beyond the seas? And the said Charles told him,
that manie stood in doubt of that iourneie, least the French-
men meant some deceit towards the king. Whereto the duke
answered, that it was to be feared, least it would come to
passe, according to the words of a certaine holie moonke.
For there is (saith he) a Chartreux moonke that diuerse
times hath sent to me, willing me to send vnto him my
chancellor: and I did send vnto him Iohn de la Court my
chapleine, vnto whome he would not declare anie thing,
till de la Court had sworne vnto him to keepe all things
secret, and to tell no creature liuing what hee should heare
of him, except it were to me.

'And then the said moonke told de la Court, that neither
the king nor his heires should prosper, and that I should
indeuour my selfe to purchase the good wils of the communaltie of England; for I the same duke and my bloud
should prosper, and haue the rule of the realme of England'
[ll. 151–71; on l. 170, cf. n.].

Sh. then reverts to Hol., p. 856 for Knevet's dismissal because of 'greeuous complaints [which] were exhibited to [Buck.] by his farmars and tenants' [ll. 171–3], and resumes with p. 864, 'Then said Charles Kneuet; The moonke maie be deceiued through the diuels illusion: and that it was euill to meddle with such matters. Well (said the duke) it cannot hurt me, and so (saith the indictment) the duke seemed to reioise in the moonks woords. And further, at the same time, the duke told the said Charles, that if the king had miscaried now in his last sicknesse, he would haue chopped off the heads of the cardinall, of Sir Thomas Louell knight, and of others' [ll. 177–86].

The rest is from an earlier part of p. 864, where we are told how Buck. 'on the fourth of Nouember, in the eleuenth yere of the kings reigne [1519], at east Greenwich in the countie of Kent, said vnto one Charles Kneuet esquier, after that the king had reprooued the duke for reteining William Bulmer knight into his seruice, that if he had perceiued that he should haue beene committed to the Tower (as he doubted hee should haue beene) hee would haue so wrought, that the principall dooers therein should not haue had cause of great reioising; for he would haue plaied the part which his father intended to haue put in practise against king Richard the third at Salisburie, who made earnest sute to haue come vnto the presence of the same king Richard: which sute if he might haue obteined, he hauing a knife secretlie about him, would haue thrust it into the bodie of king Richard, as he had made semblance to kneele downe before him. And, in speaking these words, he maliciouslie laid his hand vpon his dagger, and said, that if he were so euill vsed, he would doo his best to accomplish his pretensed purpose, swearing to confirme his word by the bloud of our Lord' [ll. 188–209].

The other subject of the scene, the rebellion of the weavers, is based on Hol., pp. 891–2: on the occasion of the king's decision 'to make wars in France', 'by the cardinall there was deuised strange commissions, and sent in the end of March [1525] into euerie shire, and commissioners appointed, and priuie instructions sent to them... that the sixt part of euerie mans substance should be paid in monie or plate to the king without delaie, for the furniture of his war. Hereof followed such cursing, weeping, and exclamation against both king & cardinall, that pitie it was to heare.'

In spite of Wol.'s efforts, 'the burthen was so greeuous, that it was generallie denied, and the commons in euerie place so mooued, that it was like to grow to rebellion'. In particular, 'The Duke of Suffolke...persuaded by courteous meanes the rich clothiers to assent therto: but, when they came home, and went about to discharge and put from them their spinners, carders, fullers, weauers, and other artificers...the people began to assemble in companies', to the number of four thousand. The Duke of Norfolk gathered a force against them, and when he came to talk with them, 'it was told him by one Iohn Greene...that Pouertie was their capteine, the which with his cousine Necessitie, had brought them to that dooing' [cf. l. 37 n.].

After the rebels had dispersed, Henry 'came to West-minster to the cardinals palace, and assembled there a great councell, in the which he openlie protested, that his mind was neuer to aske anie thing of his commons which might sound to the breach of his lawes, wherefore he willed to know by whose meanes the commissions were so streictlie giuen foorth, to demand the sixt part of euerie mans goods.

'The cardinall excused himselfe, and said, that when it was mooued in councell how to leuie monie to the kings vse; the kings councell, and namelie the iudges, said, that he might lawfullie demand anie summe by commission, and that by the consent of the whole councell it was doone; and tooke God to witnes that he neuer desired the hinderance of the commons, but like a true councellor deuised how to inrich the king. The king indeed was much offended that his commons were thus intreated, & thought it touched his honor, that his councell should attempt such a doubtfull matter in his name, and to be denied both of the spiritualtie and temporaltie. Therefore he would no more of that trouble, but caused letters to be sent into all shires, that the matter should no further be talked of: & he pardoned all them that had denied the demand openlie or secretlie. The

cardinall, to deliuer himselfe of the euill will of the commons, purchased by procuring & aduancing of this demand,
affirmed, and caused it to be bruted abrode, that through
his intercession the king had pardoned and released all
things.'

Loc. (J.D.W. after Theob., Camb.)   *Entry* (F).
2. *level* See G.

3. *full-charged* See G.; carries on the military
image.

4. *choked* Pooler quotes Beaumont and Fletcher,
The Mad Lover, 1. 1. 96–7, 'If he mount at me, |
I may chance choke his battery', for the application to
cannon.

5. *Buckingham's; in person* (J.) F '*Buckinghams,*
in perſon,'.

8. S.D. (Camb.) F 'A...the Queene, vſher'd...
Norfolke. Enter the Queene, Norfolke and Snffolke
[*sic*]: ſhe kneels. King...him'.

10. *take place* See G.

13. *Repeat* See G.   *majesty.* (F4) F 'Maieſty'.

18. *solicited* 'informed by petitioners' (Clar.)
not...few The mod. order would be 'by not a few';
cf. Abbott, §§ 305, 420.

21. *hath* Not even a grammatical irregularity, as
the true antecedent of 'which' is 'the sending of
commissions', not 'commissions'.

27–8. *breaks | The sides* Common in Sh. for the
effects of strong passion; cf. *Tw. N.* 2. 4. 93–5 [Clar.];
Ant. 4. 14. 39 [Conrad; see note on ll. 39–41 in this
ed.].

36. *to* (F2) F 'too'; cf. 1. 1. 42 n.: rarer in
prepositional place, as here; cf. l. 101 n.

37. *danger...than* Far from being deterred by the
danger of their enterprise, they welcome it, as it were,
into their ranks. Cf. the answer to Norfolk reported
in Hol., p. 891, 'that Pouertie was their capteine, the

which with his cousine Necessitie, had brought them to that dooing', singled out by a marginal note, 'Pouertie and Necessitie capteins of the rebellion' [Hunter].

42. *front* The context suggests that *O.E.D.* is right in giving this the unique sense of 'march in the front rank'. Foakes objects that *file* 'never seems to be confused with *rank*', but it can be used of a body of men abreast, especially in connexion with marching: cf. *O E.D.* 7c (extended senses in *Cor.*: see G.); and *Sh. Eng.* 1, 114 n., where the file is described as 'the unit...in which the strength of an army was expressed'. For Wolsey to admit that he was in a position analogous to that of the front man in a file (in the modern sense) would be to concede too much to the accusation. The general impression is well conveyed by J.'s 'primus inter pares'. The existence of the phrase 'the first file', which Pooler quotes from Beaumont and Fletcher, *Little French Lawyer*, 1. 1. 167—so also Massinger, *Bondman*, 4. 2 (11, 74)—tells against interpreting 'file' in the modern sense.

44–5. *frame...alike* are the organizer of what then comes to be equally known by all. She takes up Wolsey's 'know' as an evasion: 'you may not *know* more, but it is because of you that it is there to be known at all'.

47. *their acquaintance* 'acquainted with them' (Clar.).

51. *or* (F2) F 'er'.

52. *exclamation* See G.

56. *subject's* (J.C.M.) F 'Subiects' Edd. 'subjects'', but Sh.'s normal form, with the definite article, is the sing.; cf. *Ham.* G. 'subject (the)'.

57. *compels* Cf. l. 21 n.

62. *Allegiance* Four syllables [Clar.]; so *1 H. VI*, 5. 5. 43, but nowhere else in Sh.

64. *This* Singles out 'obedience' for special attention; cf. *Mac.* 1. 7. 10, 'This even-handed justice'. Clarke glosses 'this obedience of theirs'. See also Schmidt, p. 1212, second half of column 2.

67. *business* (Warb. *ap.* Han.; Southern MS.) F 'baſeneſſe'; 'primer business' = 'business which requires more immediate attention' (Clar.); 'u' and 'a' are easily confused.

70. *single* individual.

75. *place* See G.

78. *censurers* See G.; the hostile implication is only in 'malicious'.

80. *new-trimmed* See G.; 'does not explain why the ships are attractive but why they are secure' (Pooler).

82. *once* in short, in a word. Schmidt cites among instances of 'once', corresponding to German 'einmal', 'to signify that the matter spoken of is a point of fact, for which there is no remedy'. (Temporal explanations, whether 'originally' (Vaughan) or 'at one time or other' (Steev.) are less satisfactory.)

83. *oft*, (Cap.) F 'oft', which some retain, taking it closely with 'Hitting'; but the meaning must be that what he is going to describe happens as often as what he has just described.

84. *Hitting...quality* See G.

85. *shall...should* Cf. Abbott, § 371.

86. *motion* See G. (iii).

87-8. *sit,* | *Or sit* (F) Han. 'sit, or sit |'. I see no point in transferring the irregularity from one line to the other.

91. *precedent* F 'Preſident', as usual.

93-4. *rend...will* 'the figure is that of plucking up a flower from the soil in which it thrives and sticking it in one's dress for mere personal gratification' (Deighton). Perh. 'flower' and 'in one's dress' are too specific: the whole passage suggests branches rather than flowers.

94. *Sixth* F 'Sixt', as usual.

95. *trembling* See G.; 'the trembling is perhaps not merely that of those who are obliged to contribute, but of those who exact the contribution knowing how dangerous it is to drive the people to extremities' (Deighton).

97. *root,* (Warb. *ap.* Theob.) F 'roote'.   *thus hacked* when it is thus hacked (going with 'the air... sap').

101. *to't* F 'too't'; frequent in this play.

102. S.D. (Rowe).

108. S.D.'s F 'Exit Secret. | Enter Surueyor'.

110. *Is run* See G., and cf. Abbott § 295.

111. *and* om. Pope, perh. rightly.   *learned* Clar. (after Steev.) notes Buckingham's record as a patron of literature; but Sh. has prob. no more to go on than Hol.'s 'eloquent' (p. 865; see 2. 1. *Material*).

114. *out of* from outside.

116. *disposed* See G.

116–18. *The mind...fair* The general idea is that of the familiar 'corruptio optimi pessima', first recorded in Tilley (C 668) from 1630 (in Latin); the most famous Sh. expression of it is in *Son.* 94, 13–14, 'For sweetest things turn sourest by their deeds: | Lilies that fester smell far worse than weeds' (Tilley, L 297; cf. also N 317).

118. *complete* The stress 'cómplete' is common in Sh., when the word is attributive (Schmidt, p. 1413).

119–21. *and...minute* A loosely attached, but perfectly intelligible, clause.

120. *Almost...listening* 'with our attention almost ravished' (Clar.). The text seems sound, though I cannot parallel the word-order.

126. *honour* Personified.

130–1. *collected | Out of* Cf. 3. 2. 294, 'Collected from his life'.

134. *he'll* For parallels to the future instead of conditional, Dyce cites *M.N.D.* 1. 1. 191 (Q), *Err.* 1. 2. 86, *Ado*, 5. 1. 271, *Cor.* 1. 9. 2.

139. *His* (Pope) F 'This', prob. caught from the following 'his', though most edd. retain it, J. glossing 'this particular part of this dangerous design'.

139–40. *point....wish,...person* (Cap., with 'point:'). F 'point,...wiſh...perſon;'. 'Not...wish' is most naturally taken as = 'not being favoured by the fulfilment of his wish' (Clar.), and, though F's punct. of l. 140 is not impossible, 'to...person' goes best with 'malignant'.

145. *fail?* (Rowe) F 'faile;'; see G.: 'failure to have issue' is the primary sense, but the context (cf. ll. 133–4) makes clear that the title is further contingent on the king's death.

147. *Henton* From careless reading of Hol. 'Nicholas Hopkins, a monke of an house of the Chartreux order beside Bristow, called Henton'.

148. *confessor* Cf. 1. 1. 218 n.

150. *of sovereignty* 'relating to his succession to the crown' (Clar.).

156. *feared* (Pope) F 'feare'.

164. *confession's* (Theob.<Hol.) F 'Commiſſions'. The phrase in Hol. comes, not from the source of this speech, but from a slightly earlier passage (p. 863) in which the duke told the monk 'that he had doone verie well, to bind his chapleine Iohn de la Court, vnder the seale of confession, to keepe secret such matter'.

167. *demure* See G.

168. *pausingly* Cf. 1. 1. 87 n.

170. *To win* (Grant White conj.) F 'To' F4 'To gain'. Sh. seems to have conflated two phrases in Hol., 'to win the fauour of the people' (p. 863, cited by

Clar. in support of Grant White's emendation) and 'to purchase the good wils of the communaltie of England' (p. 864).

175. *nobler* The soul, as such, is nobler than a 'noble person', and so the spoiling of it is the most serious consequence of his behaviour.

176–7. *Let...forward* Divided by Pope; one line in F.

180. *To* (anon. conj. *ap.* Camb.) F 'For this to', which has all the air of an undeleted false start. Edd. have generally followed Rowe in reading 'for him to', and Cap. in transferring 'for him' to the end of l. 179; pointless tinkering.

186. *Ha!* This favourite exclamation of Henry (cf. 2. 2. 62, 65, 3. 2. 61, 5. 1. 86) is taken from Rowley's *When You See Me You Know Me*, as Elze noted; it occurs there sixteen times.   *rank* All fig. senses of this word are related to the primary sense of unchecked vegetation. Here, 'full-grown' would make good sense—'had the plot developed to that degree?'— though 'gross', 'foul', 'corrupt', which various edd. give, are no doubt also implied.

190. *Bulmer* (Clar.<Hol.) F '*Blumer*'.   *remember* Not elsewhere in Sh. followed by 'of' [Clar.].

190–1. *I...servant* Divided by Pope; one line in F.

191. *sworn* Disyllabic [Dyce].

198. *would* For ellipse of subject, cf. Abbott, § 399.

199. *giant* As often, with a glance at the rebellion of the giants against the gods: cf. *Ham.* 4. 5. 121, 'That thy rebellion looks so giant-like'.

200. *may* See G.

201. *And...prison* For the use of 'and', cf. *Tim:* 3. 1. 47, 'And we alive that lived'.   *prison?* (Rowe) F 'Prifon.'.

203. '*the...father*'...'*knife*' Marked as quotations by Cap.

209. *irresolute purpose* Not, I think, specifically a wavering, as opposed to a firm, purpose, but a purpose which, as such, is unresolved by contrast with a performance.   *period* Generally taken as 'aim'. Better, 'conclusion', but I think there may also be a word-play on the sense 'full stop'. The surveyor's account had laid stress on the punctuation of Buckingham's speech by the appropriate gestures, and Henry carries this to its conclusion.

211–12. *If...his* Perh. based on Hol., p. 865, 'Then spake the duke of Norffolke, and said: My lord, the king our souereigne lord hath commanded that you shall haue his lawes ministred with fauour and right to you' [Boswell-Stone, p. 447, n. 2].

213. *By...night* An asseveration.   *night!* (Camb., Theob. with comma) F 'night'.

214. S.D. F 'Exeunt'.

I. 3

Authorship. Fletcher.

Material. The dramatic date, preceding Buck.'s trial, is still 1521. Sir William Sands, however, did not become Lord Sands until 1523 (cf. *Material* for 1. 4 on Viscount Rochford). The Lord Chamberlain is never named in the play, but corresponds historically to two different persons: in 1521 he was Charles Somerset, Earl of Worcester, but in 1527 (the true date of the episode in 1. 4) and thereafter he was the very Lord Sands of this scene, who appears under that name only in 1. 3–4.

The satire on Frenchified fashions is prob. topical in the main, but has some basis in Hol., p. 850 [1520], recounting how 'diuerse yoong gentlemen of England' behaved in an undignified way in France. 'And when these yoong gentlemen came againe into England, they were all French, in eating, drinking, and apparrell, yea, and in French vices and brags, so that all the estates of England were by them laughed at; the ladies and gentlewomen were dispraised, so that nothing by them was praised, but if it were after the French turne, which after turned them to displesure, as you shall heare.' On complaints from the Council, the king (p. 852) answered that 'if they saw anie about him misuse themselues, he committed it vnto their reformation [l. 19]. Then the kings councell caused the lord chamberleine to call before them diuerse of the priuie chamber, which had beene in the French court, and banished them the court for diuerse considerations; laieng nothing particularlie to their charges, & they that had offices were commanded to go to their offices.'

For the last part of the sc. (from l. 49), see *Material for* I. 4.

Loc. (Camb. after Theob.)   *Entry* (F).

2. *mysteries* mysterious fashions or behaviour. Pooler notes that there can scarcely be, as J. supposed, a reference to mummers in a mystery-play, as this is an 18th-century usage.

7. *shrewd* See G.

11. *They...it* One line in Pope; two, divided after 'legs', in F.   *legs* See G.

12. *That...before* 'who had never seen them walk before they adopted this new fashion, and therefore knew that they could walk upright enough if they chose' (Deighton).   *saw* (Pope) F 'fee', which is prob. what Fletcher wrote. Pooler cites *Bonduca*, 5. 2. (VI, 150); so *Bonduca*, MS., *M.S.R.* l. 1808; 'saw' in Folio, 4. 2. (VI, 127); *Wit Without Money*, 4. 4. 231; *Scornful Lady*, 3. 1. 186; *Valentinian*, 3. 1. 366; *Humorous Lieutenant* (= *Demetrius and Enanthe*), MS., *M.S.R.* l. 691. For Sh., see *Cym.* 5. 5. 126, with note in this ed.

13. *Or* (Collier) F 'A'; perh. defensible as 'spavin —what's more, springhalt'; Collier's emendation appears in the list of notes and emendations in his copy of F2, appended to Coleridge's *Seven Lectures on Shakespeare and Milton* (1856), p. 231.

14. *to't* F 'too't', F3 'too'', F4 'too'; to't' = 'in addition'; cf. *Mac.* 3. 1. 51 [Foakes]. Collier and Symons noted that F was poss., and most recent edd. return to it (cf. 1. 2. 36, 101 nn.).

15. *worn out Christendom* 'exhausted every Christian fashion' (Deighton). S.D. Here in Dyce (1857); after 'Lovell', l. 16, in F.

18. *clapped* See G., and cf. the sb. 'clap(-bill)' (*O.E.D.* 'clap' sb.1, 13). Foakes cites 'clapt upon the court gate' from a letter by J. Chamberlain, 25 March 1613 (*Letters*, ed. N. E. McClure (1939), II, 440). *court gate* Clar. notes that a gate of Whitehall is so named in Ralph Agas's Map of London, c. 1560: 'probably that designed by Holbein...facing Charing Cross a little south of the banqueting house'.

25. *fool and feather* Apparently a cant phrase. Foakes cites John Taylor, *The Praise and Vertue of a Gallant* (1623), B8², 'There's many a Gallant, made of foole and feather', with marginal note, 'Thats an Asse'. Cf. Marston, *Malcontent* (1604), 5. 2. 136–7, 'No fool but has his feather' [F. P. Wilson, privately].

26. *points of ignorance* 'because the knowledge of things not worth knowing is no better than ignorance' (Clar.).

27. *fireworks* There may be a subordinate reference to a firework display after the Field of Cloth of Gold (Steev.], or to contemporary ones at the wedding celebrations of Princess Elizabeth [Foakes], but the primary meaning seems to be not just 'whoring or getting illegitimate children' [Foakes], but 'whores' considered as transmitters of venereal disease. This is clear in the epigram of Henry Parrot, *The Mastive* (1615), G 1ᵛ, which Foakes quotes, with its heading, 'Sine Flamma combustus'; so Marlowe, *Faustus* (ed. W. W. Greg, 1950), B 539, 'a hot whore', explained by the S.D. in A 595–6, 'a diuell drest like a woman,

with fier workes'; Massinger, *The Unnatural Combat*,
1. 1. (1, 129), 'joint purchasers | In fire and water
works'; Shirley, *The Witty Fair One*, 4. 3., in *Works*,
ed. Gifford-Dyce (1833), 1, 334, '*Flame!* I bring none
with me, and I should be sorry to meet any fireworks
here'. *O.E.D.* 'firework' 4b, cites Swift, *Answer to
a Simile* (*Poems*, ed. H. Williams, 2nd edn., 1958,
p. 618), l. 38, 'Like fire-works, she can burn in water'.
See also Pope's 'To Mr John Moore', ll. 15–16 (*Minor
Poems*, ed. N. Ault and J. Butt, 1954, p. 161); *Dunciad
Variorum*, II, 176; *O.E.D.*, 'burn', 14e, and note on
Tim. 2. 2. 75 in this ed.

28–9. *Abusing...renouncing* The apparent parallelism is deceptive: 'Abusing...wisdom' refers to the
way they have behaved up to now, and goes with 'got
in France'; 'renouncing...travel' to what they must
now do, and goes back to 'leave' in l. 24. 'Abusing'
is more prob. a participle than a gerund after 'leave',
as Deighton thinks.

30–1. *tall...breeches* Clar. refers to the portrait of
Harry, Prince of Wales, prefixed to Drayton's *Polyol-
bion* (1613)—reproduced in *Sh. Eng.*, facing II, 204,
and as frontispiece to *Cor.* in this ed.—'in short breeches
reaching to the middle of the thigh, and long stockings',
and also cites Jonson, *Tale of a Tub*, 1. 4. 11, 'long
sawsedge-hose', 2. 2. 125, 'a paire of pin'd up breech's,
like pudding bags'. See M. C. Linthicum, *Costume in
the Drama of Sh. and his Contemporaries* (1936), p. 205,
n. 8, noting that 'the puffed breeches of Edward VI
were said to be "blistered"'.

31. *types* See G.

32. *understand* See G.; the quibble, for which
Clar. cited *Tw. N.* 3. 1. 79–80, seems to me less than
certain.

34. *privilegio* (F2) F '*Pruiilegio*'.   '*oui*' (anon.
conj. *ap.* Camb.) F 'wee' F2 'wear'.

37–8. *loss…of* Cf. *1 H. IV*, 5. 4. 105, 'O, I should have a heavy miss of thee'.

38. *vanities* See G.; also *1 H. IV*, 2. 4. 446, 'that vanity in years' [Foakes] and Fletcher, *Wild-Goose Chase*, 2. 3. [IV, 343] [Pooler].

41. *fiddle* Foakes quotes a passage from Fletcher, *The Honest Man's Fortune*, 5. 1. (X, 266) in support of the view that this word may carry a bawdy suggestion carrying on the 'lay down' of l. 40.

42. *The…going* One line in Pope; two, divided after ''em', in F.   *The…'em* 'fiddle' seems to have no specific sense here—'the devil take them and their fiddles'; perh. with a glance at the prov. 'The devil rides on a fiddlestick' (Tilley, D 263; first in *1 H. IV*, 2. 4. 477–8).

44–5. *beaten…play* 'not up to the pleasing tricks I once could play' (Deighton); for the specifically sexual suggestions in 'play', Foakes cites *Wint*. I. 2. 187–8, on which see M. M. Mahood, *Sh.'s Wordplay* (1957), pp. 149–50.

47. *Held* 'have it held' (Clar.).

48. *colt's tooth* Cf. Tilley, C 525, 'He has a colt's tooth in his head' (already in Chaucer: *O.D.E.P.* p. 102).

49. *Nor…not* For double negative, cf. 2. 3. 67–8 (where Clar. cites *M.V.* 5. 1. 35), Abbott, § 406.

54. *I'll assure you* Also at *H. V*, 3. 6. 61; cf. *Tim.* I. 2. 221, 'I'll tell you', with note in this ed.

55. *That…indeed* One line in Pope; two, divided after 'churchman' in F.

59. *He…him* One line in Pope; two, divided after 'lord', in F.   *has* F 'Ha's'. Grant White, Clar. and Pooler (in note; correctly in apparatus) misquote F as reading 'h'as', and the last two say it='he has'. In fact it is common (e.g. l. 41; cf. Franz, § 55) as the third person corresponding to 'ha'' for 'have'; so

that there is simple ellipse of 'he'—cf. Abbott, § 400.

61. *Men...liberal* Noble cites 1 Tim. iii. 2 (Bishop's Bible), 'A Bishop therefore must be...a louer of hospitalitie'.

63. *But...stays* One line in Pope; two, divided after 'ones', in F. There is no reason in the length of the line for this division, which was prob. introduced so that the scene should end exactly at the foot of a column.

64. *shall along* Cf. Abbott, § 405.

66. *Guildford* F has throughout the phonetic '*Guilford*'.

67. S.D. F 'Exeunt'.

I. 4

Authorship. Fletcher.

Material. This episode is briefly mentioned by Hol. (p. 894) at the time of its occurrence, 3 January 1527. The full description used here occurs, undated, in the retro-spective account of Wol.'s career (pp. 921–2), and was taken by Hol. from Stow, and by Stow from Cavendish, an eye-witness. The initial S.D. is based on p. 922, 'the tables were set in the chamber of presence iust couered, & the lord cardinall sitting vnder the cloth of estate, there hauing all his seruice alone: and then was there set a ladie with a noble man, or a gentleman and a gentlewoman throughout all the tables in the chamber on the one side, which were made and ioined as it were but one table, all which order and deuise was doone by the Lord Sandes then lord chamber-leine to the king and by sir Henrie Gilford, comptrollor of the kings maiesties house' [ll. 1–24].

On p. 921, after telling how 'when it pleased the king for his recreation to repaire to the cardinals house...there wanted no preparations or furniture', Hol. goes on to tell how 'On a time the king came suddenlie thither in a maske with a dozen maskers all in garments like sheepheards [l. 63 S D.]'. He 'came by water to the water gate without anie noise, where were laid diuerse chambers and guns charged with shot, and at his landing they were shot off' [l. 48, S.D.]. The description of the setting of the tables, quoted above, follows: 'Then immediatlie after the great chamberleine, and the said comptrollor, sent to looke what it should meane (as though they knew nothing of the matter) who, looking out of the windowes into the Thames, returned againe and shewed him, that it seemed they were noblemen and strangers that arriued at his bridge, comming as ambassadours from some forren prince [ll. 53–6].

'With that (quoth the cardinall) I desire you, bicause you can speake French, to take the paines to go into the hall, there to receiue them according to their estates, and to conduct them into this chamber, where they shall see vs, and all these noble personages being merie at our banket, desiring them to sit downe with vs, and to take part of our fare' [ll. 56–60]. They are received, and 'At their entring into the chamber two and two togither, they went directlie before the cardinall, where he sate[,] and saluted him reuerentlie [l. 63, S.D.].

'To whom the lord chamberleine for them said: Sir, for as much as they be strangers, and can not speake English, they haue desired me to declare vnto you, that they hauing vnderstanding of this your triumphant banket, where was assembled such a number of excellent dames, they could doo no lesse vnder support of your grace, but to repaire hither, to view as well their incomparable beautie, as for to accompanie them at mum-chance and then to danse with them: and sir, they require of your grace licence to accomplish the said cause of their cōming. To whom the cardinall said he was verie well content they should so doo [ll. 65–74]....

'Then quoth the cardinall to the lord chamberleine, I praie you (quoth he) that you would shew them, that me seemeth there should be a nobleman amongst them, who is more meet to occupie this seat and place than I am, to whome I would most gladlie surrender the same according to my dutie, if I knew him [ll. 77–81].

'Then spake the lord chamberleine to them in French, and they rounding him in the eare, the lord chamberlein said to my lord cardinall: Sir (quoth he) they confesse, that among them there is such a noble personage, whome, if your grace can appoint him out from the rest, he is content to disclose himselfe, and to accept your place. With that the cardinall taking good aduisement among them, at the last (quoth he) me seemeth the gentleman with the blacke beard, should be euen he [misprinted 'be']: and with that he arose out of his chaire, and offered the same to the gentleman in the blacke beard with his cap in his hand. The person to whom he offered the chaire was sir Edward Neuill, a comelie knight, that much more resembled the kings person in that maske than anie other [ll. 82–9; the dramatist decides that the initial wrong choice is not to his purpose].' The king then 'disuisardeth his face and is verie pleasant [Marginal note]'. Wol. 'desired his highnesse to take the place of estate. To whom the king answered, that he would go first and shift his apparell, and so departed into my lord cardinals chamber, and there new apparalled him: in which time the dishes of the banket were cleane taken vp, and the tables spred againe with new cleane perfumed cloths, euerie man and woman sitting still, vntill the king with all his maskers came among them againe all new apparelled.

'Then the king tooke his seat vnder the cloth of estate... in came a new banket before the king....Thus passed they foorth the night with banketting, dansing, and other triumphs.'

Anne Bullen's father is given the title of Viscount Rochford, which he held at the true, but not at the dramatic, date of the episode. (On Lord Sands, cf. *Material* for 1. 3.) The introduction of Anne is the dramatist's invention. According to Hol. (p. 908; see *Material* for 3. 2), Henry's affection for her became known to Wolsey in 1529, but historians now regard them as having met about 1522—not long after the dramatic date of this scene.

Loc. (Cap.)   *Entry* (F).

1. *Ladies...grace* One line in Pope; two, divided after 'ladies', in F, which has the unusually elaborate sp.-pref. 'S. Hen. Guilf.'.

5. *merry* (J.) F 'merry:' F4 'merry,'.

6. *first* The contrasting 'then' (which Han. added after 'company') is not expressed.

7. S.D. (Cap.) F 'Enter L. Chamberlaine L. Sands, and Louell'.

12. *running banquet* See G. 'banquet'.

15. *confessor* Cf. 1. 1. 218 n.

20. *Place* See G.

26–9. *talk a little wild...bite none* Pooler cites Beaumont and Fletcher, *The Captain*, 1. 3. (v, 243), 'have talkt a little wildly...though they bite me not'.

30. *you* Cf. Abbott, § 220.   *with a breath* in the same breath; cf. *Ven*. 414.   S.D. (Steev.).   *Well said* See G.

31. *Gentlemen* (F2) F 'Gntlemen'.

33. *cure* See G.

34. *Let me alone* leave it to me.   S.D. (F).

38. S.D. (Theob.).

43–4. *red...cheeks* For the notion of red wine turning into blood, Foakes gives several quotations, including Marlowe, *2 Tamburlaine*, 3. 2. 107–8, 'airy wine, | That, being concocted, turns to crimson blood'.

46. *make my play* See G.

49. S.D. (F).

50. *some* one; cf. l. 60, and *Per*. 5. 1. 9.

52. S.D. (F).   53. *strangers* See G.

54. *They've* F 'th'haue'; this modernization (and 'you're' for 'y'are', etc.) is adopted throughout.

60. S.D. (after Cap.) F 'All rife, and Tables remou'd'.

61. *broken* See G.; perh. with a play on 'remains of a feast' (cf. 'broken meats'), which Pooler gives as the sole sense.

63. S.D. (F); for visiting masquers, see n. in this ed. on *Rom*. 1. 4. init. S.D.

73–4. *They...pleasures* Arranged by Pope; three lines in F, divided after 'grace', 'thanks'.

74. S.D. (Camb.) F 'Choofe Ladies, King and An. Bullen'.

76. S.D. (F).

81. S.D. (Cap.) F 'Whifper'.

84. *it* i.e. 'the place of honour' (Deighton).

85–6. *here...cardinal* See *Material* for the departure from Hol. at this point.

86. *royal choice* 'choice of a king' (Schmidt). S.D. (Cap.).

89. *unhappily* See G., and cf. Prol. 24 n.

90. *pleasant* See G.

91–6. *Prithee...you* This meeting is the dramatist's invention: see *Material* for the chronology.

94. *Sweetheart* Two words in F.; for this sp., and the stress on 'heart', cf. *Tit.* 1. 1. 481.

96. *kiss you* As customary at the end of a dance; cf. *Tp.* 1. 2. 378 (where it precedes the dance) [Clar.].

97. *Let...round* Cf. *2 H. IV,* 5. 3. 55 n.

104–5. *merry,...cardinal:* (F) But Warb.'s 'merry. ...cardinal,' has some plausibility.

108. *best in favour* handsomest.   *knock it* see G. S.D. F 'Exeunt with Trumpets'.

2. 1

Authorship. Fletcher.

Material. The trial of Buck. (13 May 1521) is described by Hol. p. 865, 'When the lords had taken their place, the duke was brought to the barre, and vpon his arreignement, pleaded not guiltie, and put himselfe vpon his peeres. Then was his indictment read, which the duke denied to be true, and (as he was an eloquent man) alledged reasons to falsifie the indictment; pleading the matter for his owne iustification verie pithilie and earnestlie. The kings attourneie against the dukes reasons alledged the examinations, confessions, and proofes of witnesses [ll. 11–17].

'The duke desired that the witnesses might bee brought foorth. And then came before him Charles Kneuet, Perke, De la Court, & Hopkins the monke of the priorie of the Charterhouse beside Bath, which like a false hypocrite had induced the duke to the treason with his false forged prophesies. Diuerse presumptions and accusations were laid vnto him by Charles Kneuet, which he would fane haue couered' [ll. 17–25]. The peers consider their verdict, and successively pronounce him guilty: 'Thus was this prince duke of Buckingham found giltie of high treason, by a duke, a marques, seuen earles, & twelue barons. The duke was brought to the barre sore chafing, and swet maruellouslie; & after he had made his reuerence, he paused a while. The duke of Norffolke as iudge said; Sir Edward, you haue heard how you be indicted of high treason, you pleaded thereto not giltie, putting your selfe to the peeres of the realme, which haue found you giltie' [ll. 26–36]. Sentence was then pronounced.

For the deeper causes of Buck.'s fall, the dramatist goes back to Hol. p. 855 [1520], just after the passage cited in *Material* for 1. 1, 'At length there was occasion offered him [Wol.] to compasse his purpose, by occasion of the Earle of Kildare his comming out of Ireland. For the cardinall knowing he was well prouided of monie, sought occasion to fleece him of part thereof...he accused him to the king, of that he had not borne himselfe vprightlie in his office in Ireland, where he was the kings lieutenant. Such accusations were framed against him when no bribes would come, that he was committed to prison, and then by the cardinals good preferment the earle of Surrie was sent into Ireland as the kings deputie, in lieu of the said earle of Kildare, there to remaine rather as an exile, than as lieutenant to the king, euen at the cardinals pleasure, as he himselfe well perceiued.'

With Buck.'s entry we revert to p. 865, 'The duke of Buckingham said, My lord of Norffolke, you haue said as a traitor should be said vnto, but I was neuer anie: but my lords I nothing maligne for that you haue doone to me, but the eternall God forgiue you my death, and I doo: I shall neuer sue to the king for life, howbeit he is a gratious prince, and more grace may come from him than I desire. I desire you my lords and all my fellowes to pray for me. Then was the edge of the axe turned towards him [l. 53, S.D.], and he led into a barge. Sir Thomas Louell desired him to sit on the cushins and carpet ordeined for him. He said nay; for when I went to Westminster I was duke of Buckingham, now I am but Edward Bohune the most caitife of the world. Thus they landed at the Temple, where receiued him sir Nicholas Vawse & sir William Sands baronets, and led him through the citie, who desired euer the people to pray for him, of whome some wept and lamented, and said: This is the end of euill life, God forgiue him....' [See also n. on ll. 107–11.]

The hints of a separation between Henry and Kath. come from Hol. p. 897 [1527], where a 'secret brute...that the marriage...was not lawfull' is mentioned: 'The king was offended with those tales, and sent for sir Thomas Seimor maior of the citie of London, secretlie charging him to see that the people ceassed from such talke' [ll. 147–53]; and p. 906 [1528], 'the king was not onelie brought in doubt, whether it was a lawfull marriage or no; but also determined to haue the case examined, cleered, and adiudged by learning, law, and sufficient authoritie. The cardinall verelie was put in most blame for this scruple now cast into the kings conscience, for the hate he bare to the emperor, bicause he would not grant to him the archbishoprike of Toledo'. He therefore sought to promote the divorce, and a marriage with the Duchess of Alençon [mentioned in the play at 2. 2. 40 and 3. 2. 85–6]. The king 'desired the court of Rome to send into his realme a legat, which should be indifferent, and of a great and profound iudgement, to heare the cause debated. At whose request the whole consistorie of the college of Rome sent thither Laurence Campeius, a preest cardinall, a man of great wit and experience...and with him was ioined in commission the cardinall of Yorke and legat of England.'

Loc. (Camb.)   *Entry* (Cap.) F 'Enter two Gentlemen at feuerall Doores'.

1. sp.-pref. F '1', '2': so throughout.

8. *Yes...upon't* One line in Pope; two, divided after 'he', in F.   *upon't* 'as the consequence of the verdict' (Clar.).

11. *in a little* See G. 'little'.

14. *defeat the law* 'and so evade the punishment' (Clar., citing *H. V*, 4. 1. 165).

15. *king's attorney* John Fitz-James, later Chief Justice of the King's Bench.

16. *Urged on* Prob., as Schmidt thinks, 'pressed his case on the evidence of', with 'urged' intrans. (as at 5. 3. 48), rather than trans., with 'on' adv.

18. *him* (F) F4, edd., 'have', unnecessarily. The construction is 'desired brought to him viva voce, to his face', with 'to his face' amplifying 'to him'. Mod. Eng. cannot say 'desired brought', but it can say 'wanted (or wished) brought', and mod. Amer. Eng. 'ordered brought'.

20. *Parke* (Foakes, sp. 'Perk') F '*Pecke*'; cf. 1. 1. 219 n.

23. *prophecies?* (Cap.) F 'Prophecies.'.

24. *which* i.e. which accusations.

27. *learnedly* Elaborating Hol.'s 'as he was an eloquent man'.

29. *Was...forgotten* 'either produced no effect, or produced only ineffectual pity' (Mal.).

40. *end* See G.

41. *attainder* (Rowe) F 'attendure'. Foakes, retaining F, notes that the sp. occurs in Hol., p. 928, though the word does not occur at all in the source of this passage.

42–3. *removed,...Surrey* F 'remou'd...*Surrey*,'.

44. *father* father-in-law.

47–9. *whoever...too* Examples of this given in Hol.

are Richard Pace (p. 872; cf. 2. 2. 120–8), and Sir William Compton (p. 878) [Vaughan].

48. *find employment* sc. for. A common type of ellipse; cf. 1. 1. 197 n.; Mal. cited *M.V.* 3. 4. 6, *J.C.* 1. 2. 311.

51. *fathom* F 'faddom'.

53. S.D. (F); 'Sir Walter Sands' (who has lost the peerage he had in 1. 3.—see *Material* there) should be 'Sir William Sands', which Theob. read.

55. *close* See G.

60. *sink* See G. As Pooler notes, the usage is common in Fletcher; but Sh. has it in *All's*, 5. 3. 180.

62–3. *The...justice* In Hol. (see *Material*) he merely says he bears no malice against his judges, not that their verdict is a fair one on the evidence.

63. *premises* *O.E.D.* cites as first example of 'previous circumstances'; the context suggests that it virtually='evidence' [Foakes].

65. *Be...will* whatever they are; cf. 5. 3. 47 n.

67. *evils* See G. and cf. *Meas.* 2. 2. 172 n.

71. *More...me* One line in Rowe; two, divided after 'faults', in F.

74. *only...dying* 'the only bitter thing; the only thing, in fact, which he feels to be a real dying' (Vaughan). Pooler cites Fletcher, *Elder Brother*, 5. 1. 244, 'The lofty noise your Greek made, only pleased me'.

77. *prayers...sacrifice* Cf. Ps. cxli. 2 (B.C.P.), 'Let my prayer be set forth in thy sight as the incense: and let the lifting up of my hands be an evening sacrifice' [Noble].

78. *And...name* One line in Pope; two, divided after 'heaven', in F.

85–6. *'Gainst...grace* Two lines in Pope; three, divided after 'with', 'grave', in F.

85. *take peace* Not elsewhere in Sh. for 'make peace' [Clar.]; cf. *Rom.* 3. 1. 156, 'take truce' [Pooler].

86. *mark* (Warb. *ap.* Han.) F 'make'; cf. *H. V*, 2. 2. 139 [Clar.], *R. III*, 2. 2. 39 n.

89. *forsake* 'Not used absolutely in Sh.' (Clar.).

93. *old time* Used for 'old age' in *L.L.L.* 1. 2. 17, though, as Foakes notes, it could be a personification here, as in *K.J.* 3. 1. 324; more apt, as involving the notion of Time *growing* old, is *Troil.* 3. 2. 184.

94. *monument* See G.

102. *lord high constable* Not mentioned by Hol. at this point, but he follows his account of Buckingham's death with a long excursus on this office, of which Buckingham was the last holder.

105–6. *seal...blood* Cf. *Sir Thomas More* (in *Sh. Apocr.*), 5. 4. 135–6, 'A very learned woorthie gentleman | Seales errour with his blood'.

106. *will* which will.

107–11. *My...fell* The source for this is a few pages further on in Hol. (pp. 869–70), 'This man [Henrie Stafford] raising warre against Richard the third vsurping the crowne, was in the first yeare of the reigne of the said Richard...betraied by his man Humfrie Banaster (to whome being in distresse he fled for succour) and brought to Richard the third then lieng at Salisburie, where the said duke confessing all the conspiracie, was beheaded without arreignement or iudgement'. Hol. goes on to note (cf. ll. 112–15) that the younger Stafford 'was by Henrie the seuenth restored to his fathers inheritance, in recompense of the losse of his fathers life'.

116. *Eighth* F 'Eight'; the normal sp. of the time, as 'sixt' of 'sixth'.

125. *from...man* i.e. from one whose words ought to carry special weight, as he is specially bound to tell the truth; cf. 4. 2. 143, *Cym.* 5. 5. 41 [Foakes]. There

may also be a hint of the different notion that dying
men are actually inspired. For examples of both
notions, cf. Tilley, M 514, 'Dying men speak true
(prophesy)'.

129–30. *fall...water* Cf. Ps. lviii. 6 (B.C.P.; =v. 7
in A.V.), 'let them fall away like water that runneth
apace' [Noble]; but the sense of 'fall away' is not the
same.

133. *long...life* He was in fact forty-three.

134–5. *Farewell...sad* Arranged by Cap.; one line
in F.

.136. *Speak...me* One line in Pope; two, divided
after 'fell', in F.   S.D. F 'Exeunt Duke and
Traine'.

146. *confident* i.e. 'of your discretion' (Deighton).

147. *shall* shall have it.

147–9. *did...Katharine* This bridges the gap between the first and the second of the play's main
themes, at the cost of telescoping the historical sequence
(see *Material*).

149. *held* See G.

155. *e'er* F 'e're'.

165. *hit the mark* Already proverbial (Tilley,
M. 667–9) [Foakes].

166. *this?* (F 3) F 'this:'.

168. *We...this* Either 'we are "in too public a
place" [Delius] here to discuss this matter', or 'we are
indiscreet in talking of such matters here' (Pooler).

169. S.D. F 'Exeunt'.

2. 2

Authorship. Fletcher.

Material. This bridge-scene takes only a few odd points,
towards the end, from Hol. For ll. 84–105, cf. p. 906 (end
of *Material* for 2. 1), where the reference to Campeius is

preceded by 'he [Henry] thought to know the truth by
indifferent iudges, least peraduenture the Spaniards, and
other also in fauour of the queene would saie, that his owne
subiects were not indifferent iudges in this behalfe. And
therefore he wrote his cause to Rome, and also sent to all
the vniuersities in Italie and France, and to the great
clearkes of all christendome, to know their opinions'.
Henry's insistence that Kath. should have the best advisers
(ll. 106–13) is from p. 907, 'he bad hir choose the best
clearks of his realme to be of hir counsell, and licenced
them to doo the best on hir part that they could, according
to the truth'. For Gardiner, see p. 907 [1528], 'the king
receiued into fauour doctor Stephan Gardiner, whose
seruice he vsed in matters of great secrecie and weight,
admitting him in the roome of doctor Pace, the which
being continuallie abroad in ambassages, and the same
oftentimes not much necessarie, by the cardinals appointment, at length he tooke such greefe therewith, that he fell
out of his right wits'. Pace's death, the dramatist's addition,
took place in 1536.

Loc. (Theob.)   *Entry* (F).
1. Chamberlain No sp.-pref. in F.
1–8. *My...sir* Usually regarded as 'the dramatist's
invention' (Foakes), but D.N.S. (p. xvi) thinks it may
have been suggested by Rowley, *When You See Me*,
M.S.R. 1266–9, 'Another Cittizen there is, com-
plaines | Of one belonging to the *Cardinall*, | That in
his Maisters name hath taken vp | Commodities,
valued at a thousand pound'.
2. *ridden* See G. 'ride'; *O.E.D.* records only as ppl.a.
9–10. *I...think* Arranged by Theob.; prose in F.
Whether verse was really intended is perh. doubtful;
Fletcher has already fallen into verse rhythms in the
letter, and ll. 7–8, 'his...sir', are perfectly regular
verse, and indeed almost entirely regular from l. 4,
'When'. S. Walker, with some tinkering, made the
whole letter verse (see Camb.).

10. S.D. (F).

16. S D. (Vaughan).

18. *doing;* (F, with colon)...*king-cardinall,* (F) Rowe, followed by many edd., unnecessarily reversed the punctuation, to make 'the king-cardinal' in apposition with 'the cardinal's doing'.

19. *blind* (*a*) as taking after his mother, Fortune; (*b*) as utterly regardless of other people (*O.E.D.* 3) [J.D.W.].

21. *Pray...else* One line in Pope; two, divided after 'do', in F.

35. *bless the king* She does so at 4. 2. 163 [D.N.S.].

41. *slept upon* See G.

42. *bold bad man* Cf. Spenser, *F.Q.* 1. i. 37. 7 [D.N.S.], and Fletcher and Massinger cited by Pooler.

47. *lump...fashioned* The image is biblical; Noble cites Rom. ix. 21; Wisd. xv. 7.

48. *pitch* See G.; the metaphor of 'lump', 'fashioned', is not carried on.

49. *creed* Here only in Sh.; first *O.E.D.* ex. in a non-religious sense [Foakes].

52. *not believe* For word-order, cf. *Tp.* 5. 1. 38, Abbott, § 305 [Clar.].

54. *the pope* Unexpectedly, instead of 'the devil'.

59. *find* find it.

60. S.D. (F, 'Exit Lord Chamberlaine, and the King...pensiuely.')

61. *sad* See G.; but obviously on the border-line of the mod. sense.

62. *ha* Cf. 1. 2. 186 n.

67. *this way* See G. 'way'.

71. S.D. (F).

74. S.D. (Theob.).

76. S.D. (J.).

77. *I...talker* 'that my professions of welcome be not found empty talk' (J.); on the contrast of words

and deeds, Steev. cites *R. III*, 1. 3. 351, 'Talkers are no good doers' [Tilley, T 64].

79. S.D. (Theob.).

80. S.D.'s (Cap.; so ll. 82, 83). *This priest* Wolsey (ironically), though Foakes oddly takes it to refer to Campeius.

81. *sick* 'with pride' (Clar.). *for his place* 'even to gain his position' (Clar.).

82–3. *If...have-at-him* Arranged by Pope; one line in F.

83. *one have-at-him* (Var., without hyphens). F 'one; haue at him', which Foakes retains, but Suffolk's 'another' is more natural with 'have-at-him' substantivally used. S.D. F 'Exeunt Norfolke and Suffolke'.

84. *precedent* F 'Prefident'; cf. 1. 2. 91.

90. *clerks* See G. I do not think the reference, in Hol. or in the play, is specifically to clerics, although the 'great clearkes of all christendome' are mentioned separately from the universities. The point is that they are experts (whether clerical or lay).

91. *I...ones, kingdoms* (Theob.) F '(I...ones... Kingdomes)', which quite mis-attaches 'in...kingdoms'.

92. *Have...voices* 'are at liberty to express their opinion freely' [Clar. after Delius].

94. *One general tongue* 'one to speak for all' (Pooler). *us* (F4) F 'vs.'.

103. *commanding,* (F4) F 'commanding.' F2 'commanding:'.

114. *secretary* Appointed 28 July 1529.

115. S.D. (F; J.D.W.) There is no need to give Wolsey an exit and a re-entry with Gardiner, as most edd. since Cap. have done. A gesture from Wolsey will be enough to have Gardiner ushered in.

116. S.D. (Cap.; so l. 117).

119. S.D.'s (i) (J.D.W.) (ii) (F; J.D.W. after Cap. 'Talk apart').

120–34. *My...persons* 'Note the strong dramatic effect of this somewhat grim conversation. After loud protestations of justice, Wolsey unblushingly scoffs at virtue, and shows himself indifferent to having caused the death of one who would not be his tool' (D.N.S.).

127. *a foreign man* 'employed in foreign embassies' (J.).

128. *died* The dramatist's addition to Hol.'s account, which itself belongs to 1528 (see *Material*); Pace did not die till 1536, six years after Wolsey.

134. *griped* See G. The exact force is not clear but it prob. means 'caught hold of disrespectfully, with improper familiarity'.

135. S.D.'s (i) (J.D.W.); (ii) F 'Exit Gardiner'.

137. *such...learning* 'hearing such learned disputations' (Deighton); or perh. 'the reception of such learned men' (Rolfe after Hunter). For placing of 'such', both edd. cite Abbott, § 423.

139. *furnished*. (F 2) F 'furnish'd,'.

140. *able* See G.

142. S.D. F 'Exeunt'.

2. 3

Authorship. Shakespeare.

Material. The only historical point here is from Hol. p. 928, 'On the first of September [1532] being sundaie, the K. being come to Windsor, created the ladie Anne Bullongne marchionesse of Pembroke, and gaue to hir one thousand pounds land by the yeare' [cf. l. 63 n.].

Loc. (Theob.)   *Entry* (F).

8. *To leave* Quite intelligible without the verb, ''s', which Theob. added; cf. Abbott, § 403.

9. *process*, (F2) F 'Proceſſe.'.

14. *quarrel*, (F2) F 'quarrell.'. See G. for J.'s, the simplest of many explanations.

16. *soul and body's* Cf. *R. II*, 2. 3. 62, 'love and labour's recompense' [Abbott, § 397]; and for the sentiment, *Ant.* 4. 13. 5–6, 'The soul and body rive not more in parting | Than greatness going off' [Mal.].

17. *stranger* See G.; not strictly true, as Tollet (*ap.* Var.) noted, since she remains princess dowager (3. 2. 70); but that is no reason for his forced interpretation, 'alienated from the King's affection'.

31. *Saving...mincing* 'in spite of your affectation' (Deighton).

32. *cheveril conscience* Proverbial; cf. Tilley, C 608.

36. *hire* Disyllabic.

40. *Pluck...little* 'come to a somewhat lower rank' (Clar. after Steev.).

43. *burden* F 'burthen'.

46. *little England* Perh. 'a secondary reference to the fact that Pembrokeshire was known as "little England [beyond Wales]", and that Anne Bullen's first promotion was to be Marchioness of Pembroke [l. 63]' (Clar. after Whalley *ap.* Var.).

47. *emballing* See G.

49. S.D. (F).

59. *note's* (Theob.) F 'notes'.

61. *Commends...opinion* 'presents his compliments' (Pooler); a variant on 'commends himself'.　　*of you* (Cap.) F 'of you, to you'. Pope 'to you'. Al. returns to F., but it seems more likely that 'to you' comes from l. 62 [Clar.].

63. *Marchioness* So Hol.: actually 'Marquess'.

67. *More...nothing* Cf. *Mac.* 1. 4. 21, 'More is thy due than more than all can pay' [Steev.].

67–8. *nor...not* Cf. 1. 3. 49 n.

75. S.D. (Pope; so l. 79).

78–9. *gem...isle* J. saw here a reference to the carbuncle, since 'any other gem may reflect light but cannot give it'; this is perh. over-literal: any gem is naturally thought of as bright, and so as 'lightening' its surroundings.

80. *spoke* = mod. 'have spoken' [Clar.; Abbott, § 347].   S.D. F 'Exit Lord Chamberlaine'.

81. *this it is* 'there you are' (Pooler); cf. *R. III*, 1. 1. 62 n.

85. *of pounds* bringing in pounds.

89. *forty* See G.

92. *mud* The source of its fertility [Steev.].

93. *with...theme* if I had the subject (your advancement) that you have [Deighton].

103. *salute...jot* 'cause my blood to rise the least in acknowledgement' (Clar.); for 'blood' as 'symbol of the fleshly nature of man' see many references in Schmidt.

107. S.D. F 'Exeunt'.

2. 4

Authorship. Shakespeare.

Material. This scene contains both the closest and the most effective use of Hol. in the play. The date is 18 June 1529. The initial S.D. draws on the retrospective account of Wol.'s career, pp. 920–1, 'Then had he his two great crosses of siluer, the one of his archibishoprike, the other of his legacie, borne before him whither soeuer he went or rode, by two of the tallest priests that he could get within the realme....Before him was borne first the broad seale of England, and his cardinals hat, by a lord, or some gentleman of worship, right solemnlie: & as soone as he was once entered into his chamber of presence, his two great crosses were there attending to be borne before him: then cried the gentlemen vshers, going before him bare headed, and

said: On before my lords and maisters, on before, make waie
for my lords grace. Thus went he downe through the hall
with a sergeant of armes before him, bearing a great mace
of siluer, and two gentlemen carieng two great pillers
of siluer'. The account of the trial itself furnishes (p. 907):
'The place where the cardinals should sit to heare the cause
of matrimonie betwixt the king and the queene, was ordeined
to be at the Blacke friers in London, where in the great
hall was preparation made of seats, tables, and other
furniture....The court was platted in tables and benches
in manner of a consistorie, one seat raised higher for the
iudges to sit in. Then as it were in the midst of the said
iudges aloft aboue them three degrees high, was a cloth
of estate hanged, with a chaire roiall vnder the same, wherein
sat the king; and besides him, some distance from him sat
the queene, and vnder the iudges feet sat the scribes and
other officers....

'Then before the king and the iudges within the court
sat the archibishop of Canturburie Warham, and all the
other bishops. Then stood at both ends within, the counsellors learned in the spirituall laws, as well the kings as the
queenes. The doctors of law for the king...had their
conuenient roomes. Thus was the court furnished. The
iudges commanded silence whilest their commission was
read, both to the court and to the people assembled. That
doone the scribes commanded the crier to call the king by
the name of king Henrie of England, come into the court,
&c. With that the king answered and said, Heere. Then
called he the queene by the name of Katharine queene of
England come into the court, &c. Who made no answer,
but rose out of hir chaire [ll. 1–12].

'And bicause shee could not come to the king directlie,
for the distance seuered betweene them, shee went about by
the court, and came to the king, kneeling downe at his feet,
to whome she said in effect as followeth: Sir (quoth she)
I desire you to doo me iustice and right, and take some
pitie vpon me, for I am a poore woman, and a stranger,
borne out of your dominion, hauing heere no indifferent
counsell, & lesse assurance of freendship. Alas sir, what
haue I offended you, or what occasion of displeasure haue

I shewed you, intending thus to put me from you after this
sort? I take God to my iudge, I haue beene to you a true
& humble wife, euer conformable to your will and pleasure,
that neuer contraried or gainesaide any thing thereof, and
being alwaies contented with all things wherein you had
any delight, whether little or much, without grudge or
displeasure, I loued for your sake all them whome you
loued, whether they were my freends or enimies [ll. 13–34].

'I haue beene your wife these twentie yeares and more,
& you haue had by me diuerse children. If there be anie
iust cause that you can alledge against me, either of dis-
honestie, or matter lawfull to put me from you; I am
content to depart to my shame and rebuke: and if there
be none, then I praie you to let me haue iustice at your
hand. The king your father was in his time of excellent
wit, and the king of Spaine my father Ferdinando was
reckoned one of the wisest princes that reigned in Spaine
manie yeares before. It is not to be doubted, but that they
had gathered as wise counsellors vnto them of euerie realme,
as to their wisedoms they thought meet, who deemed the
marriage betweene you and me good and lawfull, &c.
Wherefore, I humblie desire you to spare me, vntill I may
know what counsell my freends in Spaine will aduertise me
to take, and if you will not, then your pleasure be fulfilled.
With that she arose vp, making a lowe curtesie to the king,
and departed from thence [ll. 34–57].'

The following interchange with Wol. moves to a later
point in Hol.'s account of the trial, p. 908, 'Heere is to be
noted, that the queene in presence of the whole court most
greeuouslie accused the cardinall of vntruth, deceit, wicked-
nesse, & malice, which had sowne dissention betwixt hir and
the king hir husband; and therefore openlie protested, that
she did vtterlie abhorre, refuse, and forsake such a iudge,
as was not onelie a most malicious enimie to hir, but also
a manifest aduersarie to all right and iustice, and therewith
did she appeale vnto the pope, committing hir whole cause
to be iudged of him [ll. 74–121; on ll. 88–98, see note]'.

Sh. then reverts to the earlier passage where he had left it
at l. 55, 'The king being aduertised that shee was readie to
go out of the house, commanded the crier to call hir againe,

who called hir by these words; Katharine queene of England, come into the court. With that (quoth maister Griffith) Madame, you be called againe. On on (quoth she) ît maketh no matter, I will not tarrie, go on your waies. And thus she departed, without anie further answer at that time, or anie other, and neuer would appeare after in anie court [ll. 121–33]. The king perceiuing she was departed, said these words in effect: For as much (quoth he) as the queene is gone, I will in hir absence declare to you all, that shee hath beene to me as true, as obedient, and as conformable a wife, as I would wish or desire. She hath all the vertuous qualities that ought to be in a woman of hir dignitie, or in anie other of a baser estate, she is also surelie a noble woman borne, hir conditions will well declare the same [ll. 133–43].

'With that quoth Wolseie the cardinall: Sir, I most humblie require your highnesse, to declare before all this audience, whether I haue been the cheefe and first moouer of this matter vnto your maiestie or no, for I am greatlie suspected heerein. My lord cardinall (quoth the king), I can well excuse you in this matter, marrie (quoth he) you haue beene rather against me in the tempting heereof, than a setter forward or moouer of the same. The speciall cause that mooued me vnto this matter, was a certeine scrupu-lositie that pricked my conscience, vpon certeine words spoken at a time when it was, by the bishop of Baion the French ambassador, who had beene hither sent, vpon the debating of a marriage to be concluded betweene our daughter the ladie Marie, and the duke of Orleance, second son to the king of France [ll. 143–75].

Vpon the resolution and determination whereof, he de-sired respit to aduertise the king his maister thereof, whether our daughter Marie should be legitimate in respect of this my marriage with this woman, being sometimes my brothers wife. Which words once conceiued within the secret bottome of my conscience, ingendered such a scru-pulous doubt, that my conscience was incontinentlie accombred, vexed, and disquieted; whereby I thought my selfe to be greatlie in danger of Gods indignation. Which appeared to be (as me seemed) the rather, for that he sent vs no issue male: and all such issues male as my said wife had by me, died incontinent after they came into the world, so that I doubted the great displeasure of God in that behalfe [ll. 175–81].

'Thus my conscience being tossed in the waues of a scrupulous mind, and partlie in despaire to haue anie other issue than I had alredie by this ladie now my wife, it behooued me further to consider the state of this realme, and the danger it stood in for lacke of a prince to succeed me. I thought it good in release of the weightie burthen of my weake conscience, & also the quiet estate of this worthie relme, to attempt the law therin, whether I may lawfullie take another wife...not for anie displeasure or misliking of the queenes person and age, with whome I would be as well contented to continue, if our mariage may stand with the laws of God, as with anie woman aliue [ll. 181–202; 222–30].

'In this point consisteth all this doubt that we go about now to trie, by the learning, wisedome, and iudgement of you our prelats and pastors of all this our realme and dominions now heere assembled for that purpose; to whose conscience & learning I haue committed the charge and iudgement....Wherein, after that I perceiued my conscience so doubtfull, I mooued it in confession to you my lord of Lincolne then ghostlie father. And for so much as then you your selfe were in some doubt, you mooued me to aske the counsell of all these my lords: wherevpon I mooued you my lord of Canturburie, first to haue your licence, in as much as you were metropolitane, to put this matter in question, and so I did of all you my lords; to which you granted vnder your seales, heare to be shewed. That is truth, quoth the archbishop of Canturburie. After that the king rose vp, and the court was adiorned vntill another daie [ll. 202–22; 230–32].'

The reference to the appeal to Rome in ll. 233–5 and Henry's suspicions in ll. 235–7 draws on a later passage on p. 908, 'the legats...assaied if they could by anie meanes procure the queene to call backe hir appeale, which she vtterlie refused to doo. The king would gladlie haue had an end in the matter, but when the legats draue time, and determined vpon no certeine point, he conceiued a suspicion, that this was doone of purpose, that their dooings might draw to none effect or conclusion.' In making Campeius pronounce the adjournment, Sh. is prob. following the account later on p. 908 of the *final* adjournment (23 July) 'according to the order of the court of Rome', where Hol. repeats: 'This protracting of the conclusion of the matter, king Henrie tooke verie displeasantlie.'

Some of the details of Kath.'s attack on Wol. at ll. 105–15 are taken from Hol.'s summing-up after the fall of Wol. (p. 917), 'Here is the end and fall of pride and arrogancie of men exalted by fortune to dignitie: for in his time he was the hautiest man in all his proceedings aliue, hauing more respect to the honor of his person, than he had to his spirituall profession, wherin should be shewed all meekenes, humilitie, and charitie' and later, 'his sudden comming vp from preferment to preferment; till he was aduanced to that step of honor, which making him insolent, brought him to confusion'.

Loc. (Cap.)   *Entry* (F, except 'Archbishop' (J.; F 'Biſhop')).

6. *King* F 'K.', to avoid overrunning the line.

10–11. *Say...court* Prose in Cap.; two lines, divided after 'England', in F.

12. S.D. (F).

13. Q. Katharine No sp.-pref. in F.

13–14. *do...And to* Cf. Abbott, § 350.

17. *no more* Hol.'s 'lesse assurance' shows that this means 'no more than I have an impartial judge', and not 'no longer'.

27. *inclined.* (Rowe, with colon) F 'inclin'd?'.

28. *desire,* (Cap., with semi-colon) F 'Deſire?'.

29. *Or which* Pope om. 'Or', perh. rightly.

31. *were* For subjunctive in dependent clauses after 'know', cf. Abbott, § 301 [Deighton].

33. *gave* A negative must be supplied, not from any specific earlier line, but from the general force of the preceding questions.

40. *duty*, (Mal.) F 'dutie', which Vaughan retained, interpreting 'Against'=towards. (Mason, *ap*. Var., had noted that the sense demanded 'towards' or 'some word of a similar import'.) This is a poss. meaning of the word (*O.E.D.* 3), but would be harsh after 'against' in a more usual sense in l. 39; though the interpretation 'or aught against' which Mal.'s punctuation demands is also a little awkward.

48–9. *one | The wisest* the very wisest (though Hol. has simply 'one of the wisest'); Clar. cites *Cym*. 1. 6. 164, on which see note in this ed.; see also T. F. Mustanoja, *A Middle English Syntax*, Part 1 (1960), 297–9.

51–3. *they...lawful* I think that 'they' is the antecedent of 'that', and 'council' of 'Who' (cf. Hol. 'wise counsellors...who deemed'), and therefore (though no punctuation can really make it clear) I drop the comma after 'realm'.

62. *That...court* 'that you desire to protract the business of the court' (Mal.).

64. *What...in* 'the scruples felt by' (Deighton).

68–9. *Lord...speak* Arranged by Pope; one line in F.

69–70. *Sir...that* Arranged by Pope; one line in F.

70–3. *I...fire* Steev. noted the 'similar sentiment' of Hermione in *Wint.* 2. 1. 108–12.

79. *blown...coal* Prov. for stirring up trouble; cf. Tilley, C 465 [Foakes].

81. *abhor* See G.

86. *stood to* See G.

88–98. *Madam...truth* Foakes thinks this may owe something to Hall's account (ed. C. Whibley (1904), ii. 148; quoted in Boswell-Stone, p. 460 n. 1) of an earlier interview between Wolsey and Katharine, but the resemblances are slight, and there is nothing in the

speech that does not naturally follow from the decision
to give Wolsey a rejoinder to Katharine's charges.

91. *shall,* (Rowe) F '(Shall)'.

96. *gainsay my deed* 'deny what I have done'
(Clar.); cf., in a similar context, *Wint.* 3. 2. 56,
'gainsay what they did' [Pooler].

98–100. *If...wrong* 'if it be that he knows I do not
come within the scope of your report, he consequently
knows that I do come within the scope of your wrong,
i.e. that I have good reason to complain of being
calumniated' (Deighton, after Delius).

107. *cunning* (F 2) F 'eunning'.

108. *sign* 'set a stamp upon' (Clar.).   *in full
seeming* 'to all appearance' (Clar.).

112. *slightly* See G.

112–14. *now...will* 'You have now got *power* at
your beck, following in your retinue; and *words* therefore are degraded to the servile state of performing any
office which you shall give them' (J.). The plur. perh.
='power in its various manifestations'.

117. *spiritual;* (Theob., with colon); F 'Spirituall.'.

121. S.D. (F).

126. *Queen* F 'Q'; cf. l. 6 n.

127. sp.-pref. Gentleman Usher In Hol., the
'Griffith' of 4. 2. (see *Material*).

133. S.D. F 'Exit Queene, and her Attendants'.

138–9. *wife-like...commanding* Not entirely clear,
but prob. 'government'='self-control' and 'Obeying
in commanding'='obeying the dictates of self-restraint
even when giving commands' (Deighton).

140. *else* For position, cf. *Ham.* 1. 4. 33, 'His
virtues else'.   *speak...out* See G.

152–3. *but...lady* A parenthetical claim that he has
thanked God for such a lady. As Vaughan notes, this
would in normal grammar modify 'spake', giving quite

an absurd sense; · the anomaly, natural enough in speech, is no reason for Vaughan's 'lady spoke, or' for 'lady, spake one'.

153. *one the least* Cf. ll. 48–9 n.

155. *touch* See G.

157. *are...taught* know well already; cf. 'I am not to learn' (*O.E.D.* 'learn', 1 d).

160. *Bark...do* Cf. Tilley, D 539, citing Webster, *White Devil*, 5. 3. 95–6, 'one dog | Still sets another a-barking'.

164. *oft*, (F4) F 'oft'.

166. *speak* See G.

167. *And...to't* One line in Pope; two, divided after 'him', in F.　　*what* 'with regard to what' (Clar.).

174. *A* (Rowe) F 'And'.

178. *advertise* Always stressed on the second syllable in Sh.

182. *bosom* Thirlby's 'bottom', from Hol., 'conceiued within the secret bottome of my conscience', is tempting; but the image has already been altered by Sh.'s 'shook', and he may well have innovated further.

183. *spitting* Almost all edd. treat as a misprint for 'splitting' (F 2). But the figure of transfixing on a spit is forceful and appropriate; and I follow Kellner, *Sh. Wörterbuch* (1922), Sisson and Foakes in retaining it.

184. *which* 'refers loosely to the whole process just described' (Clar.).

185–6. *throng...pressed* Cf. *Lucr.* 1301–2, 'Much like a press of people at a door, | Throng her inventions, which shall go before', on which Mal. cited *K.J.* 5. 7. 18–20.

191. *the* (Rowe, 1714) F 'th''.

199. *throe* F 'throw', as always in Sh.

200. *wild sea* Technical for 'open sea'; cf. *Gent.*

2. 7. 32 (2nd ed.). But here the sense of 'turbulent' may well be present.

204. *yet* See G.

208. *reek* See G.

213. *state* See G. (vi), and Prol. 3 n.

214. *consequence of dread* 'issues terrible to contemplate' (Deighton).

214–15. *committed...doubt* Hol. simply makes Henry say, 'for so much as you your selfe were in some doubt'. Sh.'s 'daring'st counsel', with the implication that Linc.'s advice, if given, would have been against the marriage, seems to rest on Hol.'s account of the popular belief that it was he who first told the king that the marriage was not lawful (p. 906). If this is so, it is not necessary to adopt the contextual interpretation of Case (*ap.* Pool.), 'distrusted the advice which I should have ventured on most boldly (or with most confidence)'.

219. *summons. Unsolicited* (Theob., with colon) F 'Summons vnsolicited.'.

225. *drives* Pope's 'drive' is unnecessary; in sense, the subject is 'no dislike' [Vaughan].

230. *paragoned* See G.

235. S.D. (Cap.; so l. 240).

239. *return;...approach,* (F 4) F 'returne,...approch:'.   *return* This word in itself, quite apart from the source, and from what follows (e.g. 3. 2. 64), shows that Cranmer is not present. He was at this time abroad, collecting opinions on the marriage. His return is announced at 3. 2. 400.

241. S.D. F 'Exeunt, in manner as they enter'd'.

3.1

Authorship. Fletcher.

Material. The account of the visit of the cardinals in Hol., follows immediately on the passage cited at the end of *Material* for 2.4. The date is late July 1529. P. 908, 'the king sent the two cardinals to the queene...to persuade with hir by their wisdoms, and to aduise hir to surrender the whole matter into the kings hands by hir owne consent & will, which should be much better to hir honour, than to stand to the triall of law, and thereby to be condemned, which should seeme much to hir dishonour [ll. 93–7].

'The cardinals being in the queenes chamber of presence, the gentleman vsher aduertised the queene that the cardinals were come to speake with hir. With that she rose vp, & with a skeine of white thred about hir necke, came into hir chamber of presence, where the cardinals were attending. At whose comming, quoth she, What is your plesure with me? If it please your grace (quoth cardinall Wolseie) to go into your priuie chamber, we will shew you the cause of our comming. My lord (quoth she) if yee haue anie thing to saie, speake it openlie before all these folke, for I feare nothing that yee can saie against me, but that I would all the world should heare and see it, and therefore speake your mind. Then began the cardinall to speake to hir in Latine. Naie good my lord (quoth she) speake to me in English [ll. 16–50].

'Forsooth (quoth the cardinall) good madame, if it please you, we come both to know your mind how you are disposed to doo in this matter betweene the king and you, and also to declare secretlie our opinions and counsell vnto you: which we doo onelie for verie zeale and obedience we beare vnto your grace. My lord (quoth she) I thanke you for your good will, but to make you answer in your request I cannot so suddenlie, for I was set among my maids at worke, thinking full little of anie such matter, wherein there needeth a longer deliberation, and a better head than mine to make answer: for I need counsell in this case which toucheth me so neere, & for anie counsell or freendship that I can find in England, they are not for my profit. What thinke you my lords, will anie Englishman counsell me, or be freend to me against the K. pleasure that is his subiect? Naie forsooth. And as for my counsell in whom I will put my trust, they be not here, they be in Spaine in my owne countrie [ll. 50–91].

'And my lords, I am a poore woman, lacking wit, to answer to anie such noble persons of wisedome as you be, in so weightie a matter, therefore I praie you be good to me poore woman, destitute of freends here in a forren region, and your counsell also I will be glad to heare. And therewith she tooke the cardinall by the hand, and led him into hir priuie chamber with the other cardinall, where they tarried a season talking with the queene [ll. 175–82].'

Loc. (Theob.); cf. 1. 1, initial S.D.   *Entry* (F); this *may* have been a 'discovery' in Sh.'s theatre, but it is best not to impose it on the F text.

1. *Take...troubles* One line in Pope; two, divided after 'wench', in F.

3–14. *Orpheus...die* 'The substance of the song is found in blank verse in Beaumont and Fletcher, *The Captain*, 3. 1. [v, 263], "Music, | Such as old Orpheus made, that gave a soul | To aged mountains, and made rugged beasts | Lay by their rages; and tall trees that knew | No sound but tempests, to bow down their branches | And hear, and wonder; and the Sea whose surges | Shook their white heads in Heaven, to be as midnight | Still and attentive"' (Pooler; citation already in Craig).

9–10. *play...sea* For the rhyme, see Kökeritz, p. 198.

14. S.D. (F).

19. *near* Edd. since Cap. insert an exit here for the 'Gentleman'; but cf. 4. 2. 108 n., and *All's*, 2. 1. 91 n.

22. *their...righteous* and the business on which they come should be as righteous 'as they themselves should be good' (Clar.); but there is some attractiveness in F 2's 'are' for 'as': Kath. would then give the reason

for 'They...men'—'their business (in life) is a righteous one'.

23. *all...monks* Cf. *O.D.E.P.* p. 116, Tilley, H 586, 'The hood makes not the monk'; Sh. has the Latin 'cucullus non facit monachum' at *Meas.* 5. 1. 258.   S.D. (F, with 'Campian' (corr. Rowe) for 'Campeius'; J.C.M.); cf. l. 19 n.

24. *part of* 'to some extent' (Rolfe); cf. Hol. 'with a skeine of white thred about hir necke'.

25. *all* entirely (a housewife).

26. *reverend* (F 2) F 'reuerent'; the two forms are interchangeable at this time.

28. *chamber*, (Cap.) F 'Chamber;', which obscures for the modern reader the fact that 'May...chamber' is a conditional clause.

31. *corner* 'Perh. an echo of the proverb, "Truth seeks no corners" (Tilley, T 587), which emerges at l. 39 in the form "truth loves open dealing"' (Foakes); the whole phrase means 'deserves to be kept secret'.

38. *that...in* 'how I have behaved as a wife' (J.).

40. sp.-pref. F 'Card.', and so (or 'Car.') in the rest of the scene, though 'Wolf.' at l. 23 and 'Wol.' at l. 27. See Note on Copy, p. 114.   *Tanta... serenissima* The Latin is the dramatist's invention: Hol. merely says he 'began...to speake to hir in Latine'.

45. *strange, suspicious* strange (i.e. foreign) and therefore suspicious; S. Walker's 'strange-suspicious' (=strangely suspicious) misses part of the point.

51. *should* (F 2) F 'shoul'.

52. *And...you* Joined, as a parenthetic afterthought, with 'my integrity'.

53. *all* nothing but.

54. *by the way of* O.E.D. has no other quotations with the definite article; perh. 'come' strengthens the metaphorical colouring of the expression.

61. *your* (F 2) F 'our', caught from l. 60.

63. *still bore* has always borne.

66. *in a sign of* O.E.D. recognizes only 'in sign of' (cf. l. 54).

67. S.D. (Cap.; so l. 68).

74. *set* See G.

78. *fit* See G.; she thinks of her greatness as a disease from which she is to be freed.

82. *England* (J.) F 'England,'.

83. *profit;* (F 2, with colon) F 'profit'.

86. *desperate* 'reckless of consequences'.　　*honest* The word may suggest a reference back to l. 84—'give me honest advice' (Clar.)—but more naturally goes with 'be a known friend', i.e. 'come out honestly in public as my supporter'.

87. *live a subject* 'yet be allowed to live in England' (Deighton); the full sense of 'dare' does not carry over to this line, which is written rather as if 'can' had preceded.

88. *weigh out* The usual gloss is 'outweigh, and so compensate for' (Clar.), but this does not fit the context; what 'outweighs' in that sense is the object weighed (as O.E.D. 'weigh' 20, citing, recognizes), not the person weighing. With Hunter and Vaughan, I interpret, 'assess at their full weight'; so, as one poss. meaning, J.

100. *Heaven...yet* Cf. Tilley, H 348; G. Cross, *N. & Q.* ccvi (1961), 143–4.　　*judge* (Collier; earlier edd. with comma) F 'Iudge.'.

103. *cardinal* The 'quibble' is obvious and was noted by J., whom Foakes wrongly takes to be referring to a further, and less probable, pun on 'cardinal' and 'carnal', which seems in fact to have been first suggested by Kökeritz, p. 29.

110. *at once* all at once. I can find no support for Foakes's gloss 'at some time', though Vaughan proposed to read 'once' with that meaning.

113. *envy* See G.

115. *professors* See G.

117. *If...habits* Perh. glances again at the proverb quoted in l. 23 [cross-reference in Pooler].

119. *has* F 'ha's'; cf. 1. 3. 59 n.   *already* 'for two years before October 1528' (Clar.).

120. *old* In fact, forty-three.

123. *studies* See G.; the notion of learned research to find out such a curse seems more forcible than taking the word in the more general sense of 'diligent endeavours'.

124. *Make* let (the studies) devise for me: 'a defiance' (Pooler); others less plausibly take 'Make' as indicative.   *worse* '*i.e.* are "above this wretchedness"' (Pooler).

125–6. *let...friends* Vaughan compares *Tit.* 5. 3. 118, 'when no friends are by, men praise themselves' (Tilley, N 117, 'He dwells far from neighbors that is fain to praise himself').

134. *a constant woman to* For word-order, see Abbott, § 419a.

138. *Madam...at* One line in Rowe; two, divided after 'good', in F.

139. *My...guilty* One line in Rowe; two, divided after 'lord', in F.

145. *Ye...hearts* Foakes is prob. right in seeing an allusion to the prov. antithesis, 'Fair face, foul heart' (Tilley, F 3), as well as to the traditional 'Non Angli sed angeli', for which Steev. quoted Greene, *The Spanish Masquerado* (ed. Grosart, v, 275), '*England,* ...where as *S. Augustine* [rather, *Gregory*] saith, their be people with Angels faces'.

149. *Shipwrecked* F 'Shipwrack'd', as frequently.

151. *Almost no* scarcely any; so also *H. V,* 3. 6. 145, and cf. *R. III,* 2. 3. 39, 'You cannot reason almost with a man'.

151–2. *lily...field* Cf. Spenser, *F.Q.* II. vi. 16. 1, 'The lilly, Ladie of the flowring field' [Holt White *ap.* Var.]; and Matt. vi. 28 [Noble].

159. *For goodness' sake* Cf. Prol. 23 n.

166. *as even...calm* Craig cites Beaumont and Fletcher, *The Pilgrim*, I. I. (v, 155), 'as easie as a calm'.

168. *Madam...virtues* One line in Pope; two, divided after 'so', in F.

170. *was* (Pope) F 'was,'.

172. *lose* F 'loofe', a frequent sp. for both words.

175. *Do...me* One line in Rowe; two, divided after 'Lords', in F.   *Do...will* This suggests, though vaguely, a capitulation by Kath. which, as Vaughan noted, is unhistorical. But as she asks for counsel (after Hol.) at l. 182, perh. nothing definite should be read into this phrase.

175–6. *me;...unmannerly,* (F, Foakes) Most edd. accept 'me,...unmannerly;' from F4. But there is nothing wrong with F: 'if I have been unmannerly, it is excused by the fact that I am a woman etc.'.

179. *do my service* See G. 'service'; recorded in *O.E.D.* with 'pay', 'give', etc., but not with 'do'.

183. *set footing* Fairly common for 'set foot'; cf. *R. II*, 2. 2. 48.

184. S.D. F 'Exeunt'.

3. 2

Authorship. Shakespeare, ll. 1–203 ('have'); Fletcher, ll. 203 ('What')–458.

Material. This scene works up chronicle material fairly freely. Hol.'s account of the affair with Anne (ll. 31–45) follows immediately on the mention of Campeius's departure from England, after taking leave of Henry on 20 September 1529: pp. 908-9, 'Whilest these things were thus in hand, the cardinall of Yorke was aduised that the king had set his affection vpon a yoong gentlewoman named Anne, the daughter of sir Thomas Bullen vicount Rochford, which did wait vpon the queene. This was a great griefe vnto the cardinall, as he that perceiued afore-hand, that the king would marie the said gentlewoman, if the diuorse tooke place. Wherfore he began with all diligence to disappoint that match, which by reason of the misliking that he had to the woman, he iudged ought to be auoided more than present death. While the matter stood in this state, and that the cause of the queene was to be heard and iudged at Rome, by reason of the appeale which by hir was put in: the cardinall required the pope by letters and secret messengers, that in anie wise he should defer the iudgement of the diuorse, till he might frame the kings mind to his purpose.

'Howbeit he went about nothing so secretlie, but that the same came to the kings knowledge, who tooke so high displeasure with such his cloked dissimulation, that he determined to abase his degree, sith as an vnthankefull person he forgot himselfe and his dutie towards him that had so highlie aduanced him to all honor and dignitie. When the nobles of the realme perceiued the cardinall to be in displeasure, they began to accuse him of such offenses as they knew might be proued against him, and thereof they made a booke conteining certeine articles, to which diuerse of the kings councell set their hands. The king vnderstanding more plainlie by those articles, the great pride, presumption, and couetousnesse of the cardinall, was sore mooued against him; but yet kept his purpose secret for a while' [ll. 1–36].

For Hol.'s, and for the true, date of the marriage [ll. 38–45], see l. 42 n. The suggestion of a surreptitious departure by Campeius may (Boswell-Stone, p. 472) rest on Foxe's statement (p. 906) that he 'craftily shifted himselfe out of the Realme, before the day came appointed for determination, leauing his suttle fellow behind him, to wey with the king in the meane time, while the matter might be brought vp to the courte of Rome'; or perh. on the less full statement on p. 959, since it is the same sentence as mentions Anne's Lutheranism (see below), 'Cardinal Campeius dissembling the matter, conueied himselfe home to Rome againe', with marginal note, 'Cardinall Cãmpeius slippeth from the king'. Foakes, n. on ll. 56–60, less plausibly, cites Hall.

The following passage [ll. 63–74] again combines freely. The reference to Cranmer is from Foxe, p. 1689; Cranmer expressed himself against the Pope's dispensing power, 'And thus by meanes of Doctor Cranmers handling of this matter with the king, not only certain learned men were sent abroad to the most part of the Vniuersities in christendome, to dispute the question, but also the same beeing by commission disputed by the diuines in both the Vniuersities of Cambridge and Oxforde, it was there concluded that no such matrimonie was by the worde of God lawfull.

'Whereupon a solemne ambassage was then prepared and sent to the Bishop of Rome, then [March 1530] being at Bononie [Bologna], wherein went the Earle of Wiltshire, Doctour Cranmer, Doctour Stokesly, D. Carne, Doctour Bennet, and diuers other learned men and gentlemen.' The Pope evaded discussing the issue, whereupon all but Crànmer returned to England. He went on to the emperor and gave satisfaction on the controversy to 'diuers learned men of Germanie' (p. 1690). The account of his appointment [consecration, 30 March 1533] to the see of Canterbury immediately follows. Hol. p. 923 mentions the mission abroad, but I do not think Sh. used the passage.

For ll. 67–71, Sh. reverts to Hol. p. 929 the 'marriage was kept so secret, that verie few knew it till Easter next insuing [1533], when it was perceiued that she [Anne] was with child'....'It was also enacted the same time, that queene Katharine should no more be called queene, but princesse Dowager, as the widow of prince Arthur.'

For the episode of ll. 75–203, Sh., as Steev. was the first to observe, uses the story told of Thomas Ruthall, Bishop of Durham, under 1508, the year of Ruthall's appointment (pp. 796–7), 'this bishop hauing written two bookes (the one to answer the kings command, and the other intreating of his owne priuate affaires) did bind them both after one sort in vellame, iust of one length, bredth, and thicknesse, and in all points in such like proportion answering one an other, as the one could not by anie especiall note be discerned from the other: both which he also laid vp togither in one place of his studie.

Now when the cardinall [Wolsey] came to demand the booke due to the king: the bishop vnaduisedlie commanded his seruant to bring him the booke bound in white vellame lieng in his studie in such a place. The seruant dooing accordinglie, brought foorth one of those bookes so bound, being the booke intreating of the state of the bishop, and deliuered the same vnto his maister, who receiuing it (without further consideration or looking on) gaue it to the cardinall to beare vnto the king. The cardinall hauing the booke, went from the bishop, and after (in his studie by himselfe) vnderstanding the contents thereof, he greatlie reioised, hauing now occasion (which he long sought for) offered vnto him to bring the bishop into the kings disgrace.

'Wherefore he went foorthwith to the king, deliuered the booke into his hands, and breefelie informed the king of the contents thereof; putting further into the kings head, that if at anie time he were destitute of a masse of monie, he should not need to seeke further therefore than to the cofers of the bishop, who by the tenor of his owne booke had accompted his proper riches and substance to the value of a hundred thousand pounds. Of all which when the bishop had intelligence (what he had doon, how the cardinall vsed him, what the king said, and what the world reported of him) he was stricken with such greefe of the same, that he shortlie through extreame sorrow ended his life at London, in the yeare of Christ 1523.' Wol.'s part in this incident would make it readily come to mind at this point. Cf. the first passage from pp. 908-9 cited above.

Foxe is also used in this section, for ll. 98-9, 'the Cardinall of Yorke perceiued the king to cast fauour to the Lady Anne, whome hee knew to be a Lutheran' (p. 959).

For the next section we return to Hol. p. 909, 'And further, the seuenteenth of Nouember [1529] the king sent the two dukes of Norffolke and Suffolke to the cardinals place at Westminster, who (went as they were commanded) and finding the cardinall there, they declared that the kings pleasure was that he should surrender vp the great seale into their hands, and to depart simplie vnto Asher, which was an house situat nigh vnto Hampton court, belonging to the bishoprike of Winchester. The cardinall demanded of them their commission that gaue them such authoritie, who answered againe, that they were sufficient commissioners, and had authoritie to doo no lesse by the kings mouth. Notwithstanding, he would in no wise agree in that behalfe, without further knowledge of their authoritie, saieng; that the great seale was deliuered him by the kings person, to inioy the ministration thereof, with the roome of the chancellor for the terme of his life, whereof for his suertie he had the kings letters patents [ll. 228–51].

'This matter was greatlie debated betweene them with manie great words, in so much that the dukes were faine to depart againe without their purpose [ll. 252–349]'. The next day they return with 'the kings letters', and Wol. gives up the seal.

The charges [ll. 254–64] of Surrey, who is not in Hol. present in this scene, revert to p. 855, already used at 2. 1. 40–4 (see *Material* on that scene).

The detailed accusations of ll. 299–332 go forward to the proceedings in parliament (p. 912): 'During this parlement was brought downe to the commons the booke of articles, which the lords had put to the king against the cardinall, the chief wherof were these.

1 First, that he without the kings assent had procured to be a legat, by reason whereof he tooke awaie the right of all bishops and spirituall persons.

2 Item, in all writings which he wrote to Rome, or anie other forren prince, he wrote *Ego & rex meus*, I and my king: as who would saie, that the king were his seruant....

4 Item, he without the kings assent carried the kings great seale with him into Flanders, when he was sent ambassador to the emperour.

5 Item, he without the kings assent, sent a commission to sir Gregorie de Cassado, knight, to conclude a league betweene the king & the duke of Ferrar, without the kings knowledge....

7 Item, that he caused the cardinals hat to be put on the kings coine....

9 Item, that he had sent innumerable substance to Rome, for the obteining of his dignities, to the great impouerishment of the realme.

These articles, with manie more, read in the common house, and signed with the cardinals hand, was confessed by him.'

The next lines [337–44] revert to p. 909, 'In the meane time the king, being informed that all those things that the cardinall had doone by his power legantine within this realme, were in the case of the premunire and prouision, caused his atturneie Christopher Hales to sue out a writ of premunire against him [9 October 1529]'. On 30 October he 'confessed the action, and so had iudgement to forfeit all his lands, tenements, goods, and cattels, and to be out of the kings protection'.

Cromwell's leaving of Wol.'s service for the king's [ll. 412–27] is noted by Hol. p. 913, 'at this time diuerse of his seruants departed from him to the kings seruice, and in especiall Thomas Crumwell one of his chiefe counsell'; the careful inventory of l. 451 is in Hol. p. 909; and finally, Wol.'s famous epitaph on his own career [ll. 454–7] is from p. 917, 'if I had serued God as diligentlie as I haue doone the king, he would not haue giuen me ouer in my greie haires'.

Loc. (Theob.)   *Entry* (F).

3–4. *omit...time* 'let slip the opportunity that now presents itself' (Deighton, citing, after Rolfe, *Tp.* 2. 1. 191, 'Do not omit the heavy offer of it').

8. *duke* Buckingham.

11. *neglected* A negative before this is understood out of 'uncontemned' [Mason, *ap.* Var.].

13. *Out of* See G.   *speak your pleasures* are at liberty to say what you please; a polite way of expressing the speaker's refusal to commit himself to agreement. The shade of meaning is not quite the same in *Troil.* 3. 1. 49 (see G. in this ed.), where what is turned aside is a compliment.

16. *Gives way* See G. 'way'.

22. *he* I take this as = 'Wolsey', with a shift to 'his' = 'the king's' in l. 23. J.D.W. prefers it as 'the king', with 'settled' = 'resolved' (cf. *Mac.* 1. 7. 79), and 'come off' = 'desist' (*O.E.D.*, 'come', 61 f.).

23. *come off* See G.

26. *contrary* This perh combines 'adverse' (the most usual Sh. sense) with 'inconsistent with what appeared on the surface', which is elaborated in ll. 30–3, and which some editors take to be the primary sense.

30. *letters* See G.

38–9. *coasts...hedges* See G., and cf. Tennyson on another worldly prelate, ''e creeäpt an' 'e crawl'd along, till 'e feeäld 'e could howd 'is oän' ('The Church-warden and the Curate', st. v).

40–1. *brings...death* A variant on the proverb, 'After death the doctor (physic)' (Tilley, D 133).

42. *married* In Hol. 14 November 1532; actually about 25 January 1533 (A. F. Pollard, *Henry VIII* (1905), p. 296).

44. *all my joy* 'all the joy I can wish' (Clar.).

45. *conjunction* See G.; Pooler is prob. right in questioning the assumption (Hunter and Clar.) that there is necessarily an astrological suggestion.

47. *unrecounted* 'The only example cited in *O.E.D.*' (Foakes).

49. *complete* Cf. 1. 2. 118 n. for the contrasting stress.

51. *fall* See G.; perh., as Foakes suggests, with a quibble on 'be born', as in *K.J.* 3. 1. 90. But even without this, the nature of the blessing is clear enough.

58. *Has* F 'Ha's'; cf. 1. 3. 59 n.

61. *cried 'Ha!'* Cf. 1. 2. 186 n.

64. *in his opinions* 'that is, not in person, but, as Tyrwhitt explains, having sent in advance the opinions

he had gathered' (Clar.). Others treat the return as
literal, but 'returned in his opinions' implies that he
he has not returned in the ordinary sense of the word.
Steev.'s 'with his opinions unchanged' must be wrong:
Cranmer's own opinions are neither here nor there.

66–7. *Together...colleges* The only natural way to
take this is as a second party that the opinions collected
have satisfied. To join 'his opinions...together with
[those of] all famous colleges' [Clar., tentatively], is
impossibly harsh. See *Material* for the respective roles
of Cranmer and of those who canvassed the universities.

72. *ta'en...pain* Elsewhere in Sh. 'take pains'
[Pooler], but 'pain' = 'pains' is not uncommon; e.g.
2 *H. IV*, 4. 5. 223 (in rhyme).

75. S.D. (F).

76. *packet* Foakes notes the special application
(*O.E.D.* 1) to 'the State parcel or "mail" of dispatches
to and from foreign countries'.

78. *Presently* See G.

82–3. *Is...abroad* Divided by Han.; one line in F.

84. S.D. F 'Exit Cromwell'.

85. S.D. (Rowe).

92. *to* against.

94. S.D. (Rowe).

96–7. *This...goes* I shall be expected to remove the
difficulties in the way of this marriage, which gives me
the chance of stopping it altogether [after Vaughan].
See G. 'snuff'. Most edd. misinterpret by taking
'snuff' in its mod. sense of 'extinguish'.

102. *Hath* that hath (Abbott, § 244).

104. S.D. (F 'Enter...Scedule'; Theob. 'and
Lovell').

105–6. *string...heart* 'in old notions of Anatomy,
the tendons or nerves supposed to brace and sustain the
heart' is *O.E.D*'s definition of 'heart-strings'; cf. *K.J.*
5. 7. 52–5.

107–10. *What...together* He is commenting on the schedule before he notices the lords, and Norfolk has to call his attention to Wol.'s presence.

111. *Saw you* In present-day English, 'Have you seen'; cf. Abbott, § 347, *Cym.* 4. 2. 66 n.

112. *commotion* Cf. 'mutiny' (l. 120), and *J.C.* 2. 1. 63–9 (cited by Deighton on l. 120), with n. on l. 66 in this ed.

116. *gait* F 'gate'.

119. *be* (S. Walker conj.; Al.) F 'be,'. Most edd. 'be;'. The F punct. is ambiguous, but 'it may well be that' gives better sense than 'it...be;', followed by 'There...mind', as if the king were putting this forward as something of which he had independent knowledge, and which explained Wolsey's behaviour.

123. *There,...conscience,...unwittingly?* (Cap., with colon after 'There') F 'There (...Conſcience...vnwittingly)', which Foakes retains; but the king must be swearing that he really did find it, not to the subordinate (and conjectural) detail that it was put there unwittingly.

124. *importing:* (Theob., with semi-colon) F 'importing'.

127–8. *outspeaks...subject* 'speaks of that which is beyond the usual possession of a subject' (Clarke).

132. *object* For the sing., without article, cf. Marvell, *Definition of Love*, l. 2, 'As 'tis for object strange and high'.

134. *below the moon* worldly; with special emphasis **on** the impure (sublunary) nature of the objects of his thought.

135. S.D. (F).

137. *stuff* See G. Whether there is a quibble on household stuff (l. 126), as Foakes thinks, is doubtful; the fig. 'inventory' perh. supports the idea.

140. *spiritual leisure* 'time withdrawn from earthly

business and devoted to religious duties' (Clar. after Vaughan).

142. *glad* (F2) F 'gald'.

144. *a time; a time* The repetition suggests that Sh. is thinking of Eccles. iii. 1–8, and the prov. 'There is a time for all things' (cf. Tilley, T 314–16).

153–4. *'tis...deeds* See Tilley, D 402, and other proverbs contrasting words and deeds cited there.

155–6. *with...word* Cf. *Mac.* 4. 1. 149, 'crown my thoughts with acts' [Steev.].

157. *kept* (F2) F 'kcpt'.

159. *havings* Here only plur. in Sh., except for the doubtfully authentic *Comp.* 235 [Clar.].

160. S.D. (Rowe). *should* Cf. Abbott, § 325, *Tim.* 4. 3. 400 n.

161. S.D. (Rowe).

168. *purposes* Subject of 'requite' and antecedent of 'which'.

171. *filed* (Han.) F 'fill'd'; for the corruption, cf. *Wint.* 4. 4. 607 [Clar.], and Fletcher, *Wit Without Money*, 3. 4. 7, where 'filed' (Q1) is corrupted to 'filled' in Q2, F [Dyce]. See G. for the meaning, and 1. 2. 42 n. for the corresponding sense of the noun.

172. *so that* only to the extent that; Latin 'ita ut' can have this same restrictive sense.

181. *honour* The antithetic 'foulness' shows, as Vaughan pointed out, that the reference is to an intrinsic quality, not='reputation', though the choice of word may have been prompted by the already current proverb (cited by Foakes), Tilley H 571, 'Honor is the reward of virtue'. There is a transition, though not a sharp one, to 'honour' as something bestowed in l. 185.

186. *any* on any.

188. *notwithstanding* No sense but 'in spite of' is attested, though Schmidt here gives 'over and above'

and J. 'besides'. There is clearly a contrast between 'duty' and 'love', and I take the sense to be 'though duty is normally the prime motive, yet here the special force of love should have even more effect'. This is a little forced, but is better than treating 'bond of duty' as that to the Holy See [Foakes], which has not been mentioned or implied in the dialogue.

190. *any* 'a loose expression for "than the hand... &c., of any"' (Clar.).

192. *am* Ellipse of a first pers. sing. is not common, but can be paralleled (cf. Abbott, §401), and is natural in rapid speech (so 'have' for 'have been'). With the whole phrase 'am...be', cf. *Troil.* 1. 3. 288, 'That means not, hath not, or is not in love' [Hunter].

193. *crack* Used of a bond also in *Lr.* 1. 2. 112.

198. *break* 'stem, as in "breakwater"' (Foakes).

201. S.D. (Pope).

202. *after*, (Theob.) F 'after'.

203. S.D. (F, with 'Exit King' for 'King departs'). *should* Cf. 3. 2. 160 n.

208. *makes...nothing* annihilates him [Delius].

209. *fear*, (Rowe) F 'feare'.

222–7. *Nay...more* Foakes sees in this an echo of Speed's *History of Great Britain* (1611), p. 769, 'Cardinall *Wolsey* fell likewise in great displeasure of the King...but now his Sunne having passed the Meridian of his greatnesse, began by degrees againe to decline, till lastly it set under the cloud of his fatall eclipse'.

226. *exhalation* See G.; the figure is common in the drama of the time: see esp. citations in Symons and Pooler.

227. S.D. (F, with 'Enter'; Cap. 'Re-enter').

228. One line in Pope; two, divided after 'cardinal', in F.

231. *my...Winchester's* Hol. has 'belonging to the

bishoprike of Winchester' (p. 909). Wolsey was himself still Bishop of Winchester; no doubt, as Boswell-Stone suggests (p. 474 n. 2), we are meant to think of the later Bishop, Stephen Gardiner (4. 1. 101 etc.).

236. *to do it* If this links with 'deny it' in l. 238, 'to render up the great seal' (Vaughan and later edd.) is preferable to J.'s 'to carry authority so weighty'.

237. *officious* The mod. sense was not yet common: *O.E.D.* has only one earlier quotation (1602), referring, oddly enough, to Wolsey.

239. *coarse* F 'courſe'.

241. *it* following my disgraces [Vaughan].

244. *Christian warrant* warrant in the habitual behaviour of Christians.

250. *Tied* See G.

255. *scarlet* Alludes both to the colour of the cardinal's robes and to the traditional notion of scarlet sins as in Isaiah i. 18 [Hunter].

260. *Ireland* Trisyllabic.

272. *That* Relative: the construction is 'I...that... dare'.

276. One line in Pope; two, divided after 'you', in F. *you; thou* The move from the formal to the familiar coincides with that from the office to the man.

281. *Farewell nobility* For 'the same expression and meaning' Pooler cites Fletcher, *Elder Brother*, 4. 1. 58; also below, 5. 3. 27.

282. *dare* See G.

291. *issues* See G.

292. *Who* (F2) F 'Whom', perh. the author's slip, as Dyce and Grant White remarked, but too violent to be retained, as no 'attraction' in the normal sense can explain it.

293. *articles* See G.

300. *Thus much* 'thus much I may say' (Clar., after Delius).

309. One line in Rowe; two, divided after 'head', in F.

313. *or else* This use (=simple 'or') is quite common in Sh. (see Schmidt, 'else'), though *O.E.D.* 'or', 5, does not record it after 1577.

314. *Ego...meus* Not in the original articles, which read 'had joyned himself with your Grace, as in saying and writing, *The king and I would ye should do thus*'. Pooler notes that the order of words in the phrase (which originated in Hall and was copied by Hol.) is normal in Latin, and that 'Wolsey's offence, if any, consisted in mentioning himself at all, not in putting himself first'. But Hall's use of the story (whether he invented it or found it current) surely implies that he knew this, but that he saw how the word-order could seem an offence to less skilled Latinists, as his addition of 'as who would saie, that the king were his seruant' shows.   *et* F '&'.

315. *inscribed* Foakes notes that the word is not found elsewhere in Sh., and that it is in origin a geometrical term.

322. *allowance* See G. Foakes notes that, though *O.E.D.* does not record this sense before 1628, it occurs elsewhere in Sh. (cf. Schmidt, 1). But the distinction from *O.E.D.* 2, 'approbation,...sanction', is a nice one.

325. *to* om. Pope, perh. rightly.

326. *innumerable substance* Hol.'s phrase; 'innumerable' with a sing. sb. is common (*O.E.D. a*).

339. *legatine* (Rowe) F 'Legatiue', which Foakes retains. But as Hol.'s form is regularly 'legantine', a misreading in F seems more likely than a deliberate alteration of the ending as well as of the second syllable.

343. *Chattels* (Theob.) F 'Caſtles'. Hol.'s form is 'cattels', so that perh. the form most likely to have stood in the MS. is 'Cattles'.

344. *of* (F2) F 'of'.

349. S.D. F 'Exeunt all but Wolſey'.

351. *Farewell!* (Var.; earlier edd. with comma) F 'Farewell?'. Some (following Hunter *ap.* Clar., which itself follows Var.) have retained F's punctuation, ='Did I say "Farewell"?...Yes, it is surely so'. But this is forced, and it is much more probable that the question-mark, as often, represents an exclamation-mark. Pooler quotes several instances of repeated 'farewell' in Fletcher, such as *Little French Lawyer*, 5. 1. 126–7, 'Farewell, wench, | A long farewell'; for the stylistic trick he also cites 'a frost, a killing frost' (l. 355).

353. *blossoms* Best taken as a vb., though F's capital suggests that the transcriber or compositor took it as a noun.

354. *honours* *O.E.D.* cites as first ex. of 6*b*, 'decoration, adornment'. It is thus applicable within the metaphor, to a tree, as well as directly to Wolsey. J. W. Mackail, citing this line in his note on *Aeneid*, 1, 591 (ed. of 1930), notes the usage as a Latinism.

359. *Like...bladders* Pooler, among other Fletcher parallels for the general run of ll. 358–61, follows Craig in citing *Wit at Several Weapons*, 1. 1. (ix, 67), 'a long great Ass that swims with bladders'. Cf. also Donne, *Sermons* (ed. Potter and Simpson), vi, 15. 619–20, 'and so, that bladder is pricked, upon which thou swommest'.

360. *This* Cf. Abbott, § 87.

365. *Vain...world* Renounced in the name of the child in the Anglican baptismal service [Noble].

369. *aspect* Always stressed 'aspéct' in Sh. *their ruin* the ruin they produce [Mal.].

371. *like Lucifer* Cf. Isa. xiv. 12, 'how art thou fallen from heaven, O Lucifer' [Douce]. Mal. noted that Churchyard attributed this comparison to Wolsey

himself: *Mirror for Magistrates,* ed. L. B. Campbell (1938), p. 507, ll. 358–9, 'my pryde, | For which offence, fell *Lucifer* from skyes'.

372. S.D. (F).

378. *know myself* 'Recognize my limitations and my sins and am able to transcend them' (Foakes, noting the popularity of the 'know thyself' catchword: cf. Tilley, K 175).

386. One line in Pope; two, divided after 'grace', in F.   *made...of* drawn that good lesson from.

387. One line in Pope; two, divided after 'have', in F.

393. *Sir Thomas More* The three events referred to in ll. 393–406 were in fact widely spaced in time. More became Chancellor on 24 November 1529 (Hol. p. 910), Cranmer was consecrated Archbishop on 30 March 1533 (though a reader of Hol. might readily place it in 1532), and Henry and Anne were secretly married, according to Hol. (but see note on l. 42) on 14 November 1532.   *More* F '*Moore*', as often.

399. *tomb...tears* J. stigmatized the phrase as 'very harsh'. Steev. noted the parallel in W. Drummond, *Tears on the Death of Maeliades* (1614), in *Poetical Works,* ed. L. E. Kastner (1913), I, 84, 'The Muses... haue raised of their Teares | A chrystall Tombe'. *orphans'* F 'Orphants'.   *him* (F) Cap., most edd., ''em', but the shift to the person is natural enough.

403. *hath...married* Cf. l. 42 n.

404. *in open* See G. Steev. takes this as a Latinism ('in aperto'); *O.E.D.* does not note it as such, though it does so treat the opposite 'in hid' ('in occulto', 'in abscondito').

407. One line in Pope; two, divided after 'down', in F.

415. *sun I pray* (Foakes) F 'Sun, I pray'. Edd. 'sun, I pray,'. The construction is 'that sun which I

pray may never set'. Foakes retains F's brackets round
'That...set', but dashes are clearer in a modern text.

420. *make use now* 'do not let the present advantage
slip' (Deighton, after Schmidt).

424. *hearts of iron*. Cf. *Tim.* 3. 4. 84 [Conrad].

433. *dull* Foakes suggests that this combines the
notions of 'inanimate' and 'gloomy, cheerless'.

441. *that sin* The sin of the angels is normally
called 'pride', but cf. Raleigh, *History of the World*
(1614), ii. xiii. 7, p. 432, 'ambition, which begetteth
euery vice, and is it selfe the childe and darling of
Satan....It was the first sinne that the world had, and
beganne in *Angels*'. Foakes (on ll. 358–64) notes that
earlier in Hol. (p. 837), Wolsey is led by 'ambition...
a diuelish and luciferian vice'. Milton, *P.L.* iv, 40,
joins 'Pride and worse Ambition'.

443. *cherish...Thee* Cf. Matt. v. 44 (Geneva),
'Love your enemies...doe good to them that hate you'
[Foakes].

449–50. *Thou...in* Arranged by Rowe; F divides
after 'martyr'.

451–2. *have...penny;* (Cap., with comma) F 'haue,...
peny,'. Theob. 'have;...penny,', which is equally
possible.

455–7. *Had...enemies* See *Material* for Hol.'s
version.

459. S.D. F 'Exeunt'.

4. 1

Authorship. Fletcher.

Material. The information in the opening dialogue
comes from Hol. p. 930, 'In the beginning of Maie [1533],
the king caused open proclamations to be made, that all
men that claimed to do anie seruice...at...the coronation...
should put their grant...before Charles duke of Suffolke,
for that time high steward of England, and the lord chan-

cellor and other commissioners. The duke of Norffolke claimed to be erle marshall, and to exercise his office at that feast' [ll. 15–19]. Then from pp. 929–30, 'the ladie Katharine Dowager...persisted still in hir former opinion, and would reuoke by no meanes hir appeale to the court of Rome. Wherevpon the archbishop of Canturburie, accompanied with the bishops of London, Winchester, Bath, Lincolne, and diuers other learned men in great number, rode to Dunstable, which is six miles from Ampthill, where the princesse Dowager laie, and there by one Doctor Lee she was cited to appeare before the said archbishop in cause of matrimonie in the said towne of Dunstable, and at the daie of appearance she appeared not, but made default, and so she was called peremptorie euery daie fifteene daies togither, and at the last, for lacke of appearance, by the assent of all the learned men there present, she was diuorsed from the king [23 May], and the marriage declared to be void and of none effect' [ll. 22–33].

The 'Order of the Coronation' [1 June], with ll. 37–55, is from p. 933, 'First went gentlemen, then esquiers, then knights, then the aldermen of the citie in their cloks of scarlet, after them the iudges in their mantels of scarlet and coiffes....After them [earls etc.] came the lord chancellor in a robe of scarlet open before, bordered with lettise: after him came the kings chapell and the moonks solemnelie singing with procession...then...the maior of London with his mace and garter in his cote of armes, then went the marquesse Dorset in a robe of estate which bare the sceptre of gold, and the earle of Arundell which bare the rod of iuorie with the doue both togither.

'Then went alone the earle of Oxford high chamberleine of England which bare the crowne, after him went the duke of Suffolke in his robe of estate also for that daie being high steward of England, hauing a long white rod in his hand, and the lord William Howard with the rod of the marshalship, and euerie knight of the garter had on his collar of the order. Then proceeded foorth the queene in a circot and robe of purple veluet furred with ermine in her here coitte and circlet as she had the saturdaie, and ouer hir was borne the canopie by foure of the fiue ports, all crimson with points of blue and red hanging on their sleeues, and the bishops of London and Winchester bare vp the laps of the queenes robe. The queenes traine which was verie long was borne by the old duches of Norffolke: after hir folowed ladies being lords wiues, which had circots of scarlet.' Items 9 and 10 in the 'Order' draw on a later passage, 'euerie duches had put on their bonets a coronall of gold wrought with flowers,...and euerie king of armes put on a crowne of coper and guilt, all which were worne till night'.

The description in ll. 62–94 continues to follow on p. 933, 'When she was thus brought to the high place made in the middest of the church, betweene the queere and the high altar, she was set in a rich chaire. And after that she had rested a while, she descended downe to the high altar and there prostrate hir selfe while the archbishop of Canturburie said certeine collects: then she rose, and the bishop annointed hir on the head and on the breast, and then she was led vp againe, where after diuerse orisons said, the archbishop set the crowne of saint Edward on hir head, and then deliuered hir the scepter of gold in hir right hand, and the rod of iuorie with the doue in the left hand, and then all the queere soong *Te Deum*, &c. Which doone, the bishop tooke off the crowne of saint Edward....

'When the queene had a little reposed hir, the companie returned in the same order that they set foorth...then she was brought to Westminster hall, & so to hir withdrawing chamber.'

Loc. (Theob.)   Entry (F).

8. *royal* 'well affected to their king' (Mal.).

9. *As* For this usage, to introduce a parenthesis, cf. *Per.* 4. 2. 14 n.   *let...rights* 'to give them their due' (Clarke).

12. *I'll assure you* Cf. 1. 3. 54 n.

20. sp.-pref. 2 Gentleman (F4, '2') F '1'.

33. *late* former; cf. 3. 2. 94 [Deighton]; it is true that it is not now regarded as having been a marriage, but it is laying too much stress on that to gloss 'late' as 'lately considered as valid', with Steev. and Clar.

34. *Kimbolton* F 'Kymmalton'. Foakes notes similar 16th-century phonetic spellings in the *Victoria County History of Huntingdonshire*, III (1936), 75. Hol. has 'Kimbalton', so perh. the form in F suggests personal knowledge.

35. S.D. (Cap.)

36. One line in Pope; two, divided after 'close', in F. S.D. *hautboys...flowers* (F); The Order, item 5, *gilt copper* W. J. Lawrence (*T.L.S.* 18 December 1930, p. 1085) notes the reference to this in the metaphor of *Troil.* 4. 4. 105. The Order, item 8, *Cinque-ports* see G.; cited by *O.E.D.* 1 *b*, as only ex. of this usage, but in fact it comes from Hol.'s margin. *in her hair* with her hair hanging loose. The phrase is Hol.'s. *As...them* (J.D.W. after Camb.) F '*Exeunt*, firſt paſſing ouer the Stage in Order and State, and then, A great Flourish of Trumpets'; Cap. first transferred the exit to follow l. 55: see note there.

42. S.D. (J.).

45. *Indies* Cf. 1. 1. 21 n.

50. One line in Pope; two, divided after 'happy', in F.

55. 1 Gentleman *And* (S. Walker conj.) F 'And'. This is a neater solution than transferring 'No...that' to '1 Gentleman', with F 3.   *falling* For the quibble, Foakes cites E.A., *Stɪange Foot-Post* (1613), B 2ʳ, 'falling Starres, whereunto wantons may bee compared'.   S.D. (J.D.W. after Cap.); for position in F of 'and...trumpets', see l. 36 S.D. n. Entry (F).

59. *rankness* See G.; sense (*a*) is primary; Foakes compares *Cor.* 3. 1. 66, 'The...rank-scented meiny', and Deighton *J.C.* 1. 2. 247 'stinking breath'. The reference need not be exclusively to breath.

59–60. *You...ceremony* Divided by Han.; one line in F.

74–5. *Had...lost* This suggests such mod. expressions as 'you would lose your head if it weren't fixed on'; Tilley, A 387, has a similar saying with 'arse'.

87. *makings* See G. Foakes notes that the mod. use of 'the makings of' is 19th century (*O.E.D.* first from Dickens, *Pickwick Papers*).

88. *as* namely; cf. Abbott, § 113.

94. *York Place* Mentioned to give occasion for the correction in ll. 95–7. The feast was actually in Westminster Hall, which a reader of Hol. could fail to distinguish from the palace of Westminster, though 'Westminster hall' and 'Whitehall' are distinguished in the passage immediately preceding the account of the coronation (p. 932).

95–7. *You...Whitehall* Cf. Hol. p. 923, 'after Christmas [1530] he [Henry] came to his ·manour of Westminster, which before was called Yorke place: for after that the cardinall was attainted...he made a feoffement of the same place to the king...& then the king changed the name and called it the kings manor of Westminster, and no more Yorke place'.

101. *Stokesley* Consecrated on 27 November 1530. Hol. mentions the appointment on p. 909.   *Gardiner* Consecrated on 3 December 1531.

102. *secretary* Cf. 2. 2. 114 n.

110–11. Arranged by Collier, 2nd ed.; F divides after 'him'.

110–12. *The...council.* So Hol., p. 929, 'Thomas Cromwell, maister of the kings iewell house [14 April 1532], & councellor to the king, a man newlie receiued into high fauour'.

117. S.D. F 'Exeunt'.

4.2

Authorship. Fletcher.

Material. The occasion is fictional, and links two widely separated events: the death of Wol. (29 November 1530) and that of Katharine (7 January [8 in Hol.], 1536].

The Wol. part begins with Hol. pp. 916–17. Wol. was arrested by the Earl of Northumberland on 4 November 1530, and taken ill on 22 November at Sheffield Park from which he set out on 24 November for Hardwick Hall (Notts.). 'The next daie [25 November] he rode to Notingham, and there lodged that night more sicke: and the next daie he rode to Leicester abbeie, and by the waie waxed so sicke that he was almost fallen from his mule; so that it was night before he came to the abbeie of Leicester, where at his comming in at the gates, the abbat with all his conuent met him with diuerse torches light, whom they honorablie receiued and welcomed.

'To whom the cardinall said: Father abbat, I am come hither to lay my bones among you, riding so still untill he came to the staires of the chamber, where he allighted from his mule, and master Kingston led him vp the staires, and as soone as he was in his chamber he went to bed. This was on the saturday at night, and then increased he sicker and sicker, vntill mondaie, that all men thought he would haue died: so on tuesdaie saint Andrewes euen, master Kingston came to him and bad him good morrow.' Two hours later he died as 'the clocke stroke eight...which caused some to call to remembrance how he said the daie before, that at eight of the clocke they should loose their master [ll. 11–30]'.

The account of Wol.'s character is drawn from two places. It begins with p. 922, 'This cardinall...was of a great stomach, for he compted himselfe equall with princes, & by craftie suggestion gat into his hands innumerable treasure: he forced little on simonie, and was not pittifull, and stood affectionate in his owne opinion: in open presence he would lie and saie vntruth, and was double both in speach and meaning: he would promise much & performe little: he was vicious of his bodie, & gaue the clergie euill example' [ll. 33–44]. Then it reverts to p. 917, 'This

cardinall...was a man vndoubtedly borne to honor: I think
(saith he [Campian]) some princes bastard, no butchers
sonne, exceeding wise, faire spoken, high minded, full of
reuenge, vitious of his bodie, loftie to his enimies, were they
neuer so big, to those that accepted and sought his freendship woonderfull courteous, a ripe schooleman, thrall to
affections, brought a bed with flatterie, insatiable to get,
and more princelie in bestowing, as appeareth by his two
colleges at Ipswich and Oxenford, the one ouerthrowne with
his fall, the other vnfinished, and yet as it lieth for an house
of students, considering all the appurtenances incomparable
thorough Christendome, whereof Henrie the eight is now
called founder, bicause he let it stand. He held and inioied
at once the bishopriks of Yorke, Duresme, & Winchester,
the dignities of lord cardinall, legat, & chancellor, the
abbeie of saint Albons, diuerse priories, sundrie fat benefices
In commendam, a great preferrer of his seruants, an aduancer
of learning, stout in euerie quarell, neuer happie till this his
ouerthrow. Wherein he shewed such moderation, and ended
so perfectlie, that the houre of his death did him more
honor, than all the pompe of his life passed [ll. 48–68]'.

For the vision, see n. on l. 82. For ll. 99–108, Boswell-
Stone suggests as a source p. 936: on 17 December 1533,
Henry sent to Katharine the Duke of Suffolk who 'discharged a great sort of hir houshold seruants, and yet left
a conuenient number to serue hir like a princesse, which
were sworne to serue hir not as queene, but as princesse
Dowager. Such as tooke that oth she vtterlie refused, and
would none of their seruice, so that she remained with the
lesse number of seruants about hir.'

The last episode goes on to p. 939, 'The princesse
Dowager lieng at Kimbalton, fell into hir last sicknesse,
whereof the king being aduertised, appointed the emperors
ambassador that was legier here with him named Eustachius
Caputius, to go to visit hir, and to doo his commendations
to hir, and will hir to be of good comfort. The ambassador
with all diligence did his duetie therein, comforting hir the
best he might: but she within six daies after, perceiuing hir
selfe to wax verie weake and feeble, and to feele death
approching at hand, caused one of hir gentlewomen to

write a letter to the king, commending to him hir daughter
and his, beseeching him to stand good father vnto hir: and
further desired him to haue some consideration of hir
gentlewomen that had serued hir, and to see them bestowed
in marriage. Further, that it would please him to appoint
that hir seruants might haue their due wages, and a yeeres
wages beside. This in effect was all that she requested, and
so immediatlie herevpon she departed this life the eight of
Ianuarie at Kimbalton aforesaid, and was buried at Peter-
borow.'

Loc. (Theob.)　　　*Entry* (F).

4. *So*— (Rowe) F 'So'; see G.

7. *think* (F 2) F 'thanke'.

10. *me happily* (F) Rowe, most edd., 'me, happily,',
interpreting 'happily' as 'haply'. But it may mean
'appropriately' (Foakes), and F's punctuation leaves
the decision to the reader.

17. *roads* See G.

19. *covent* A common form of 'convent' (cf.
'Covent Garden') up to about 1650 (*O.E.D.*).

31. One line in Pope; two, divided after 'rest',
in F.

32. *thus far* Cf. *Cym.* I. I. 24, 'You speak him
far' [Delius].

35–6. *by...kingdom* The Hol. passage that lies
behind this reads 'by craftie suggestion gat into his
hands innumerable treasure'. What Hol. meant by
'suggestion' is not entirely clear, nor what the dramatist took him to mean. The context suggests 'underhand
practice' (Schmidt). J.'s 'by giving the king pernicious
counsel' is also possible.

36. *Tied* F 'Ty'de'; Han. 'Tith'd', which is
attractive. If it is right, it may have been suggested by
Hol., p. 874, 'Order was taken by the cardinall, that
the true value of all mens substance might be knowne,
and he would haue had euerie man sworne to haue

vttered the true valuation of that they were woorth,
and required a tenth part thereof to bee granted towards
the kings charges now in his warres, in like case as the
spiritualtie had granted a fourth part' [cited by
Vaughan]. But in that case the dramatist would be
departing from Hol.'s 'gat into his hands', unless he
was assuming that Wolsey got a rake-off from the procedure described. On the whole, it seems best to
retain F, and interpret 'brought the whole kingdom
into a condition of bondage' [Clar.], even though this
makes the charge more remote from that in the sentence in Hol. which is the starting point.

38–9. *double...meaning* The exact contrast between
'words' and 'meaning' is obscure. The next line suggests that 'double in words' = 'using ambiguous expressions' and 'double in meaning' = 'performing
actions (e.g. 'pitiful' ones) with an intention other than
what appeared on the surface'. But the dramatist may
have taken over Hol.'s 'double both in speach and
meaning' without much reflection.

43. *Of...body* i.e. in sexual morals (Hol., 'vicious
of his bodie'); cf. 3. 2. 295–6.

45. *live in brass* Cf. Tilley, I 71, 'Injuries are
written in brass'.

45–6. *virtues...water* Cf. Beaumont and Fletcher,
Philaster, 5. 3. 83–4, 'all your better deeds | Shall be
in water writ, but this in marble' (on which Theob.
cited the present passage); Tilley, W 114.

50. *honour...cradle.* (Theob., with semicolon) F
'Honor. From...cradle'. The hyperbole conveyed by
the F punctuation seems out of place. The main, and
perh. the only, Hol. source is that cited in *Material*. Some
have thought the dramatist also used the slightly later
passage 'being but a child, verie apt to be learned',
which might give some slight support to F.

54. *sought him* Hol. 'sought his freendship'.

55. *unsatisfied* See G.; for this sense of negative participial adjj., cf. 'unavoided' (*R. II*, 2. 1. 268), 'unvalued' (*R. III*, 1. 4. 27) [Delius].

59. *Ipswich and Oxford* Wol.'s college at Ipswich did not survive him, as the dramatist noted, following Hol. p. 913, 'for bicause the college of Ipswich was thought to be nothing profitable, therefore he [the king] left that dissoloued'. The projected college at Oxford became Henry's foundation of Christ Church.

60. *good* Apparently abstract for concrete; 'goodness' = 'good man'.

70. *living* while alive; On. cites, *inter alia*, *R. II*, 5. 1. 39, 'thy last living leave'.

74. *religious...modesty* See G.

80. S.D. (F).

82. S.D. (F). *bays* bay-leaves, as symbols of triumph. *golden vizards* 'probably to indicate spirits' (Foakes, citing Dekker, *Old Fortunatus*, 1. 3. init. S.D., 'wearing gilded visards, and attirde like deuils'). *reverent* F 'reverend', as often; cf. 3. 1. 26 n. There is no chronicle source for this vision. Mrs E. E. Duncan-Jones, *N. & Q.* ccvi (1961), 142–3, suggests that it may be indebted to a dream dreamt just before her death by Margaret of Navarre, and recorded in her funeral oration. Margaret was the Duchess of Alençon mentioned at 3. 2. 85.

89. *thousand* Cf. Prol. 29 n. [Foakes].

94. *music* See G.

95. S.D. (F).

98. *And...eyes* It requires charity to see an effective 'dramatic pause' (Foakes) in the metrical irregularity, but the text may be sound. The most attractive correction is 'Mark you her eyes?' (Cap.)

99. S.D. (F).

101. *to* F 'too', as frequently in this phrase; cf. *Err.* 4. 1. 47 n.

108. S.D. (J.C.M.) F 'Exit Messeng. | Enter Lord Capuchius'. My version follows Foakes's comment—against the traditional (Cap.) exit and re-entry for Griffith—that 'there is no need for him to leave the stage in order to fetch or beckon for the waiting ambassador'; cf. 3. 1. 19 n.   Capucius F 'Capuchius' throughout.

113. One line in Rowe; two, divided after 'me', in F.

123. *here* in this world.

128. S.D. (Mal.).

132. *model* See G.   *loves*, (F4) F 'loues:'.

138. One line in Rowe; two, divided after 'dearly', in F.

141. *both my fortunes* my good and bad fortunes. Cf. Massinger, *Duke of Milan*, 1. 3. (I, 257), 'both fortunes', Beaumont and Fletcher, *Sea Voyage*, 5. 1. (IX, 61), 'either fortune'; and the title of Petrarch's *De Remediis utriusque Fortunae*.

143. *now...lie* Cf. 2. 1. 125 n.

145. *decent* Not elsewhere in Sh.

146. *let him be* even if he should be (cf. 1. 3. 4); that is, even nobles should not be left out of consideration, as if they were too high in rank to marry my women.

159. *fashion* See G.; the implication is that he would have no right to human shape if he behaved so inhumanly.

169. *maiden flowers* Cf. *Ham.* 5. 1. 227, 'maiden strewments' [Clar.]. Foakes cites the lists in *Wint.* 4. 4. 113–29 and *Cym.* 4. 2. 218–24.

171. *forth;...unqueened,* (Pope) F 'forth (...vn-queen'd)'.

173. S.D. F 'Exeunt leading Katherine'.

5. 1

Authorship. Shakespeare.

Material. Except for the announcement of the birth of Elizabeth, and the passing reference to Cromwell at ll. 133–5 (see note on ll. 34–5), entirely from Foxe, in his long biographical account of Cranmer, the actual date (not in Foxe) being 1544. The introductory dialogue [ll. 1–39] is fictitious, up to Gardiner's speech, which draws on Foxe, pp. 1693–4, 'certaine of the Counsaile, whose names neede not to be repeated[,] by the intisement & prouocation of his ancient enemie the Bishop of Winchester, and other of the same sect, attempted the king against him, declaring plainely, that the Realme was so infected with heresies and heretickes, that it was daungerous for his highnesse, farther to permit it vnreformed…[For passage omitted here, see *Material* for 5. 3.]…The king perceiuing their importunate sute against the archbishop (but yet meaning not to haue him wronged, and vtterly giuen ouer vnto their handes) graunted vnto them that they should the next day commit him to the Tower for his triall [ll. 39–54]. When night came, the king sent Sir Anthonie Denie about midnight, to Lambeth to the Archbishop, willing him forthwith to resort vnto him at the Court. The message done, the Archbishop speedily addressed himselfe to the Court, and comming into the Galerie where the king walked, and taried for him, his highnesse saide: Ah my Lorde of Canturbury, I can tell you newes. For diuers waighty considerations it is determined by me, and the Counsaile, that you to morrowe at nine of the clocke shall be committed to the Tower,…the Counsell haue requested me, for the triall of the matter, to suffer thẽ to commit you to the tower, or else no man dare come forth, as witnesse in these matters, you being a Counsellor.

'When the king had said his mind, the Archb. kneeled downe and said: I am content if it please your grace, with al my hart, to go thither at your highnes commandement, and I moste hũbly thank your maiesty that I may come to my triall, for there be that haue many waies slandered me, and nowe this way I hope to trie my selfe not worthy of such report.

'The king perceiuing the mans vprightnesse, ioyned with such simplicitie, saide: Oh Lorde, what maner a man be you? What simplicitie is in you? I had thought that you would rather haue sued to vs to haue taken the paines to haue heard you, and your accusers together for your triall, without any such induráce. Do not you know, what state you be in with the whole world, and how many great enemies you have? Do you not consider what an easie thing it is, to procure three or foure false knaues to witnesse against you? Thinke you to haue better lucke that waie, then your maister Christ had? I see by it, you will run headlong to your vndoing, if I would suffer you. Your enemies shall not so preuaile against you, for I haue other-wise deuised with my selfe to keepe you out of their handes. Yet notwithstanding to morrow when the Counsaile shall sit, and send for you, resort vnto them, and if in charging you with this matter, they do commit you to the tower, require of them, because you are one of them, a Counsailor, that you may haue your accusers brought before them without any further indurance, and vse for your selfe as good perswasions that way as you may deuise, and if no intreatie or reasonable request will serue, then deliuer vnto them this my ring, (which then the king deliuered vnto the Archbishop) [see *Material* on 5.3 for omission]...for... so soone as they shall see this my ryng, they knowe it so well that they shall vnderstande that I haue resumed the whole cause into mine owne handes and determination, and that I haue discharged them thereof.

'The Archbishop perceiuing the kinges benignity so much to him wards, had much ado to forbeare teares. Well, said the K. go your waies my Lorde, and do as I haue bidden you. My L. humbling himselfe with thankes, tooke his leaue of the kinges highnesse for that night.'

The final episode, ll. 157–76, is based on the bare announce-ment in Hol. p. 934, 'The seuenth of September [1533], being sundaie, betweene three & foure of the clocke in the afternoone, the queene was deliuered of a faire yoong ladie'.

Loc. (Camb.)   *Entry* (F).

9. *go* The subjunctive is commoner in Sh. after 'before' than the indicative (Franz, § 643).

13. *late* See G.

19. *feared* Prob. the passive form of 'they fear her that she will die' [Abbott, § 414].

24. *the* Anon. conj. *ap.* Camb. 'ye'; Al. 'thee' (but both speakers use 'you' throughout); 'the amen'='the appropriate amen' is good sense.

25. *sweet lady* Hyphenated in F.

28. *way* 'opinion in religion' (J.). They are both anti-Lutheran. Craig cites Acts ix, 2, 'any of this way'.

30. *of* from.

33. *As for* This does not affect the construction of the sentence (see *O.E.D.* 'as', 33 *b*), hence 'is', not 'he's', in l. 34.

34. *Beside that* as well as; irregular with no immediately following verb, but colloquially natural.

34–5. *jewel...secretary* Hol. (p. 929), refers to Cromwell as already 'maister of the kings iewell house' in 1533 (the appointment was made 14 April 1532), records his being sworne as Master of the Rolls on 19 October 1534 (p. 938), and mentions him as secretary in 1536 (p. 940), a post he had held since 1534 [Boswell-Stone].

36. *gap* 'the opening through which preferments pass' (Clar.).   *trade* See G. These two words together virtually form (as Conrad notes, p. 255) a hendiadys; 'the trodden path with the opportunities it offers'.

37. *time* (F4) F 'Lime'.   *Th'* Some edd. expand to 'The', but the stress 'árchbishop' is common in Sh., as in l. 80.

43. *Insensed* (Rann, ed. of 1791) F 'Incenſt'. See G.; it seems prob., and *O.E.D.* agrees, that this is the word intended; but there may well be word-play on 'incense'.

44. *For*, (Vaughan) F 'For'. Vaughan interprets, 'since I know it they are persuaded of it'. More

exactly, 'so' = 'provided that' [Deighton]: it is only
necessary for me to know it for them to know it too;
i.e. I can make them 'know' what I know. This is far
more pointed than taking 'so' as adv., and making
'I know', 'they know', two parallel clauses with
asyndeton.

45. *arch heretic* (Theob.) F 'Arch-Heretique'. The
hyphen is contrary to mod. usage: 'most' modifies
'arch'.

46. *moved* See G.

47. *broken* See G. 'break (with)'.

50. *hath* that he hath: impressionistic syntax.

54. S.D. F 'Exit Gardiner and Page'. Cap. post-
poned this to follow l. 55, but that line can be spoken
to a departing Gardiner.

55. S.D. (F).

56. *Charles* See 1. 1. 197 n.

61. *news?* (Rowe) F 'Newes.'.

64. *who* and she (the queen) [Vaughan].

66. *ha* Cf. 1. 2. 186 n.

72. *midnight* the middle of the night (not in con-
tradiction with l. 1). Foakes notes that the word was
more loosely used than now.

75–6. *that...to* 'subjects to which company would
not be favourable' (Deighton).

78. S.D. F 'Exit Suffolke'.   *Entry* Here in J.,
after 'follows' (l. 79) in F.

83. S.D. (after Rowe).

84. S.D. (Rowe).

85. S.D. (F).

86. One line in Cap.; two, divided after 'gallery',
in F.   S.D. (F).

87. S.D.'s (i) F 'Exeunt Louell and Denny';
(ii) (Cap.).

89–90. *How...you* Arranged by Rowe; three lines,
divided after 'lord' and 'Wherefore', in F.

90. S.D. (J.).

94. One line in Pope; two, divided after 'you', in F.

97. *unwillingly*, (F4) F 'vnwillingly'.

98. *grievous*, (F4) F 'greeuous.'.

104–5. *take…you* Cf. *Wint.* 3. 2. 230 [Clar.].

106. *you…us*, (F2) F 'you,…vs'. The meaning is, in Foxe's words (see *Material*), 'you being a Counsellor'; for omission of 'being', cf. Abbott, § 381.

108. S.D. (J.).

110–11. *winnowed…asunder* For this biblical figure cf. *Troil.* 1. 3. 28 (with note on ll. 22–30 in this ed., citing Luke xxii. 31, where 'winnow' is peculiar to the Geneva version [Noble]).

121. *indurance* See G. The word occurs twice in Foxe (see *Material*). In the first passage, the main source of these lines, the relevant words are 'any such indurăce'; 'further' comes from a few lines later, where Henry advises Cranmer to ask the next day (when he will have been a night in the Tower) to be allowed to answer the accusations 'without any further indurance'. The conflation is enough to account for the rather anomalous use of 'further' here, and there is no need to suppose that Sh. is thinking of the ordinary word 'endurance', or that 'further' means 'in addition' [Pooler], or that there should be a comma after 'indurance', so that 'further' goes with 'heard' [Cap.].

125. *Being…vacant* 'if it is devoid of truth and honesty' (D.N.S.).

129. *not ever* See G. 'ever'. Clar. is wrong in saying that 'not ever' is not found elsewhere in Sh.: cf. *Ado*, 2. 1. 323 (where the Q, F text must be retained).

131. *at what ease* how easily.

134. *potently opposed* The adv. is used rather as in *Ham.* 2. 2. 272, 'I am most dreadfully attended'.

139. *precipice* (F2) F 'Precepit', regarded by O.E.D. as a variant form rather than an error.

142. *is* which is.

152. *good man* F 'goodman', implying stress on the first syllable (as still in 'madman').

156. S.D. F 'Exit Cranmer'.   *He...strangled* Placed here by Han.; begins l. 157 in F.

157. S.D. (Cap.) F 'Enter Olde Lady'.   sp.-pref. F. 'Gent. within'.

163-4. *Ay...boy* She does not venture to disobey the king's instructions what to say; but she must then correct herself [J.D.W.].

168-9. *as...to cherry* In Sh.'s time, as now, the usual comparison is in terms of peas: Tilley, P 136; also E 66, 'eggs' (*Wint*. 1. 2. 130, cited by Conrad).

170. One line in Pope; two, divided after 'marks', in F.   S.D. F 'Exit King'.

173. *or scold* even if I have to scold.

174. *Said...him?* Cf. Rowley, *When You See Me*, ll. 288-90, 'shee that brings the first tydings howsoever it fall out, let her be sure to say the Childs like the father, or els she shall haue nothing' [Elze].

174-6. *Said...issue* With Al. and Foakes, I retain F's lineation. Steev. rearranged as three complete lines, divided after 'him' and 'now', by dint of expanding 'I'll' to 'I will' and ''tis' to 'it is'. This is arbitrary in the extreme.

175. *While...hot* Cf. Tilley, I 94, 'It is good to strike while the iron is hot'.

176. S.D. (after Cap.) F 'Exit Ladie'; Lovell's exit is ignored, as was his entry at l. 157, though he speaks at l. 169.

5. 2

Authorship. Fletcher.

Material. Foxe, p. 1694, continuous with that quoted on 5. 1: 'On the morrow about 9. of the clocke before noone, the Counsaile sent a gentleman Vsher for the Archbishop, who when hee came to the Counsaile chamber doore, could not be let in, but of purpose (as it seemed) was compelled there to waite among the Pages, Lackies, and seruing men all alone. D. Buts the kings phisition resorting that way, and espying how my lord of Cant. was handled, went to the kings highnesse and said: My Lorde of Cant. if it please your grace is well promoted: for nowe he is become a Lackey or a seruing man, for yonder hee standeth this half hower at the Counsaile Chamber doore amongste them. It is not so (quoth the king) I trowe, nor the Counsaile hath not so little discretion as to vse the Metropolitaine of the Realme in that sort, specially being one of their own number. But let them alone (saide the King) and wee shall heare more soone.'

Loc. (Cap.)   *Entry* (F).

4. S.D. (J.D.W.) F 'Enter Keeper'.

7. S.D. (F).

8. S.D. (Dyce).   *piece* (F 2) F 'Peere'.

10. S.D.'s (i) F 'Exit Buts'; (ii) (J.)   *Butts*, (F 3) F '*Buts*.'.

13. *sound* Disputed, but I think it is clearly a fig. use of 'sound'='fathom' [Schmidt]. There is prob. also a reference, as Delius thought, to the physician's profession: the vb. in medical contexts='probe' (*O.E.D.* 8).

14. *of purpose* Cf. *Tim*. 3. 1. 26 n.

17. *at door* For the omission of definite article, Clar. (on 5. 3. 140) cites *Lr*. 3. 7. 17 'at gate'; cf. also *Cor*. 3. 3. 138.

18. One line in Rowe; two, divided after 'lackeys', in F.

19. S.D. (F).

20. *sight*— (Rowe) F 'ſight.'.

21. *saw* has seen; cf. *Cym*. 4. 2. 66 n.

22. *Body o' me* An exclamation of Henry's also in Rowley, *When You See Me*, ll. 2601, 2678 [Clar.].

24. *pursuivants* F 'Purſeuants', as at *2 H. VI*, I. 3. 33, representing pronunciation.

25. *Ha* Cf. I. 2. 186 n.

31. *dance attendance* Cf. Tilley, A 392 (first in Skelton).

35. S.D. (J.C.M. after Cap.). For upper stage curtains, see J. C. Adams, *The Globe Playhouse* (1942), pp. 135–45 [Foakes, who also cites 'They draw the curtaines' from Massinger, *The Picture* (1630), L1ᵛ: a play from the rebuilt Globe]. Richard Hosley, *Sh. Survey*, 10 (1957), 78, notes that no action aloft in Sh. 'require[s] a curtain for a discovery', and comments in note 14 on the mention in l. 34, 'this may be regarded as fictional colouring appropriate to the situation of spying from a window'. But it is surely more natural if there really was a curtain; and in his more recent article on the music-room, Hosley cites this passage as possible evidence for 'the existence of a music-room at the First Globe between 1609 and 1613' (*Sh. Survey*, 13 (1960), 119). F has no exit here, and no new scene noted, though the scene is conceived as shifting to within the Council-chamber, taking Henry and Butts, as spectators, with it. As Henry reappears on main-stage level, the move is not obtruded on the audience; Cranmer must withdraw so that he can be brought in from 'without' (5. 3. 5). W. W. Greg, *The Sh. First Folio* (1955), p. 425, describes the procedure as 'clumsy', and writes, 'one would suppose that at the Globe there must have been a "discovery"'; but clearly the whole of the main stage is required for this elaborate scene.

5. 3

Authorship. Fletcher.

Material. The opening passage introduces Cranmer, as in the passage immediately following that quoted on 5. 2 (p. 1694), 'Anone the Archbishop was called into the Counsaile chamber, to whom was alleadged, as before is rehearsed'. The details of the accusation, after a passage from a far distant passage of Foxe, or from Hall (see ll. 10–15 n.), proceed to draw on a part of Foxe, 1694, omitted in the interview between Cranmer and Henry in 5. 1: 'permit it vnreformed, least peraduenture by long suffering, such contention should arise, and ensue in the Realme among his subiects, that thereby might spring horrible commotions, and vprores, like as in some partes of Germanie, it did not long ago: The enormitie whereof they could not impute to any so much, as to the Ar[c]hbishop of Canturbury, who by his own preaching, and his Chapleins[,] had filled the whole Realme full of diuers pernicious heresies' [ll. 15–31].

The main narrative (p. 1694) continues, 'The Archb. aunswered in like sort, as the king had aduised him: and in the end when he perceiued that no maner of perswasion or intreatie could serue, he deliuered them the kings ring, reuoking his cause into the kings hands. The whole Counsaile being thereat somewhat amazed, the Earle of Bedford with a loud voice confirming his words with a solemne othe, said: when you first began the matter my Lordes, I told you what would come of it. Do you thinke that the king will suffer this mans finger to ake? Much more (I warrant you) will hee defend his life against brabling varlets. You doe but cumber your selues to heare tales and fables against him. And so incontinently vpon the receipt of the kings token, they all rose, and caried to the K. his ring, surrendring that matter as the order and vse was, into his owne hands [ll. 32–113]'.

As before, some details are taken from the source of the earlier scene, Henry's injunctions to Cranmer, 'saie vnto them, if there be no remedie my Lords, but that I must needes go to the tower, then I reuoke my cause from you, and appeale to the kinges owne person by this his token vnto you all [ll. 92–101]'. The play then substitutes an entry of the King for the departure of the council into the King's presence, and Foxe continues (p. 1694), 'When they were all come to the kings presence, his highnes with a seuere countenance, said vnto them: Ah my Lordes, I thought I had had wiser men of my counsaile then now I find you. What discretion was this in you, thus to make the Primate of the realme, & one of you in office, to waite at the counsaill chanber doore amongst seruing men? You might haue considered that he was a counsellor as wel as you, and you had no such commission of me so to handle him. I was content that you should trie him as a Counseller, and not as a meane subiect. But now I well perceiue that things be done against him maliciouslie, and if some of you might haue had your mindes, you woulde haue tried him to the vttermost. But I doe you all to wit, and protest, that if a Prince may bee beholding vnto his subiect (and so solemnelie laying his hand vpon his brest) said: by the faith I owe to God, I take this man here my Lord of Canturburie, to bee of all other a most faithfull subiect vnto vs, and one to whome wee are much beholding, giuing him great commendations otherwise. And with that one or two of the chiefest of the Counsaile, making their excuse, declared, that in requesting his induraunce, it was rather ment for his triall, and his purgation against the common fame, and slander of the worlde, then for any malice conceiued against him. Well, well my Lordes (quoth the king) take him and well vse him, as hee is worthy to be, and make no more adoe. And with that euery man caught him by the hand, and made faire weather of altogethers, which might easilie be done with that man [ll. 114–58]'.

The saying of ll. 175–77 comes from Foxe's earlier remark (p. 1691), 'it came into a common prouerbe: Doe vnto my lord of Canturbury displeasure or a shrewd turne, and then you may bee sure to haue him your friend whiles he liueth'.

Loc. (J.D.W., after Camb., plus F 'A Councell Table brought in with Chayres and Stooles, and placed under the State'). The bringing in of the properties constitutes the change of scene. For F's 'state' see G. 'state' (ix); this must be the sense, which *O.E.D.* first records from Bacon's *New Atlantis*, a few years later.

Entry (F; Camb. 'Keeper...door').

4. *knowledge* See G.

7. S.D. (F; Camb.) The addition of 'enters and' is consequential on the introduction of a new scene; see note on 5. 2. 35 S.D.

9. *present* present time; cf. *Wint*. 1. 2. 192 [Clar.].

10–15. *but...laws* One of the oddest uses of source material in the play. It originates in Hall (1809 ed. p. 783), 'My frendes all, you knowe well that we be men frayle of condicion and no Angels, and by frailtie and lacke of wysedome wee haue misdemeaned our selfe toward the King our Soueraygne Lord and his lawes, so that all wee of the Cleargy were in the Premunire'. This passage (first noted by W. Lloyd, *N. & Q.* 7 Ser. VII (1889), 203–4) is in Bishop Stokesley's speech to his clergy in 1531. Foxe, as Foakes notes, quotes it verbatim from Hall, but in a part not otherwise used.

11–12. *capable...flesh* 'liable to...the weaknesses belonging to flesh and blood' (Collier); 'capable of' ='susceptible to' is normal—what is unusual is that 'our flesh' is conceived on the analogy of a solicitation from outside.

16. *chaplains'* Cap. added the apostrophe, which modern usage would demand also in the source in Foxe, 'by his own preaching, and his Chapleins'. Whether the distinction was consciously made by either author is doubtful.

22. *Pace...hands* 'do not put them through their paces while leading them by the bridle' (Clar.).

27. *Farewell...physic* Cf. 3. 2. 281 n.

30. *upper Germany* Foxe has merely 'diuers partes
of Germany'. Grey (*ap.* Var.) saw a reference to the
insurrection of Münzer in Saxony and Thuringia
(1524–5), and Clar. adds the Anabaptist sedition at
Münster (1535). It may be relevant that Hall's
examples of civil dissension in his Introduction include
'the manifolde battails that were fought in the realme
of Beame [Bohemia], betwene the catholikes and the
pestiferus sectes of the Adamites and others'. D.N.S.
p. xvi cites Rowley, *When You See Me*, ll. 2201–5,
'Much bloodshed there is now in Germanie, | About
this difference in religion, | With Lutherans, Arians,
and Anabaptists, | As halfe the Prouince of *Helvetia*, |
Is with their tumults almost quite destroyde'.

38. *single heart* Cf. Acts ii. 46, 'singleness of heart'
[Reed].

46. *case* Foakes 'case,', with 'of justice'='in fair-
ness'. He argues that 'case of justice' is 'pointless';
but cf. *Cym.* 1. 6. 41, 'case of favour'. The meaning
seems to be 'case where justice is involved'.

47. *Be...will* Cf. 2. 1. 65, *1 H. VI*, 5. 3. 45 [Clar.].

48. *urge* Not used absolutely elsewhere in Sh., acc.
to Pooler, but cf. 2. 1. 16 n.

50. *by that virtue* 'by virtue of that' (Clar.).

53. *our consent* 'what we have consented to'
(Clar.).

58. *Winchester,* (Rowe)...*you;* (Collier) F '*Win-
cheſter*:...you,'.

60. *both* For position, cf. Abbott, §§ 420–1.

67. *make...conscience* have scruples about. This
expression has two opposite applications when followed
by an infinitive: 'to regard it as wrong to' and 'to
regard it as right (or obligatory) to'; they are well
illustrated in successive quotations in *O.E.D.* 'conscience', 11, 'make...conscience to break a Fast',
'I make conscience to say thou lyest'. This line belongs

with the former (and commoner) usage. Foakes confuses matters by citing an example of the latter.

73. *you are* (Pope) F 'y'are', but there seems no purpose in metrical irregularity here.

75. *faulty* (F2) F 'faultly'.

77. *load...man* Cf. 3. 2. 333 [Steev.].

78. *worst* with least justification.

81. *not sound* May owe something to Rowley, *When You See Me* (*M.S.R.*), ll. 1499–1501, 'I doe suspect that *Latimer* and *Ridly* | ...Are not sound Catholickes' [D.N.S. p. xvii].

85. sp.-pref. Chancellor (Cap.) F 'Cham.', i.e. Chamberlain; but it is the Chancellor who is conducting the business.

87. sp.-pref. Chancellor (Theob. conj.) F 'Cham.'.

95. S.D. (F).

99. *ring* For this incident, cf. Rowley, *When You See Me*, ll. 2703–8 [Elze].

103. *'Tis* (F2) F ''Ts'.

104–5. *put...ourselves* Cf. Prov. xxvi. 27, 'he that rolleth vp a stone, it will returne vpon him' [Noble]; Tilley, S 889.

108. *in value with* highly esteemed by.

112. *only* With 'the devil...disciples' [Clar., comparing l. 60].   *envy* See G.; the mod. sense would be quite inappropriate.

113. *blew...ye* Cf. 1. 1. 140–1 n.   S.D. (F).

114. One line in Pope; two, divided after 'sovereign', in F.

122. *sudden* See G.

125. *They* flatteries of this kind. *bare* (Mal. conj.) F 'bafe'; cf. *1 H. IV*, 1. 3. 108 for the corruption [Clar.], and *Oth.* 1. 3. 108, 'thin habits' for the metaphor.   *offences.* (Rowe) F 'offences,'.

126. *reach* (J., with comma) F 'reach.'; 'me...reach'='me whom you cannot reach'. F's punct. in

ll. 125–6 would join 'To...reach' with 'hide offences',
and this is prob. what copyist or compositor intended.
But none defend F's comma after 'offences', and it is an
unsatisfactory compromise to take 'To...reach' as an
independent statement. 'You...spaniel' calls for speci-
fication of the object of flattery.   *play the spaniel*
Cf. *J.C.* 3. 1. 43, 'base spaniel-fawning'; Tilley,
S 704, 'As flattering (fawning) as a spaniel'; *Ham.*
3. 2. 58–60 n.

130. S.D. (Rowe).

130–1. *proudest,* | *He* (Collier) F 'proudeſt | Hee,',
which most edd. retain, with 'He'='man', as in
3 H. VI, 1. 1. 46, 'The proudest he' [Delius]. I agree
with Abbott, § 216, that this is 'intolerably harsh'—
it is, in particular, unFletcherian—and it is not even
clear that it is what F intended. Omission of punctuation at the end of a line is not uncommon in this play
(1. 1. 78, 92, 133; 2. 1. 79; 2. 2. 74; 3. 2. 381;
4. 2. 145), and the comma between a pronoun and a
relative is quite normal.

133. *this* (F4) F 'his', unconvincingly defended
by Mal. as='the office of privy-councillor'.

140. *At chamber door* Cf. 5. 2. 17 n.

167 *spoons* Christening-spoons, given by the spon-
sors (see *Sh. Eng.* II. 143).

172. *brother-love* (Mal.) F 'Brother; loue': cf.
Cym. 3. 3. 40 n.

174. *heart* (F2) F 'hearts'.

179. *made a Christian* Not recorded as a stock
expression, but Sir Henry Sidney, 30 June 1569, writes
to Cecil, 'I most heartily thank you for the great honour
you did me in helping me to make a Christian of my
little son' (quoted by Mona Wilson, *Sir Philip Sidney*
(1950 ed.), p. 41).

181. S.D. F 'Exeunt'.

5.4

Authorship. Fletcher.
Material. Invented.

Loc. (Theob.; J.D.W.)　　*Entry* (F with 'within' (the normal theatrical form) for 'outside').

1–11. *You'll...rascals* Cap. arranged as verse; cf. l. 32 n.

2. *Parish* (F) F4 substituted the more normal 'Paris', but the F spelling was widely current. On the garden, see Chambers, *E.S.* ii. 450 ff. Jonson, *Epicoene*, 4. 4. 15, cites '*Paris*-garden' as one of the noisiest places in London [Foakes].

3. *gaping* See G.

4. S.D. (J.D.W.) F 'Within', as sp.-pref.; cf. n. on init. Entry.

8. *are...'em* i.e. 'make no impression on their hides' (Deighton).

9. *scratch your heads* Bullen, *ap.* Variorum Beaumont and Fletcher, *Maid's Tragedy*, 1. 2. 42, 'do your heads itch? I'll scratch them for you', cited this passage.

10. *ale and cakes* Traditionally served at weddings, christenings, etc.; cf. *Tw. N.* 2. 3. 121–2 n.

15. *May-day morning* 'when it was the custom to rise early and gather May-dew, which was believed to be of great virtue as a cosmetic' (Clar., citing Pepys's Diary, 28 May 1667).

16. *Paul's* F 'Powles', hence some edd. 'Powle's', but the sp. is a perfectly normal one.

20. *poor remainder* He holds up either a broken remnant of a cudgel, or, perh. more probably (since 'four foot' sounds an excessive weapon for the occasion), a cudgel of more moderate size, with the jocular pretence that the rest of it is worn away.

22. *Guy* See G.

24. *see a chine* eat meat; 'spoken like a beafeater' (Clar.).

27. *not for a cow* Dyce, 2nd ed., cites *Literary Gazette*, 25 January 1862, to the effect that 'I would not do that for a cow, save her tail' was still to be heard in Devon; Foakes cites 'not for a cow god save her' from *The Tell-tale* (Dulwich College MS.), p. 20 (=*M.S.R.* l. 1052).

28. S.D. (J.D.W.) F 'Within', as sp.-pref. (cf. l. 4).

29. *I...you* See G., 'with'.

29–30. *I...sirrah* Prose in Rowe; two lines of verse, divided after 'puppy', in F. ('Puppy' ends what would be a full prose line, but the cap. in 'Keepe' shows that verse was intended.)

32. *What...do* Prose in Rowe; one line of verse in F. Perh. 'What...dozens' was intended as verse (so Cap., in the process of turning the whole of ll. 32–65 into verse; some parts, esp. ll. 55–8, 'when...work', sound much like verse).

33. *Moorfields* Foakes notes that there seems to be no other evidence that Moorfields was used as a training ground, though edd. since J. have said it was. Clar. cites Stow, *Survey of London* (ed. C. L. Kingsford (1908), ii, 76–7), 'In the yeare 1498. all the Gardens which had continued time out of mind, without More-gate, to witte, aboute and beyonde the Lordship of Finsbery, were destroyed. And of them was made a playne field for Archers to shoote in'.

34. *tool* (Pope) F '*Toole*', apparently taking it for a proper name; see G.

37. *this...thousand* Perh. on the analogy of the prov. (Tilley, W 231), 'One wedding begets another', though the causal process implied is not the same.

43. *under the line* on the equator; cf. *Tp.* 4. 1. 237–8, and n.

43–4. *fire-drake* O.E.D. cites under 4*b*, 'a man with a fiery nose'; it is hard to be sure which of the more literal senses is being used metaphorically; 'discharged' suggests sense 3, 'a kind of firework'.

46–7. *haberdasher's...wit* Most simply taken literally, as by Deighton. The idea that it='who dealt in small wit, and had a ready tongue' (Clar.), is not adequately supported by the citation of Jonson, *Magnetic Lady*, Ind. 12, 'all Haberdashers of small wit' [Mal; earlier noted by Z. Grey, *Critical...Notes on Shakespeare* (1754), II, 99].

50. '*Clubs!*' See G.

52. *Strand* F 'Strond'.

54. *to th'broomstaff* i.e. to close quarters.   *with* (Pope) F 'to', prob. caught from the preceding 'to'.

56. *loose shot* See G., 'loose', 'shot', and *Sh. Eng.* I, 115 n. 1.

61. *tribulation...Limehouse* Sugden, p. 308, suggests that these were 'two gangs of young hooligans' infesting the two districts; the names seem to be chosen largely for the sake of alliterative jingle; see G., 'tribulation' (conjectural), 'limb'.

63. *Limbo Patrum* See G. Foakes (privately) points out the application to the Fleet Prison in Nashe, I, 300, McKerrow's note on which adds to *O.E.D.* an earlier (1587) quotation.

64–5. *running...beadles* 'a public whipping' (J.), as the dessert to their confinement [Steev.]. Cf. Doll Tearsheet's 'whipping-cheer' in *2 H. IV*, 5. 4. 5 [J.D.W.].

65. S.D. (F).

69. *made...hand* See G. 'hand'; cf. *Cor.* 4. 6. 118 [Clar.].

71. *friends* (F 2) F 'ftiends'.   *suburbs* See G.

78. *suddenly* See G.

80. *baiting...bombards* See G.; 'of'=from.

83. *a way* (F2) F 'away'.

85. *Marshalsea* See G.

88. *camlet* F 'Chamblet'.   *get...rail* Regarded
by J. W. Saunders, *Sh. Survey*, 7 (1954), 70–1, as
addressed to a member of the audience, the rail being
the low railing round the stage represented on some
title-pages. He notes, against J. C. Adams, *The Globe
Playhouse* (1942), p. 100, who postulates a 'crowd of
citizens congregated about one of the stage doors', that
the stage-crowd is off-stage. But as Foakes notes, l. 89
implies that the person addressed is on the same side
of the rails as the speaker; and since he can be identified
by his 'camlet' he must be an actor.

89. *peck* See G.   S.D. (J.D.W.) F 'Exeunt'.

5. 5

Authorship. Fletcher.

Material. Hol. p. 934, the christening 'was appointed
on the wednesdaie next following [the birth], and was
accordinglie accomplished on the same daie, with all such
solemne ceremonies as were thought conuenient. The godfather at the font, was the lord archbishop of Canturburie,
the godmothers, the old dutches of Norffolke, & the old
marchionesse Dorset, widow;...the child was named
Elizabeth.

'Vpon the daie of the christening, the maior sir Stephan
Peacocke, in a gowne of crimsin veluet, with his collar of
SS, and all the aldermen in scarlet, with collars and chaines,
and all the councell of the citie with them, tooke their barge
after dinner, at one of the clocke, and the citizens had
another barge, and so rowed to Greenwich, where were
manie lords, knights, and gentlemen assembled.' Then
'the child was brought to the hall, and then euerie man set
forward; first the citizens two and two, then gentlemen,
esquiers and chapleins, next after them the aldermen and
the maior alone: next the maior the kings councell, the
kings chappell in copes: then barons, bishops, earles, then

came the earle of Essex, bearing the couered basins gilt, after him the marquesse of Excester with the taper of virgin wax, next him the marquesse Dorset bearing the salt.

'Behind him the ladie Marie of Norffolke, bearing the creesome which was verie rich of pearle and stone, the old dutches of Norffolke bare the child in a mantell of purple veluet, with a long traine furred with ermine. The duke of Norffolke with his marshall rod went on the right hand of the said dutches, and the duke of Suffolke on the left hand, and before them went the officers of armes. The countesse of Kent bare the long traine of the childs mantell, and betweene the countesse of Kent and the child went the earle of Wilshire on the right hand, and the earle of Darbie on the left hand, supporting the said traine: in the middest ouer the said child was borne a canopie, by the lord Rochford, the lord Husoe, the lord William Howard, and by the lord Thomas Howard the elder, after the child followed manie ladies and gentlewomen. When the child was come to the church doore, the bishop of London met it with diuerse bishops and abbats mitred.

'When the ceremonies and christening were ended, Garter cheefe king of armes cried aloud, God of his infinite goodnesse send prosperous life & long to the high and mightie princesse of England Elizabeth: & then the trumpets blew. Then the archbishop of Canturburie gaue to the princesse a standing cup of gold: the dutches of Norffolke gaue to hir a standing cup of gold, fretted with pearle: the marchionesse of Dorset gaue three gilt bolles, pounced with a couer: and the marchionesse of Excester gaue three standing bolles grauen, all gilt with a couer....Then they set forwards, the trumpets going before in the same order towards the kings palace, as they did when they came thitherwards, sauing that the gifts that the godfather and the godmothers gaue, were borne before the child by foure persons, that is to saie. First Sir Iohn Dudleie bare the gift of the ladie of Excester, the lord Thomas Howard the yoonger bare the gift of the ladie of Dorset, the lord Fitzwater bare the gift of the ladie of Norffolke, and the earle of Worcester bare the gift of the archbishop of Canturburie....

'In this order they brought the princesse to the Q.
chamber, & tarried there a while with the maior & his
brethren the aldermen, and at the last the dukes of Norffolke & Suffolke came out frō the K. thanking them
hartilie, who commanded them to giue thanks in his name:
which being doone with other courtesies they departed,
& so went to their barges. From that time forward (God
himselfe vndertaking the tuition of this yoong princesse,
hauing predestinated hir to the accomplishment of his
diuine purpose) she prospered vnder the Lords hand, as a
chosen plant of his watering, & after the reuolution of
certeine yeares with great felicitie and ioy of all English
hearts atteined to the crowne of this realme, and now
reigneth ouer the same: whose heart the Lord direct in his
waies, and long preserue hir in life, to his godlie will and
pleasure, and the comfort of all true and faithfull subiects.'

Clar. (after Reed) notes that the christening actually took
place at **Grey Friar Church**, Greenwich (10 September
1533).

Entry (F).
1–3. Prose in Cap., four lines, divided after
'heaven', 'life', 'mighty', in F.
3. S.D. (F).
4. S.D. (J.).
5. *partners* See G.
9. S.D. (J.).
23. *Saba* See G.; the sp. of pre-1611 English
versions (<Vulgate), except Geneva, and of B.C.P.
(Ps. lxxii. 10) [Clar.].
26. *piece* See G.
32. One line in Rowe; two, divided after 'sorrow',
in F.
34. *Under...vine* Biblical; Steev. cites I Kings iv.
25; Reed adds Micah iv. 4, and Pooler II Kings xviii.
31 and Isa. xxxvi. 16.
37. *read* See G.   *ways* (F4) F 'way'.
42. *admiration* See G.

44. *this...darkness* 'this world in which we wander for a time in darkness' (Deighton).

47. *fixed* Carries on the figure of 'star-like'; the fixed stars are contrasted with mere planets, comets and 'exhalations' (3. 2. 226).   *Peace...love* P. A. Jorgensen, *Sh.'s Military World* (1956), p. 201, notes that these are specified by James I in 1607 as three of·the 'Commodities' brought by the union of England and Scotland (*Political Works of James I*, ed. C. H. McIlwain (1918), p. 297).

50–4. *Wherever...him* Noted by Foakes as 'based on the prophecy in Gen. xvii. 4–6, "a father of many nations have I made thee...I will make thee exceeding fruitfull, & will make nations come of thee" (Geneva)'. He also notes that it 'was frequently cited in reference to the marriage of Princess Elizabeth in 1613'.

52. *new nations* Mal. first suggested a reference to the settlement of Virginia, for which a lottery was held in 1612.

65. *get* 'achieve, quibbling on "beget"' (Foakes).

69. *mayor* F 'Maior' [=major], a common 17th-century form.

70. *your* (Thirlby *ap.* Theob.) F 'you'.

74. *no...think* 'let no man think' (Clar.).

75. *Has* he has; F ''Has'.

76. S.D. F 'Exeunt'.

Epilogue

Authorship. See on Prologue.

4. *trumpets* (F2) F 'Tumpets'.

5–6. *hear...extremely* Foakes sees this as perhaps 'a glance at the private theatres', where 'abuse of citizens was a stock theme', and cites N. Field, *Woman is a Weathercock* (1612), ed. W. Peery (1950), 2. 1. 275–6, 'Such a Cittizen | As the Playes flout still'.

8. *hear* (Pope) F 'heare.' F 2 'heare,'.

9–10. *in...women* For the rhyme, cf. Prol. 25–6 n.

14. *clap* This is by far the earliest example quoted in *O.E.D.* for the vb. used absolutely; the next is 1676. Bawdy wordplay on terms of archery (e.g. *L.L.L.* 4. 1. 117–38) is so common as to make one suspect a pun on the sense *O.E.D.* 10, 'put...with promptness and effect', esp. 10*c*, ellipt. for 'clap an arrow', for which the only quotation is *2 H. IV*, 3. 2. 48, 'clapped i'th'clout'. E. Partridge, *Sh.'s Bawdy* (2nd ed., 1955, p. 87), notes the innuendo, but without specific *O.E.D.* reference.

ADDITIONAL NOTE

The publication of F. P. Wilson's Presidential Address of the Modern Humanities Research Association, 1961, *The Proverbial Wisdom of Shakespeare*, makes it possible to give dates earlier than those in Tilley's *Dictionary* for these proverbs cited in the notes: 1. 1. 84, Tilley L 452 (1576); 4. 2. 45, Tilley I 71 (*c.* 1513); 5. 3. 126, Tilley S 704 (1585); the last is in *O.D.E.P.*, p. 209.

GLOSSARY

Note. Where a pun or quibble is intended, the meanings are distinguished as (*a*) and (*b*). Notes such as 'here only', 'first here', refer to what *O.E.D.* records. 'Hol.' or 'Foxe' indicates that the word is used exactly as in Holinshed or Foxe; it does not imply that the sense is not also found elsewhere in Shakespeare.

ABHOR, protest against (technical in canon law; Hol.); 2. 4. 81

ABJECT, contemptible; 'abject object', object of contempt; 1. 1. 127

ABLE, (i) vigorous, lusty; 2. 2. 140; (ii) sufficient; 4. 2. 153

ABODE, forebode; 1. 1. 93

ABOUND, be rich; 1. 1. 83

ABROAD, (i) out of one's house (room, etc.); 1. 4. 5; 3. 2. 83; (ii) in the world, current; 3. 2. 391

ABUSE, revile; 1. 3. 28

ACQUAINT, inform; 2. 2. 106

ADMIRATION, power of exciting admiration (cf. *Tp.* 3. 1. 38) [Foakes]; 5. 5. 42

ADMIRER (of), one filled with wonder (by); 1. 1. 3

ADMIT, allow; 4. 2. 107

ADVERTISE, inform; 2. 4. 178

ADVISED, 'be advised', take care; 1. 1. 139, 145

AFFECT, love; 1. 1. 39; 2. 3. 29

AGAINST, (i) in preparation for; 3. 1. 25; (ii) towards; 3. 2. 118

AIR, expose to the air; 2. 4. 193

ALLAY, abate, restrain; 1. 1. 149; 2. 1. 152

ALLEGE, bring forward (Hol.); 2. 1. 13

ALLEGIANT, loyal (here only before 19th century); 3. 2. 176

ALLIED, associated in work (with); 1. 1. 61

ALLOW, (i) approve; 1. 2. 83; (ii) acknowledge; 2. 4. 4; (iii) assign as a right, accord; 2. 2. 111

ALLOWANCE, permission; 3. 2. 322

ANON, presently, after a short time; 1. 2. 107; 1. 4. 49; 3. 2. 117; 5. 2. 35

ANSWER, (i) reply made to a charge; 5. 1. 104; (ii) 'to his answer', to answer the charges against him; 4. 2. 14

A-PIECES, to pieces; 5. 4. 75

APPLIANCE, medicinal application, remedy; 1. 1. 124

APPOINTMENT, direction; 2. 2. 132

APPROBATION, sanction; 1. 2. 71

APPROVE, confirm; 2. 3. 74

APT, inclined; 2. 4. 122

ARCH, pre-eminent; 3. 2. 102; 5. 1. 45

A-RIPENING, about to ripen; 3. 2. 357

ARROGANCY, arrogance; 2. 4. 110

ART, learning; 4. 2. 62

ARTICLE, (i) clause of an agreement; 1. 1. 169; (ii) item (in an indictment); 3. 2. 293, 299, 304

AS, as if; Prol. 27; 1. 1. 10; 3. 1. 7; 5. 3. init. S.D.

ASHER HOUSE, a residence of the Bp. of Winchester, near Hampton Court; Asher now 'Esher'; 3. 2. 231

ASPECT, look (bestowed on another); 3. 2. 369; 5. 1. 88

ASPIRE, rise; 3. 2. 368

ASSISTANT, associate; 1. 1. 62

ATTACH, (i) seize (goods); 1. 1. 95; (ii) arrest (person); 1. 1. 217; 1. 2. 210

ATTAINDER, disgrace; 2. 1. 41

ATTEMPT, make an attack; 3. 2. 17

ATTEND, (i) accompany (trans.) 1. 4. 60; 5. 5. 27; (with 'on') 1. 1. 75; (ii) await; 3. 2. 82; 5. 1. 83, 91; (iii) (abs.) wait; 5. 2. 19

AUDIT, statement of accounts; 3. 2. 141

AVAUNT, dismissal; 2. 3. 10

AVOID, leave; 5. 1. 86

BAIT, refresh oneself; 5. 4. 80

BANQUET, hasty, slight repast; 1. 4. 61, 98; so fig. 'running banquet' (with bawdy quibble) 1. 4. 12; (jocularly, for 'public whipping') 5. 4. 64

BARE, threadbare (fig.); 5. 3. 125

BASE, (a) low-born, (b) morally base; 2. 1. 104

BEHOLDING, beholden; 1. 4. 41; 4. 1. 21; 5. 3. 156; 5. 5. 70

BENEFICIAL, beneficent; 1. 1. 56

BESIDE, besides; Prol. 19

BEVIS, Saxon knight, Bevis of Southampton, hero of E.E. metrical romance, 'Sir B. of Hampton', with his legendary exploits; 1. 1. 38

BEVY, company (of ladies); 1. 4. 4

BLACK, malignant; 1. 3. 58

BLISTERED, puffed; 1. 3. 31

BLOW, blow up; 5. 4. 46

BOMBARD, large leathern bottle; 5. 4. 80

BOOK (sb.), concr. for abstract, learning; 1. 1. 122

BOOTLESS, useless; 2. 4. 61

BORE (vb.), cheat; 1. 1. 128

BOSOM (sb.), fig. inward recesses; 2. 4. 182

BOSOM UP, take to heart; 1. 1. 112

BOUND, under obligation; 1. 2. 112; 3. 2. 165; 5. 3. 114

BOWED, bent; 2. 3. 36

BRAKE, thicket; 1. 2. 75

BRAZIER, worker in brass; 5. 4. 40

BREAK (WITH), make a disclosure (to); 5. 1. 47

BREEDING, upbringing; 4. 2. 134

BRING OFF, rescue; 3. 2. 220

BROKEN, interrupted; 1. 4. 61

BROW, fig., aspect; Prol. 2

BUD OUT, develop; 1. 1. 94

BUY, (i) gain; 1. 1. 65; (ii) 'buy and sell', barter, traffic in (proverbial, in a bad fig. sense); 1. 1. 192

BUZZING, rumour; 2. 1. 148

BY (adv.), see 'lie by'; 3. 1. 11

BY (prep.), for; 2. 4. 49

CALL, 'call back', revoke; 2. 4. 234

CAMLET, costly fabric (of various materials); 5. 4. 88

CAN, can do; 4. 2. 173

CAPABLE (OF), susceptible (to the weaknesses of); 5. 3. 11

CAPACITY, power of receiving; 2. 3. 31

CARDER, one who 'cards', i.e. combs out, impurities from wool; 1. 2. 33

CARDINAL (virtues, sins), chief; 3. 1. 103, 104

CARRIAGE, behaviour; 3. 1. 161; 4. 2. 145

CARRY, (i) manage; 1. 1. 100; 1. 2. 134 ('carry it' = 'manage things'); (ii) refl., behave; 2. 4. 143

CATCH, captivate; 2. 3. 77

CAUSE, (i) case under judicial examination; 5. 3. 121; (ii) case (for or against a person); 3. 2. 269

CAUTION, warning; 2. 4. 186

CENSURE, (i) judgment (neutral); 1. 1. 33; (ii) unfavourable opinion, adverse judgment; 3. 1. 64

CENSURER, one who passes judgment; 1. 2. 78

CERTAIN, certainly; 2. 4. 71

CERTES, assuredly; 1. 1. 48

CHAFED, angered; 1. 1. 123; 3. 2. 206

CHALLENGE (legal term), objection raised, exception taken, to a person or things in a trial; 2. 4. 77

CHAMBER, small piece of ordnance; 1. 4. 49 S.D.

CHANCELLOR, secretary to a great nobleman or lord; 1. 1. 219; 2. 1. 20

CHANGE, figure in a dance; 4. 2. 82 S.D.

CHARGE (sb.), (i) expense; 1. 1. 77; (ii) order; 3. 2. 344

CHARGE (vb.), accuse; 1. 2. 174

CHARTREUX, the Carthusian monastery in Smithfield; here = a Carthusian monk; 1. 1. 221; (adj.) Carthusian; 1. 2. 148

CHEER, entertain; 1. 4. 41

CHERISH, foster; 3. 2. 443

CHERUBIN, cherub (Sh.'s usual form); 1. 1. 23

CHEVERIL, flexible; 2. 3. 32

CHIDING, fig., brawling; 3. 2. 197

CHINE, joint from the backbone of an animal, here 'beef', prob. sirloin; 5. 4. 26

CHOICE, chosen; 1. 2. 162

CHOKE, obstruct; 1. 2. 4

CHRISTENDOM, Christianity; here, = Christian fashion of dress; 1. 3. 15

CHRONICLE, chronicler; 1. 2. 74

CHURCHMAN, ecclesiastic; 1. 3. 55; 1. 4. 88; 3. 1. 117

CINQUE-PORTS, barons of the Cinque Ports (Hol.); 4. 1. 36 S.D.

CIRCUMSTANCES, adjuncts of a fact constituting circumstantial evidence (cf. *Oth.*, G.); 2. 4. 76

CLAP, (i) stick up; 1. 3. 18; (ii) impose; 5. 4. 79

CLERK, scholar (Hol.); 2. 2. 90

CLINQUANT, glittering with gold or silver; 1. 1. 19

CLOSE, (i) out of sight, screened from view; 2. 1. 55; 4. 1. 36; (ii) shut; 5. 4. 30

CLOTH OF STATE, canopy for the throne (Hol. 'estate'); 2. 4. init. S.D.

CLOTHARIUS, Prob. Clotaire (497–561), son of Clovis, early king of the Merovingian dynasty; 1. 3. 10

CLUBS, the call to London prentices to start or stop a fight; 5. 4. 50

COARSE, inferior; 3. 2. 239

COAST, vb., fig., 'proceed circuitously' (*O.E.D.* 2 *d*, citing as only ex.); 3. 2. 38

COLBRAND, see 'Guy'; 5. 4. 22

COLD, coldness; 4. 2. 98

COLLAR, ornamental chain, part of the insignia of the order of knighthood; 'c. of SS', because it consisted of a series of S's (first instituted 1407); 4. 1. 36 S.D.

COLLECT, gather (information); 1. 2. 130

COLOUR, pretext; 1. 1. 178

COLT'S TOOTH, fig., youthful tastes, wanton inclination; 1. 3. 48

COMBINATION, alliance; 1. 1. 169

COMBUSTION, conflagration, i.e. (fig.) commotion; 5. 4. 49

COME HOME, accrue; 3. 2. 158

COME OFF, escape (if 'he'= Wolsey), or desist (if 'he' = the King); 3. 2. 23

COMFORTLESS, disconsolate; 2. 3. 105

COMMEND, (i) entrust; 5. 1. 17; (ii) commit to the care (of); 4. 2. 131; (iii) 'commend…opinion', present… compliments; 2. 3. 61

COMMENDATION, greetings; 4 2. 118

COMMISSION, warrant, mandate; 1. 2. 20, 92, 101;

2. 4. 1; 3. 2. 233, 320; 5. 3. 141

COMMIT, send to prison; 1. 2. 193; 5. 1. 146

COMMONALTY, common people (Hol.); 1. 2. 170

COMMOTION, (i) perturbation; 3. 2. 112; (ii) insurrection, sedition; 5. 3. 28

COMPASS, range, reach; 1. 1. 36; 3. 2. 340

COMPELLED, forced (on one) unsought; 2. 3. 87

COMPLETE, fully endowed; 1. 2. 118

COMPOUNDED, composite; 1. 1. 12

COMPTROLLER, household officer, whose duty consisted chiefly in checking expenditure; 1. 3. 67

CONCEIT, opinion; 2. 3. 74

CONCEIVE, 'conceive of', form a conception of; 1. 2. 105

CONCEPTION, design; 1. 2. 139

CONCLAVE, the body of Cardinals (first here in this sense); 2. 2. 98

CONDITION, disposition; 1. 2. 19

CONDUCT, guidance; 1. 4. 70

CONFEDERACY, conspiracy; 1. 2. 3

CONFERENCE, conversation; 2. 3. 51

CONGEE (vb.), bow ceremoniously; 4. 2. 82 S.D.

CONJUNCTION, union in marriage; 3. 2. 45

CONSCIENCE, (i) inmost conviction; 3. 2. 123; (ii) 'make conscience', have scruples; 5. 3. 67

CONSISTORY, (meeting of) College of Cardinals (Hol.); 2. 4. init. S.D.

CONSTABLE, 'Lord High Constable', principal officer in the royal household in France and England; 2. 1. 102

CONSTANCY, persistence (here only in this sub-sense); 3. 2. 2

CONSTRUCTION, interpretation; Epil. 10

CONTENT (vb.), please; 3. 1. 132

CONTRARY (sb.), opposite side (in a trial); 2. 1. 15

CONVENT, summon; 5. 1. 52

COPE, encounter; 1. 2. 78

CORDIAL (fig.), restorative medicine; 3. 1. 106

CORNER, place of concealment (cf. mod. 'hole-and-corner'); 3. 1. 31

CORNET, instrument resembling a horn; 1. 2. init. S.D.; 2. 4. init. S.D.

COUNCIL, 'board of council', the Privy Council; 1. 1. 79

COUNTENANCE, demeanour; 2. 4. 26

COURSE, (i) 'course of the sun', year; 2. 3. 6; (ii) line of action; 5. 3. 35

COVENT, old form of 'convent', hence 'Covent Garden'; 4. 2. 19

CREATURE (OF), one who owes his or her position (to), 3. 2. 36

CREDIT, reputation; 3. 2. 265

CROSS (adj.), perverse, thwarting one's purposes; 3. 2. 214

CROSS (vb.), oppose; 3. 2. 234

CROWN (vb.), consummate; 3. 2. 155

CRY, 'cry down', put down, overcome, by greater vehemence; 1. 1. 137; 'cry up', praise; 1. 2. 84

CUM PRIVILEGIO, with acknowledged or sanctioned right; 1. 3. 34

CURE (sb.), (a) cure of souls, (b) remedy; 1. 4. 33

CURE (vb.), remedy; 3. 2. 216

CURRENT, genuine, sterling; 1. 3. 47

DARE, (i) fascinate and daze (by mirror, red cloth, etc.), and so entrap; 3. 2. 282; (ii) defy; 3. 2. 307

DASH, splash; 1. 1. 93

DEAR, (used as intensive) heartfelt; 5. 3. 119

DEARLY, at high cost; 5. 3. 30

DEATH, (imprecation or oath) ellipt. for 'Christ's (God's) death'; 1. 3. 13

DECEIVED, cheated of one's expectation; Prol. 17

DECLINE, fall; 3. 2. 375

DEEP, subtle; 2. 1. 45

DEFACER, destroyer; 5. 3. 41

DELIVER, relate; 1. 2. 143; 2. 2. 135; 2. 3. 106; 5. 1. 62

DEMAND, question; 2. 3. 52

DEMICORONAL, small coronet (Hol.); 4. 1. 36 S.D.

DEMURE, grave; 1. 2. 167

DENY, refuse; 2. 2. 109; 3. 2. 238

DEPUTY, Lord Lieutenant (of Ireland); 2. 1. 42; 3. 2. 260

DERIVE (TO), direct (towards); 2. 4. 32

DESIRE, request; 2. 1. 17; 5. 1. 167

DETERMINATE, decisive; 2. 4. 176

DETERMINE, decide; 1. 1. 214

DEVICE, plot; 1. 1. 204

DIFFERENCE, (i) disagreement; 1. 1. 101; 3. 1. 58; (ii) 'difference in', distinction between; 1. 1. 139

DIGEST, put up with, 'swallow'; 3. 2. 53

DIRECTLY, (i) unequivocally; 1. 3. 8; (ii) immediately; 1. 4. 63 S.D.

DISCERNER, one who passes judgment; 1. 1. 32

DISCOVER, reveal; 5. 3. 71

DISCRETION, good judgment; 5. 3. 137

DISPLEASURE, (i) disapproval; 3. 2. 23; (ii) loss of favour; 3. 2. 392

DISPOSE, put to use; 1. 2. 116

DISPOSING, management; 1. 1. 43

DISTINCTLY, separately; 1. 1. 45

DISTRACTION, (fit of) madness; 3. 1. 112

DISTRIBUTE, deal out shares (of blows); 5. 4. 20

DIVERS, various; 5. 3. 18

DIVORCE (sb.), separation ('of' =caused by); 2. 1. 76

DIVORCE (vb.), remove: 3. 1. 142

Do, (i) fare; 1. 1. 1; (ii) make; 4. 2. 60

DOCTOR, doctor of law; 2. 4. init. S.D., 206

DOG-DAYS, supposedly the hottest period of the year, 13 July–15 August, when Sirius, the dog-star, rises nearly at the same time as the sun; 5. 4. 41–2.

DOMESTIC, household servant

(here first in this sense); 2. 4. 114

DOUBLET, men's close-fitting body garment (14th–18th centuries); 4. 1. 74

DRAW, (i) make liquor flow by turning a tap, here fig.; Prol. 4; (ii) frame, draw up; 1. 1. 169; (iii) (a) assemble; (b) draw (a weapon; here, the 'truncheon'); 5. 4. 51.

DROP, (fig., fr. rain falling) rain, shed; 2. 3. 18 (intrans.); 3. 2. 185 (caus.).

DUE (sb.), justice, 'due of the verdict'=just verdict; 5. 1. 131

DUTY, homage to a sovereign, act of homage, reverence, etc.; 1. 2. 61, 198; 1. 4. 80; 2. 2. 67; 2. 4. 40; 3. 2. 188, 193, 196

EAGERLY, sharply; 4. 2. 24

EARTHY, death-like; 4. 2. 98

EASINESS, indulgent temper; 5. 3. 25

EASY, easygoing; 3. 2. 356

ELEMENT, ?component part; 1. 1. 48

EMBALLING, here only; O.E.D. suspects an 'indelicate sense'; usually explained as investing with the royal emblem of the 'ball'; 2. 3. 47

EMBRACEMENT, embrace; 1. 1. 10

END, (i) result; 1. 1. 171; (ii) ultimate cause, 'at the bottom of' (Clarke); 2. 1. 40; (iii) purpose, object; 2. 1. 124; 2. 2. 39; 3. 1. 154; 3. 2. 171, 212; (iv) manner of death; 3. 2. 268

ENVIOUS, malicious; 2. 1. 45; 3. 2. 243, 446

ENVY (sb.), malice, hatred; 2. 1. 85; 2. 2. 87; 3. 1. 36, 113; 3. 2. 239; 5. 3. 44

ENVY (vb.), hate; 2. 2. 125; ('envy at') 5. 3. 112

EQUAL, fair, impartial; 2. 2. 106; 2. 4. 18; as adv., equally; 1. 1. 159

ESTATE, (i) state, government; 2. 2. 68; (ii) condition; 5. 1. 74; (iii) 'robe of estate', state robe (Hol.); 4. 1. 36 S.D.

EVEN, (i) uniform (in its uprightness); 3. 1. 37; (ii) equable; 3. 1. 166

EVENT, outcome; 1. 2. 36

EVER, 'not ever', not always; 5. 1. 129

EVIL, ? privy (see *O.E.D.* 'evil', sb.²); 2. 1. 67

EXAMINATION, deposition; 1. 1. 116; 2. 1. 16

EXAMPLE, precedent; 1. 2. 90

EXCLAMATION, vehement reproach (Hol.); 1. 2. 52

EXHALATION, meteor; 3. 2. 226

FACULTY, personal quality; 1. 2. 73

FAIL (sb.), (i) (contextually) death without issue; 1. 2. 145; (ii) failure; 2. 4. 198

FAIL (vb.), die; 1. 2. 184

FAIN, obliged; 5. 4. 57

FAINT, depress; 2. 3. 103

FAIR, favourable; 2. 3. 74

FAIRLY, properly; 1. 4. 31; 5. 3. 109

FAIR-SPOKEN, of courteous or pleasing speech; 4. 2. 52

FAITH, (i) (='in faith') truly, indeed; 1. 1. 167; 1. 3. 16; 1. 4. 17; (ii) trustworthiness, loyalty; 2. 1. 143, 145; 3. 1. 53

FAITHFUL, loyal; 2. 1. 61

FALL, (i) come to pass; 2. 1. 141; 3. 2. 51; (ii) 'fall to himself again', recover self-possession; 2. 1. 35; (iii) 'fall into', come within (the range of); 3. 2. 340; (iv) 'fall off', withdraw, retire; 4. 1. 64; (v) 'fall on', (abs.) make an attack; 5. 4. 53

FAME, report; 1. 4. 66

FANCY, inclination; 5. 1. 60

FAR, 'was too far', mod. went too far; 3. 1. 65

FASHION, form; 4. 2. 159

FAST, shut; 5. 2. 3

FATHER, priest; 2. 4. 58, 205

FAULT, offence; 3. 2. 262, 334; 'make faults', commit offences; 2. 1. 71

FAVOUR, (i) leave, 'give me favour', give me leave (to go on speaking); 1. 1. 168; (ii) looks; 1. 4. 108

FEAR (vb.), doubt; 3. 2. 16

FEARFUL, afraid; 5. 1. 87

FEATHER, plume in a hat; 1. 3. 25

FEE, pay; 3. 2. 213

FEEL, truly know; 4. 2. 65

FELLOW, (i) (used contemptuously or abusively); 1. 1. 138; 4. 2. 100, 107; (ii) equal; 1. 3. 41

FELLOWSHIP, intercourse; 3. 1. 121

FIERCE, extravagant; 1. 1. 54

FILE (sb.), (i) list; 1. 1. 75; (ii) body of persons; 1. 2. 42; 5. 4. 55

FILE (vb.), keep pace; 3. 2. 171

FIRE-DRAKE, man with fiery nose; 5. 4. 43–4

FIREWORK, fig. for 'whore' (in ref. to venereal disease); 1. 3. 27

FIRST, foremost; Prol. 24

FIT (sb.), 'fit of the face', grimace; 1. 3. 7; (ii) attack (of a disease; here fig.); 3. 1. 78

FIT (vb.), be fitting; 5. 1. 107

FITNESS, something demanded by propriety; 2. 4. 231

FLAW, break; 1. 1. 95; 1. 2. 21

FLOOD, sea; 3. 2. 197

FLOURISH, short tune, call (on trumpet, etc.), 'fanfare' to announce approach of a distinguished person; 4. 1. 36 S.D., 55 S.D.

FLOWING, abundant; 2. 3. 62

FOR ALL, in spite of; 2. 3. 26

FORCE (sb.), validity; 1. 2. 101

FORCE (vb.), urge; 3. 2. 2

'FORE, before; 2. 4. 120

FOREGO, forsake; 3. 2. 422

FORSAKE, leave the body; 2. 1. 89

FORSOOTH, in fact; 3. 2. 124

FORTY, used for an indefinite number; 2. 3. 89; 3. 2. 253

FORWARD (adj.), eager; 4. 1. 9; (adv.), on his way; 4. 2. 13

FRANKLY, unreservedly; 2. 1. 81

FREE (adj.), (i) uncoerced; 2. 2. 92; (ii) unaffected; 2. 4. 99; (iii) innocent; 3. 1. 32; (iv) frank; 3. 1. 60

FREE (adv.), unreservedly; 2. 1. 82

FREE (vb.), acquit; 2. 4. 157

FREEDOM, ease; 5. 1. 102

FREELY, unreservedly; 1. 4. 36; 2. 2. 85, 111

FRESH FISH, fig., novice; 2. 3. 86

FRET, wear away; 3. 2. 105

FRIEND (vb.), assist; 1. 2. 140

FRIGHT, frighten; Epil. 4

FRONT, march in the front rank; 1. 2. 42

FROM, (i) at variance with, alienated from; 3. 1. 161; (ii) of; 3. 2. 268

FRY, swarm; 'fry of fornication'=crowd of would-be fornicators; 5. 4. 35–6

FULL, 'at full', (i) fully; 4. 1. 8; (ii) at the full; 1. 4. 60

FULL-CHARGED, fully loaded, fig., fully prepared; 1. 2. 3

FULLER, one who cleanses cloth; 1. 2. 33

FURNISH, (i) equip; 2. 2. 3; (ii) fit up (room) with all requisite things; 2. 2. 139

FURNITURE, equipment; 2. 1. 99

FURTHER, later; 2. 4. 232

'GAINST, (aphetic form) against; in opposition to; 3. 1. 85

GALL (sb.), rancour; bile was the supposed seat of malicious or bitter feelings; 1. 1. 152

GALL (vb.), wound; 3. 2. 207

GALLANT, vague epithet of praise, 'fine, splendid'; 3. 2. 49

GAMESTER, frolicsome person; 1. 4. 45

GAPING, bawling; 5. 4. 3

GARTER, Garter King at arms, the chief herald; 4. 1. 36 S.D.; 5. 5. init. S.D

GENERAL, common to, made by, shared by, all; 1. 1. 92; 1. 4. 1; 2. 2. 94; 5. 3. 28

GENERALLY, by all; 2. 1. 47

GENTLE, kind, kindly; 2. 3. 54, 57; 4. 2. 122

GET, have begotten on one; 2. 3. 44

GIVE, (i) attribute; 3. 2. 262; (ii) 'my mind gave me', I had a misgiving; 5. 3. 109

GLAD, gladden; 2. 4. 196

GLADDING, gladdening; 5. 1. 71

GLISTERING, glittering; 2. 3. 21

GLOSS, specious appearance (*O.E.D.* notes tendency to confuse with 'gloss'=(sophistical) interpretation); 5. 3. 71

GO, (i) 'go to', expression of remonstrance, reproach, etc., 2. 2. 70; 4. 2. 103; 5. 1. 138; (ii) 'go beyond', overreach; 3. 2. 408; (iii) be pregnant (with); 5. 1. 20; (iv) 'go about', undertake; 1. 1. 131; (v) 'go forward', go on as before; 3. 2. 281

GOING OUT, expedition; 1. 1. 73

GOOD, goodness; 4. 2. 60

GOSSIP, fellow-sponsors (regarded as spiritually related to natural parent); 5. 5. 12

GOVERNMENT, self-control; 2. 4. 138

GRACE, (i) honour; 1. 1. 59; (ii) charm; 1. 2. 122; (iii) 'do grace', embellish; 1. 4. 73; (iv) favour; 2. 4. 22; 3. 2. 166, 174

GRIEF, grievance; 1. 2. 56

GRIEVANCE, distress; 1. 2. 20

GRIEVED, aggrieved; 1. 2. 104

GRIPE (sb.), clutch; 5. 3. 100

GRIPE (vb.), grasp; 2. 2. 134

GROOM, menial servant; 5. 1. 172; 5. 2. 18

GROW TO, cling to (cf. the opposite 'grow from', 3. 1. 161); 3. 1. 89; 5. 5. 49

GROW TOGETHER, form one body; 1. 1. 10

GUARDED, trimmed; Prol. 16

GUY, of Warwick, famed in romance as the slayer of the Danish giant Colbrand before King Athelstan (v. Drayton, *Polyolb.* XIIth Song); 5. 4. 22

HA (exclamation) expressing surprise, indignation, etc.; 'hallo!', eh?, what!, etc.; 1. 1. 115; 1. 2. 186; 2. 2. 62, 65, 71; 5. 1. 66, 81, 86; 5. 2. 25

HABIT (sb.), dress; 1. 2. 122; 2. 4. init. S.D.; 3. 1. 117

HABIT (vb.), dress; 1. 4. 63 S.D.; 5. 5. init. S.D.

HALBERD, halberdier; 2. 1. 54 S.D.

HALL, 'the Hall', Westminster Hall; 2. 1. 2

HAND, (i) signature; 2. 4. 222; (ii) 'made a hand', made a success (of something), freq. with 'fair', 'fine', etc.; here iron. (as often: see Tilley, H 99); 5. 4. 69; 'in (someone's) hands', led by (someone); 5. 3. 22

HAP, luck; Epil. 13

HAPPY, favourable; Prol. 24

HAPPILY, fortunately; 4. 2. 10 (? or='haply'); 5. 1. 85; 5. 2. 9

HARD, 'too hard for'='too much for'; 5. 1. 57

HARDLY, harshly; 1. 2. 105

HARD-RULED, difficult to manage; 3. 2. 101

HAUTBOY, oboe; 1. 4. init. S.D., 34 S.D., 63 S.D.; 4. 1. 36 S.D.

HAVE-AT-HIM (sb.), blow ('have at you', words of warning before a fight or attack); 2. 2. 83

HAVE AT YOU, 'look out!', 'here goes!', etc.; 3. 2. 309; 5. 3. 113

HAVING, possession; 2. 3. 23; (plur.) 3. 2. 159

HEAD, armed force; 2. 1. 108

HEART, core; 1. 2. 1, 21

HEAVEN, God; 2. 4. 22, 187; 3. 1. 100

HEAVY, tedious; 4. 2. 95

HEDGE, creep along secretly; 3. 2. 39

HEELS, 'lay by the heels', put in the stocks; 5. 4. 77–8

HEIGHT, highest degree; 1. 2. 214

HENCE, as a result of this; 1. 2. 192

HIGH, (i) eminent; 1. 1. 61; (ii) extreme; 1. 1. 107

HIGH-BLOWN, (fig.) inflated to the utmost degree; 3. 2. 361

HIGH STEWARD, Lord High Steward, official in charge of the coronation ceremony, or presiding at a peer's trial; 4. 1. 18

HIT, fit in with, appeal to; 1. 2. 84

HOLD, (i) last; 2. 1. 149; (ii) refrain; Epil. 14

HOLIDAME, 'by my holidame', asseveration (freq. in Sh.); 5. 1. 116

HONEST, (i) sincere; 3. 2. 430; (ii) possessing integrity; 5. 3. 82

HONESTY, truth, integrity, goodness; 1. 1. 40; 3. 2. 271, 306, 444; 4. 2. 145; 5. 1. 122; 5. 2. 28; 5. 3. 111

HONOUR, (i) reputation; 4. 2. 71; (ii) fact of being honourable; 3. 2. 181

HOT, fresh; 5. 1. 175

HOW, what!; 2. 2. 124

HOW NOW, exclamation of surprise, etc., or as greeting, 'hallo!', etc.; 1. 3. 15; 1. 4. 53; 3. 1. 15; 3. 2. 372; of simulated anger, 'well!'; 5. 1. 89

HULL (vb.), drift; 2. 4. 199

HUSBAND, manager of financial affairs; 3. 2. 142

ILLUSION, deception; 1. 2. 178

IMPORT, convey (information); 3. 2. 124

IN, with reference to; 2. 4. 103

INCREASE, make thrive; 3. 2. 161

INDIAN, N. American Red Indian; 5. 4. 34

INDIES (fig.), wealth of the East; 4. 1. 45

INDIFFERENT, impartial (Hol.); 2. 4. 17

INDUCEMENT, incentive; 2. 4. 169

INDURANCE, imprisonment (Foxe); 5. 1. 121

INFECT, contaminate; 1. 1. 162

INSENSE, inform; 5. 1. 43

INSTANT, now present; 1. 1. 225

INTELLIGENCE, information received; 1. 1. 153

ISSUE, child; 3. 2. 291

ITEM, likewise (used in making a detailed list); 3. 2. 320

JADE, befool; 3. 2. 280

JEWEL, piece of jewelry; 2. 2. 30

JUGGLE, trick; 1. 3. 1

JUST, honest; 3. 1. 60

JUSTIFY, confirm; 1. 2. 6

KEECH, animal fat rolled into a lump by the butcher, 'lump of fat'; 1. 1. 55

KEEPER, door-keeper; 5. 2. 4 S.D.

KNELL (fig.), sound betokening death (here, death-sentence); 2. 1. 32

KNOCK IT, strike up (first here); 1. 4. 108

KNOWLEDGE, 'have knowledge', be informed; 5. 3. 4

LACKEY, running footman; 5. 2. 18

LAG-END, remainder; 1. 3. 35

LARGE, wide in scope; 3. 2. 320

LATE, (i) recent; 4. 1. 27, 31; (ii) performed at a late hour; 5. 1. 13; (iii) former; 3. 2. 94; 4. 1. 33

LAY, (i) 'lay down', bring to child-bed; 1. 3. 40; 'lay forth', lay out (for burial); 4. 2. 171; (iii) arrange in order to entrap; 5. 2. 14

LEAGUE, alliance, treaty; 1. 1. 182; 2. 2. 23; 3. 2. 323

LEAVE, leave off, desist from; (trans.) 3. 1. 2, 92; 5. 4. 1, 3; (intrans.) 4. 2. 94

LEG, (a) lit. sense, (b) obeisance by drawing back one leg and bending the other; here, a 'new' way of doing this; 1. 3. 11

LEGATINE, belonging to a legate; 3. 2. 339

LETTERS, letter; 3. 2. 30

LETTERS-PATENTS, official documents, conferring some authority or privilege (Hol.); 3. 2. 250

LEVEL, range, aim; 'i'th'level', in the direct aim; 1. 2. 2

LEWDNESS, vicious habits; 1. 3. 35

LIE, (i) pass the night; 4. 1. 28; (ii) 'lie by', come almost to a stand (*O.E.D.* 'by', prep., adv., B 2 *b* (citing)); 3. 1. 11

LIGHT (sb.), 'by this light', freq. asseveration,=by the light of the sun; 5. 1. 171

LIGHT (vb.), alight; 1. 1. 9

LIGHTEN, give light to; 2. 3. 79

LIKE (adj.), likely; 1. 2. 182

LIKE (vb.), please; 5. 3. 148; 'like it', ellipt., if it pleases, i.e. if you will allow me (to say so); 1. 1. 100; similarly, 'an't like'; 4. 2. 100

LIMB (fig.), (i) member; 1. 1. 220; (ii) young imp; 5. 4. 61

LIMBO PATRUM (from Lat. *limbus patrum*) in mediev. theol. the place between heaven and hell where the righteous and Patriarchs living before Christ waited till his 'descent into hell', i.e. Hades, the place of departed spirits; here, for 'prison' (oftener, simply 'Limbo'); 5. 4. 63

LIMEHOUSE, a dockyard town on the N. bank of the Thames; 5. 4. 61

LIST (vb.), choose; 2. 2. 20

LITTLE, 'in a little', in a few words; 2. 1. 11

LIVER, person living (a particular mode of life); 2. 3. 20

LOFTY, haughty; 4. 2. 53

'LONG, (i) (aphetic form) belong; 2. 3. 48; (ii) ''longing', belonging, i.e. dependent on them as employers; 1. 2. 32

LOOK, (i) take heed; 1. 2. 101; 2. 1. 66; (ii) expect; 5. 1. 117

LOOSE, (i) carelessly indulgent; 2. 1. 127; (ii) irregular; 5. 4. 56.

LOP, smaller branches which can be lopped off; 1. 2. 96

LOSE, forget; 2. 1. 57

LOUVRE, seat of the French Court in Sh.'s time; 1. 3. 23

Low, recumbent; 4. 2. 76

LUCIFER, properly, the morning star; then, the Devil (erron. interpretation of Isa. xiv. 12, here alluded to); 3. 2. 371

MACE, staff of office; here, royal sceptre; 2. 4. init. S.D.; 4. 1. 36 S.D.

MADAM, lady; 1. 1. 23

MADE, created; 2. 2. 50

MAIDEN, befitting a maiden (i.e. white); 4. 2. 169

MAIDENHEAD, virginity; 2. 3. 23, 25

MAIN, (i) exerted to the full (still in 'main force'); 2. 2. 6; (ii) very important; 2. 2. 39; 3. 1. 93; 3. 2. 215; (iii) general; 4. 1. 31

MAKE, make one's way; 1. 4. 55

MAKINGS OF, what goes to make; 4. 1. 87

MANAGE, training (of a horse); 5. 3. 24

MARK, a silver coin, worth 13s. 4d.; 5. 1. 170

MARRY, interj., orig. the name of the Virgin Mary used as an oath or invocation; 1. 1. 97; 1. 3. 38; 3. 2. 47, 54

MARSHALSEA, prison in Southwark used for debtors and also for those charged with contempt of court; 5. 4. 85

MASTER, teacher; 1. 1. 17

MASTER-CORD, principal string; 3. 2. 106

MATE, vie with; 3. 2. 274

MAY, can; 1. 2. 200; 2. 4. 235

MAZED, bewildered; 2. 4. 185

MEAN, means; 5. 3. 146

MEASURE, dance, usually a grave, stately one; 1. 4. 106

MEMORIZE, make memorable; 3. 2. 52

MEND, (i) set right; 1. 2. 201; (ii) improve (with play on 'broken'); 1. 4. 61; (iii) reform; 3. 1. 105

MERCY, 'cry (one) mercy', beg one's pardon; 5. 3. 78

MERE, utter; 3. 1. 112; 3. 2. 329

MERIDIAN, fig., highest point; 3. 2. 224

MINCING, affectation; 2. 3. 31

MINDED, inclined; 3. 1. 58

MINISTER (sb.), (i) agent, instrument; 1. 1. 108; (ii) servant; 5. 1. 137

MINISTER (vb.), provide; 1. 1. 86

MIRROR (fig.), paragon; 2. 1. 53

MISCARRY, go astray; 3. 2. 30

MISTAKE (vb.), misjudge; 1. 1. 195; 3. 1. 101

MODEL, image; 4. 2. 132

MODEST, moderate; 4. 1. 82; 5. 3. 69

MODESTY, moderation; 2. 2. 135; 4. 2. 74; 5. 3. 64

MOE, more; 2. 3. 97; 3. 2. 5, 55; 5. 1. 36

MOIETY, half; 1. 2. 12

MONSIEUR, (Fr., 'Mr', 'sir') gentleman affecting French fashions; 1. 3. 21

MONSTROUS, unnatural; 1. 2. 122

MONUMENT, grave; 2. 1. 94

MORROW, morning, 'good morrow', good morning; 1. 1. 1; 2. 3. 50

MORTAL STATE, natural life; 2. 4. 228

MORTARPIECE, mortar; 5. 4. 46

MOTION, (i) lit. a movement of the soul; hence, impulse; 1. 1. 153; (ii) proposal; 2. 4. 233; (iii) (a) movement (as opposed to standing still); (b) (ii); 1. 2. 86

MOTLEY, parti-coloured, 'motley coat', the dress of the professional fool; Prol. 16

MOULD UP, go to form; 5. 5. 26

MOUNT, raise, cause to rise; 1. 1. 144; 1. 2. 205

MOVE, (i) appeal to, 2. 4. 209, 217; (ii) induce, prompt; 2. 4. 167; 5. 1. 100; (iii) provoke, anger; 5. 1. 46

MUSIC, band of musicians; 4. 1. 36 S.D., 91; 4. 2. 94

MYSTERIES, mysterious fashions; 1. 3. 2

NAUGHT (adj.), worthless; Epil. 5

NAUGHTY, wicked; 5. 1. 138

NEW, (i) newly; 3. 2. 366; (ii) over again; 5. 5. 41

NEWLY, recently; 4. 1. 102

NEW-TRIMMED, newly fitted out for sea; 1. 2. 80

NOISE (vb.), report; 1. 2. 105

NOT APPEARANCE, failure to appear; 4. 1. 30

NOTE (sb.), (i) notice; 1. 1. 63; 1. 2. 48; (ii) tune; 4. 2. 78

NOTE (vb.), observe; 2. 1. 46; 4. 2. 95

NOTHING (adv.), not at all; 1. 1. 207; 5. 1. 125

NURSE (fig.), fosterer; 2. 2. 92

O', (i) in; 2. 1. 78; (ii) by; 2. 4. 230; (iii) off; 5. 4. 88

OBJECTION, accusation; 3. 2. 307

OCCASION, opportunity; 3. 2. 7; 5. 1. 109

O'ERMOUNT, soar higher than; 2. 3. 94

O'ERTOP, surpass; 2. 4. 88

OF, 'of purpose', on purpose; 5. 2. 14

OFFER (sb.), 'offer of this time' = opportunity now offered; 3. 2. 4

OFFER (vb.), make an attempt or show of intention (to do something); 2. 4. 121 S.D.

OFFICE, (i) officers, 1. 1. 44; (ii) duty of an official position; 1. 1. 198; (iii) function; 2. 4. 115, 190; 3. 2. 144; (iv) official position; 3. 2. 156; 4. 1. 15

OMIT, let slip; 3. 2. 3

ON, of; 1. 1. 94; 2. 3. 102; 2. 4. 151; 3. 1. 21; 3. 2. 106; 5. 3. 109

ONCE, (i) in short; 1. 2. 82;
(ii) all at once; 3. 1. 110

OPEN (sb.), 'in open', in public; 3. 2. 404

OPEN (adj.), in a public place;
2. 1. 168

OPEN (vb.), (i) make freely
available; 3. 2. 184; (ii) disclose; 3. 2. 201

OPINION, reputation; Prol. 20

OPPOSE, expose; 4. 1. 67

OPPRESSION, distress; 2. 4. 208

OR...OR, either...or; 2. 4. 192

ORDER (sb.), (i) regulated ar-
rangement; 1. 1. 44; (ii)
ecclesiastical status (bishop,
priest, etc.); 4. 1. 26

ORDER (vb.), arrange; 1. 1. 50

ORPHEUS, mythical poet and
lyre-player, son of the Muse
Calliope; 3. 1. 3

OTHERWHERE, elsewhere; 2. 2.
58

OUI, '"oui" away', spend in
speaking French (saying
'oui'); 1. 3. 34

OUT (adv.), (i) not concerned;
1. 1. 79; (ii) at an end;
3. 2. 20

OUT (prep.), (i) 'out of', from
outside; 1. 2. 114; (ii) 'out
of', except; 3. 2. 13

OUT, 'out upon', interj., exclamation of indignant reproach; 3. 1. 99

OUTGO, surpass; 1. 2. 207

OUTRUN, run beyond; 1. 1. 141

OUTSPEAK, speak of what is
more than; 3. 2. 127

OUTWORTH, be more highly
valued than (here only);
1. 1. 123

OVER-RUNNING, running too
far, beyond one's object;
1. 1. 143

PACE (vb.), train (a horse in its
paces); 5. 3. 22

PACK, depart; 1. 3. 33

PACKET, (official) mail; 3. 2.
76

PAINTED, specious; 5. 3. 71

PAINTING, rouge on the
cheeks; 1. 1. 26

PALE, paling; 5. 4. 89

PANG (vb.), cause pangs; 2. 3.
15

PAPER, set down on paper;
1. 1. 80

PARAGON (vb.), hold up as a
perfect model (here only in
this sense); 2. 4. 230

PARCEL, item; 3. 2. 125

PARE, cut down; 3. 2. 159

PARISH GARDEN, Paris Garden,
a bear garden on Bankside,
near the later Globe Theatre,
Southwark; 5. 4. 2

PART (sb.), quality (physical
and mental); 2. 3. 27; 2. 4.
139

PART (vb.), (i) depart; 3. 1. 97
(with 'away'); 3. 2. 205;
4. 1. 92; (ii) separate
(intrans.); 4. 2. 153; (iii)
share; 5. 2. 28

PARTICULAR (sb.), special intimacy; 3. 2. 189

PARTICULAR (adj.), (i) of each
person; 2. 4. 221; (ii) private; 2. 3. 101

PARTNER, fellow-godparent;
5. 5. 5

PASS (vb.), (i) be acceptable, be
accepted; Prol. 11; 5. 3. 59;
(ii) proceed; 2. 1. 10

PASSAGE, (i) passing; 1. 1. 114
S.D.; (ii) proceeding; 2. 4.
165

PAUL'S, St Paul's Cathedral;
5. 4. 16

PEACE, 'take peace', make peace; 2. 1. 85

PECK, pitch; 5. 4. 89

PEPIN, son of Charles Martel, founder of the Carlovingian dynasty, father of Charlemagne; 1. 3. 10

PERK UP, make spruce or smart; 2. 3. 21

PERNICIOUSLY, so as to desire his death; 2. 1. 50

PERSUADE (refl.), be convinced; 3. 2. 50

PERSUADING, persuasive; 4. 2. 52

PERUSE, scrutinize; 2. 3. 75

PHOENIX, fabulous Arabian bird, only one in the world, but when it dies, it is reborn out of its own ashes; 5. 5. 40

PIECE, masterpiece (of person); 5. 5. 26

PILLAR, portable pillar, borne as an emblem of dignity, here of cardinals; 2. 4. init. S.D.

PINCH, afflict; 2. 3. 1

PINKED, ornamented with perforations; 5. 4. 48

PITCH, height (fig.); 2. 2. 48

PITY, subject for pity; 2. 3. 10

PLACE (sb.), (high) position or office, dignity, rank; 1. 1. 66, 161; 1. 2. 75; 2. 2. 81, 110; 2. 4. 108; 3. 1. 156; 3. 2. 248; 5. 2. 30; 5. 3. 40

PLACE (vb.), put (guests) in their places on; 1. 4. 20

PLAGUE OF (imprec.), curse; 3. 2. 259

PLAIN-SONG, simple melody; 1. 3. 45

PLAY (sb.), 'fair play', a just practice; 4. 2. 36; 'make one's play', win one's game; 1. 4. 46; 'hold play', keep engaged; 5. 4. 85

PLEASANT, facetious; 1. 4. 90; 2. 3. 93

PLEASURE, (i) desire (shading into 'command'); 1. 2. 68; 3. 2. 228, 337; 5. 2. 18; 'speak your pleasures', say what you think; 3. 2. 13

PLUCK OFF, come down; 2. 3. 40

POMP, magnificence; 1. 1. 15, 163; 2. 3. 7; 3. 2. 365

PORRINGER, cap looking like a porringer; 5. 4. 48

POSSESS, imbue; 2. 1. 158

POST (sb.), courier (see *2 H. IV*, G.); 5. 2. 32

POST (vb.), hasten (with auxil. 'to be'); 3. 2. 59

PRACTICE, plot, trickery; 1. 1. 204; 1. 2. 127; 3. 2. 29; 5. 1. 128

PRÆMUNIRE, statute limiting the power of the Pope in England, here probably that of R. II, 1393, forbidding legal suits outside the country, and naming Rome in partic.; the word is the 1st in the legal writ issued to sheriffs to summon offenders against the statute (Hol.); 3. 2. 340

PREFER, promote; 4. 1. 102

PREJUDICE, detriment; 1. 1. 182; 2. 4. 154

PREMISES, previous events (regarded as evidence); 2. 1. 63

PRESCRIPTION, advice (perh. fig. fr. medical sense); 1. 1. 151

PRESENCE, (i) the fact of being present; 1. 1. 30; (ii) presence-chamber, place of audience; 3. 1. 17; 4. 2. 37

PRESENT, immediate; 1. 2. 211

PRESENTLY, immediately, at once; 1. 2. 157; 3. 2. 78, 229; 5. 2. 10; 5. 4. 29

PRESS, crowd; 4. 1. 78; 5. 4. 83

PRESUME, venture to say; 3. 2. 183

PRETENCE, pretext; 1. 1. 177; 1. 2. 59

PRICK, qualm; 2. 4. 171

PRIDE, magnificent adornment; 1. 1. 25

PRIME (adj.), foremost; 1. 2. 67; 2. 4. 229; 3. 2. 163

PRIMERO, fashionable gambling card-game, c. 1530–1640; 5. 1. 7

PRIVATE, (i) alone; 2. 2. 13; (ii) not invested with a public function; 5. 3. 55

PRIVITY, participation in something private (cf. 'privy to'); 1. 1. 74

PROCESS, proceeding; 2. 3. 9; 2. 4. 38

PROFESS, affirm; 2. 4. 84; 3. 2. 44, 190

PROFESSOR, one who professes (a religion); 3. 1. 115

PROGRESS, course; 5. 3. 32

PRONOUNCE, declare; 1. 1. 196; 2. 3. 4; 3. 2. 163

PROOF, experience (as corroborating an assertion); 1. 1. 197

PROPER, fine (iron.); 1. 1. 98

PROPORTION, size; 5 1. 129

PROUD, high; 3. 2. 127

PUBLISH, proclaim publicly; 3. 2. 68

PUPPY, contempt. term of address; 5. 4. 30

PURGATION, clearing from suspicion of guilt; 5. 3. 152

PURGE, exonerate; 5. 1. 102

PURSE, bag containing the .Great Seal of the Lord High Chancellor; 1. 1. 114 S.D.; 2. 4. init. S.D.

PURSUIVANT, junior officer attendant on a herald; 5. 2. 24

PUT, (i) incite; 1. 1. 58; (ii) 'put off', dismiss, discard; 1. 2. 32; 2. 4. 21; (iii) 'put from', take from; 2. 2. 55–6

PUTTER-ON, instigator; 1. 2. 24

QUALITY, person of such and such a character; 1. 2. 84

QUARREL, (abstr. for concr.) quarreller; 2. 3. 14

QUARTER (vb. pass.), dwell; 5. 4. 53

QUEEN IT, play the part of a queen; 2. 3. 37

QUESTION (sb.), (i) doubt; 2. 4. 151; (ii) case at issue; 5. 1. 130

QUESTION (vb.), dispute; 1. 2. 99; 2. 4. 50

QUIT, rid; 5. 1. 70

RAM, battering ram; 4. 1. 77

RANGE, occupy a position; 2. 3. 20

RANK, full-grown; 1..2. 186

RANKNESS, (a) strong smell; (b) exuberance; 4. 1. 59

RATE, price; 1. 1. 99; 3. 2. 127

READ, learn; 5. 5. 37

RECEIPT, reception; 2. 2. 137

REEK, smoke with heat (here fig. for sweating under a mental load); 2. 4. 208

RELIGIOUS, strict, conscientious; 4. 2. 74

REMARKED, remarkable; 5. 1. 33

REPAIR, restore; 5. 1. 3

REPEAT, state; 1. 2. 13

REPUTE (FOR), consider (to be); 2. 4. 45

REQUIRE, request, demand; 2. 4. 144, 177; 3. 2. 122

RESPECTING, in view of; 2. 4. 180

RESPITE, delay; 2. 4. 177, 181

REST, remain; 5. 1. 55

RESTORE, bring back to mental calm; 2. 2. 28

RETAIN, take as one's servant; 1. 2. 192

REVOKEMENT, revocation (first here; one other instance); 1. 2. 106

RIDE, break (of horse); 2. 2. 2

RIPENESS, full development; 5. 5. 20

ROAD, stage (in a journey); 4. 2. 17

ROAR, behave rowdily; 5. 4. 7

ROD, sceptre; 4. 1. 89

ROME, the Roman Church, hence, the Pope as Head of it; 3. 2. 328

ROSE, The Red Rose, the Duke of Buckingham's manor, which from 1561 became the Merchant Taylors' School; 1. 2. 152

ROUND, heavy; 5. 4. 79

RUB, impediment; 2. 1. 129

RUDE, violent; 3. 2. 364

RUIN, destruction; 3. 2. 205

RUN, 'is run in', has incurred; 1. 2. 110

SABA, Sheba, here the Queen of Sheba; 5. 5. 23

SACRING, =consecrating; 'sacring bell', bell rung at the elevation of the host in the Mass; 3. 2. 295

SAD, (i) serious; Prol. 3; 2. 2. 56, 61; (ii), (i) with quibble on 'sorrowful' as opposed to 'happiest'; Prol. 25

SALUTE, exhilarate; 2. 3. 103

SAUCY, insolent; 4. 2. 100

SAVING, with all respect to; 2. 3. 31

SCHEDULE, scroll of paper; 3. 2. 104 S.D.

SEAL, ratify; 2. 1. 105

SECOND, support; 3. 2. 60

SECTARY, member of a (heretical) sect; 5. 3. 70

SEE, (i) (abs.), meet; 1. 1. 2; (ii) 'see away', spend on seeing (nonce-use); Prol. 12

SELF-DRAWING, drawn out of itself (cf. *O.E.D.* 'draw', 54='spin (a thread)'); 1. 1. 63

SELF-METTLE, one's own high spirit; 1. 1. 134

SEMBLANCE, pretence; 1. 2. 198

SENNET, set of notes played on a trumpet as a signal for the approach or departure of a procession; 2. 4. init. S.D.

SERVICE, 'do (one's) service', remember (one) respectfully; 3. 1. 179

SET, (i) 'set on', set forth; 2. 4. 241; (ii) (pass.), be seated (Hol.); 3. 1. 74

SETTING (sb.), fig., downfall; 3. 2. 225

SETTLED, permanently placed (if 'he'=Wolsey), or resolved (if 'he'=the King); 3. 2. 22

SEVERAL, various; 3. 2. 125

SHAME (vb.), be ashamed; 5. 2. 16

SHARP, (i) acute, subtle; 2. 1. 14; (ii) fierce in attack; 5. 3. 74

SHINE DOWN, surpass in brilliance (first here; one other, 19th century, example); 1. 1. 20

SHOAL, shallow; 3. 2. 436

SHORE, 'shore of rock', ? rocky shore; 1. 1. 158

SHOT, coll. sing., body of shooters; 5. 4. 56

SHOULD, would; 3. 2. 198

SHOW (sb.), spectacle; Prol. 10

SHREWD, (i) intensive term in describing something bad; 1. 3. 7; (ii) ill-natured, bad (Foxe); 5. 3. 177

SHRINK (FROM), desert; 4. 1. 107

SHROUDS, sail-ropes; 4. 1. 72

SICK, unsound; 1. 2. 82

SICKEN (fig.), impoverish (here first trans.); 1. 1. 82

SIGN, mark; 2. 4. 108

SINGLE, (i) (a) unmarried; (b) ? small; 1. 1. 15; (ii) 'with a single heart', single-mindedly; 5. 3. 38

SINK, destroy, ruin; 2. 1. 60, 131

SIR, term of address, used of a cleric; 2. 1. 20

SIRRAH, term of address, used to an inferior; 5. 4. 30

SLEEK, oily, plausible; 3. 2. 241

SLEEP, (i) fig., cease; 5. 5. 39; (ii) 'sleep upon', be blind to; 2. 2. 41

SLIGHTLY, easily; 2. 4. 112

SNUFF, free the wick of a candle from its snuff (cf. *O.E.D.* 1). The mod. sense

'extinguish' not found before the end of the 17th century; 3. 2. 96

So (conj.), provided that; 5. 1. 44

So (interj.), (i) good!; 4. 2. 4; (ii) (of resignation), very well; 5. 2. 7

SOIL, taint; 1. 2. 26

SOME, some one; 1. 4. 50, 60

SOMETHING, to some extent; 1. 1. 195

SOMETIMES, formerly; 2. 4. 181

SOOTH, truth; 2. 3. 30

SOUND (adj.), loyal; 3. 2. 274; 5. 3. 81

SOUND (vb.), fathom; 3. 2. 436; 5. 2. 13

SOUR, morose; 4. 2. 53

SPAN, measure out (first here; rare); 1. 1. 223

SPANIARD, Spanish nation; 2. 2. 88

SPARE (sb.), frugal use; 5. 4. 21

SPAVIN, prop. a disease of horses, a bony tumour at joints; here extended to men, of a new-fangled mode of walking; 1. 3. 12

SPEAK, (i) 'speak to', ask, engage; 1. 3. 66; (ii) 'speak out', describe fully; 2. 4. 140; (iii) bear witness in favour of; 2. 4. 166; 3. 1. 125; 4. 2. 63; (iv) speak of; 4. 1. 61; 4. 2. 32, 47

SPEAKING, thing spoken; 2. 4. 104

SPEED, usu. in invocation with 'God' or 'Heaven', prosper; here with 'the devil', as an imprecation, 'help him to Hell'; 1. 1. 52

SPEEDING, effective; 1. 3. 40

SPICE, dash (of some quality); 2. 3. 26

SPINSTER, spinner; 1. 2. 33

SPITTING, transfixing on a spit; 2. 4. 183

SPLEEN, regarded as the seat of the strong passions, anger, hatred, etc.; 1. 2. 174; 2. 4. 89, 110

SPLEENY, splenetic, ill-humoured; 3. 2. 99

SPOIL, destroy; 1. 2. 175

SPRINGHALT, affection of the hind legs of a horse, causing certain muscles to contract spasmodically; 1. 3. 13

STAND, (i) remain (steadfastly); 2. 2. 50; 3. 2. 3 (with 'under'=against); 4. 2. 157; (ii) 'stand to', support; 2. 4. 86; (iii) 'stand under', be subject to; 5. 1. 122; (iv) 'stand on', take one's stand on; 5. 1. 122

STANDING BOWL, bowl resting on a foot; 5. 5. init. S.D.

STARVE, die; 5. 3. 132

STATE, (i) dignity; Prol. 3; (ii) ruler (here, king); 1. 1. 101; (iii) chair of state, a raised chair surmounted by a canopy; 1. 2. 8 S.D.; 1. 4. 34 S.D.; (iv) 'keep state', maintain a demeanour of dignity or grandeur; 1. 3. 10; (v) high rank, official position; 2. 1. 101; 5. 1. 127; (vi) condition of things; 2. 4. 213; (vii) pomp; 4. 1. 36 S.D.; (viii) position of dignity; 5. 2. 24; (ix) canopy; 1. 4. init. S.D.; (x) 'trick of state', see 'trick'; (xi) 'mortal state', see 'mortal'

STATE-STATUE, mere image of a statesman (nonce-word); 1. 2. 88

STAY, (i) keep (in); 1. 1. 5; (ii) wait; 1. 1. 129; 1. 3. 63; 3. 2. 232; 4. 2. 105; 5. 3. 97; (iii) stop (intrans.); 2. 1. 53; 5. 5. 75; (iv) stop (trans.); 3. 2. 33

STEEL, weapon of iron or steel (here, axe); 2..1. 76

STICK, scruple; 2. 2. 125

STILL (adj.), quiet, silent; Prol. 11.

STILL (adv.), always, continually; 1. 1. 31; 2. 1. 13; 2. 2. 127; 2. 3. 7; 3. 1. 63, 130; 3. 2. 315, 445; 5. 5. 17, 29

STIR, (i) be active; 5. 3. 39; (ii) move, shift (people) on; 5. 4. 16

STOCK, trunk of a tree, here fig., parent, mother; 5. 1. 22

STOMACH, arrogance (Hol.); 4. 2. 34

STRAIGHT, immediately; 3. 2. 115

STRAIN, embrace; 4. 1. 46

STRANGER, foreigner; 1. 4. 53 (Hol.); 2. 2. 100; 2. 3. 17; 2. 4. 15 (Hol.)

STROKE, blow; 2. 2. 34

STUBBORN, stiff; 5. 3. 23

STUDIED, diligent; 3. 2. 168

STUDY, (i) diligent endeavour; 3. 1. 174; 5. 3. 34; (ii) learned enquiry (or perh. as (i)); 3. 1. 123

STUFF, (i) matter (fig.), capabilities; 1. 1. 58; 3. 2. 137; (ii) cloth (robe or upholstery); 3. 2. 126

SUBJECT (sb.), body of subjects; 1. 2. 56

SUBJECT (TO) (adj.), under the influence (of); 2. 4. 26

SUBSTANCE, treasure, money; 1. 2. 58; 3. 2. 326 (Hol.)

SUBURBS, in 16th–17th-century England the disorderly quarters of London, with brothels, etc.; 5. 4. 71

SUCCESSOR, descendant; 1. 1. 60

SUDDEN, (i) immediate; 1. 1. 94; (ii) extempore; 5. 3. 122

SUDDENLY, (i) immediately; 5. 4. 78; (ii) extempore; 3. 1. 70 (Hol.)

SUE, apply for; 3. 2. 341

SUFFERANCE, suffering, pain; 2. 3. 15; 5. 1. 68

SUGGEST, incite; 1. 1. 164

SUGGESTION, underhand practice (Hol.); 4. 2. 35

SUIT (sb.), petition; request; 1. 1. 186; 1. 2. 10, 197; 2. 3. 85; 5. 3. 160

SUPERFLUOUS, extravagant; 1. 1. 99

SUPERSTITIOUS, idolatrously devoted (to); 3. 1. 131

SURE (adv.), (i) assuredly; 1. 3. 15; 2. 1. 37; 3. 2. 141; 4. 2. 147; (ii) as excl. of surprise or query, 'surely'; 5. 2. 4

SURVEYOR, overseer, of household, estate, etc.; 1. 1. 115, 222; 1. 2. 172; 2. 1. 19

SWELL, grow angry; 3. 1. 164

TAINT (sb.), corruption; 5. 3. 28

TAINT (vb.), sully; 3. 1. 55

TAINTED, disgraced; 4. 2. 14

TAKE, (i) 'take out', lead out for a dance; 1. 4. 95; (ii) 'take right', have the right

effect; 3. 2. 219; (iii) 'better taken', more acceptable; 4. 1. 12; (iv) 'take place', take one's seat; 1. 2. 10; 2. 4. init. S.D.; (v) 'take up', obstruct; 1. 1. 56

TALL, long; 1. 3. 30

TANTA EST ERGA TE MENTIS INTEGRITAS, REGINA SERENISSIMA, such integrity of mind is there towards thee, most serene Queen; 3. 1. 40–1.

TARGET, shield; Prol. 15

TELL, count; 2. 1. 91; hence, 'tell steps', march in step; 1. 2. 43

TEMPER, disposition; 3. 1. 165

TEMPERANCE, self-control; 1. 1. 124

TEMPORAL, worldly; 2. 2. 71; 2. 3. 13

TEMPT, put to the test; 1. 2. 55

TENDANCE, attention; 3. 2. 149

TENDER, (i) offer; 2. 3. 66; (ii) be concerned for; 2. 4. 116

TENNIS, the older game, played in an enclosed court (see H. V, G.); 1. 3. 30

TERROR, 'of terror', intended to terrify; 5. 1. 88

THAT, so that; 1. 1. 25, 36, 38; Epil. 7

THICK, numerous; 3. 2. 195

THINKINGS, thoughts; 3. 2. 134

THIS, 'by this', by this time; 3. 2. 83

THROUGHLY, thoroughly; 5 1. 110

TIE, (i) ratify; 3. 2. 250; (ii) bring into bondage; 4. 2. 36

TIME, (i) 'good time', good fortune; 5. 1. 22; (ii) present state of affairs; 5. 1. 37

TIPSTAVES, officers whose staffs are tipped with silver, who take prisoners into custody, bailiffs; 2. 1. 53 S.D.

To, (i) for; 3. 2. 108; (ii) as to (after 'so'); 1. 2. 135; 3. 1. 86, 140

TOOL, membrum virile; 5. 4. 34

TOOTH, 'to the teeth', in open defiance; 1. 2. 36

TOP-PROUD, proud to the highest degree (only ex.); 1. 1. 151

TOUCH (sb.), (i) sullying; 2. 4. 155; (ii) hint; 5. 1. 13

TOWER-HILL, hill to the W. and N. of the Tower of London, where state offenders were executed; 5. 4. 61

TRACE, follow; 3. 2. 45

TRACT, course (perh. with subordinate sense 'description'); 1. 1. 40

TRACTABLE, docile; 1. 2. 64

TRADE, trodden path; 5. 1. 36

TRAIN, retinue; 4. 1. 37

TREMBLING, accompanied with trembling; 1. 2. 95

TRIBULATION, trouble-maker ('app. a cant name for a gang of disturbers', *O.E.D.*); 5. 4. 61

TRICK, 'trick of state', stroke of policy; 2. 1. 44

TRIM, (iron.) fine; 1. 3. 38; 5. 4. 70

TROOP, company; 1. 4. 53; 4. 2. 87; (in procession) 5. 4. 84

TROTH, (i) loyalty, 'by my troth' (assever.); 2. 3. 23; (ii) 'good troth', 'troth', used exclamatorily; 2. 3. 33, 34

TROW, feel sure; 1. 1. 184

TRUE, loyal; 1. 2. 19

TRUNCHEONER, one armed with a truncheon (nonce-word); 5. 4. 51

TRUST, 'in trust', trusted; 1. 2. 125

TYPE, badge; 1. 3. 31

UNDERSTAND, (*a*) have comprehension, have views, in general; ? (*b*) stand up (under clothes); 1. 3. 32

UNDERSTANDING, (*a*) comprehending, (*b*) standing below the level of the stage; Prol. 22

UNDERTAKE, take charge of; 2. 1. 97

UNDO, ruin; 2. 1. 159; 3. 2. 210

UNFOLD, disclose; 3. 2. 27

UNHANDLED, not dealt with; 3. 2. 58

UNHAPPILY, unfavourably; 1. 4. 89

UNPARTIAL, impartial (not elsewhere in Sh.); 2. 2. 105

UNQUEEN, depose from being queen (cf. 'unkinged', *R. II*, 4. 1. 220); 4. 2. 171

UNSATISFIED, insatiate; 4. 2. 55

UNSETTLED, undecided; 2. 4. 64

UNWITTINGLY, unintentionally; 3. 2. 123

UPROAR, insurrection; 5. 3. 28

UPWARD, upwards; 2. 4. 36

URGE, press one's case; 2. 1. 16; 5. 3. 48

USE (sb.), 'make use', take advantage, profit by the opportunity; 3. 2. 420

USE (vb.), (i) (refl.), behave oneself; 3. 1. 176; (ii) treat; 4. 2. 168

VACANT, devoid; 5. 1. 125

VAIN, worthless; 1. 2. 147; 3. 2. 365

VALUE (vb.), be worth; 1. 1. 88; 2. 3. 52

VANITY, (i) foolish extravagance; self-conceit; 1. 1. 85; (ii) vain creature; 1. 3. 38

VENT, utter; 1. 2. 23

VISITATION, visit (which as sb. is post-Sh.); 1. 1. 179; 5. 1. 167

VIZARD, mask; 4. 2. 82 S.D.

VOICE, (i) vote; 1. 2. 70; 5. 3. 88; (ii) (expression of) opinion; 2. 2. 86 (cf. *Ham.* 5. 2. 247, again with 'precedent'), 92; (iii) general talk, report; 3. 2. 405; 4. 2. 11; 5. 3. 175

VOID, empty; 5. 3. init. S.D.

VOUCH (sb.), attestation; 1. 1. 157

VOUCHSAFE, deign to accept; 2. 3. 43

WANTON, insolently triumphant; 3. 2. 241

WAY, (i) course (of life); 1. 3. 61; 3. 1. 157; 5. 1. 28; (ii) 'this way', in respect of this; 2. 2. 67; so 'any way', in any respect; 3. 1. 56; (iii) 'ways' (in 'come, go, thy ways'); old gen. sing., used adverbially; go; 2. 4. 133; (iv) 'give way', be propitious; 3. 2. 16; allow;

5. 1. 143; (v) 'in the way of', as regards; 3. 2. 272

WEAR, spend; 2. 4. 228

WEEN OF, dream of, expect to have; 5. 1. 135

WEIGH, (i) be equal in weight to; 1. 1. 11; 3. 2. 259; (ii) 'weigh out', assess at full weight; 3. 1. 88; (iii) attach value to; 5. 1. 124

WELL SAID, well done; 1. 4. 30

WHAT!, exclam. of impatience; 5. 1. 87

WHICH, (after 'such') as; 1. 2. 27

WHILES, while; 5. 1. 137

WHOLESOME, salutary; 1. 1. 113; 1. 2. 45; 3. 2. 99

WHORESON, coarse term, here used mockingly, 'sly dog'; 1. 3. 39

WILL (sb.), (i) desire; 1. 2. 13; (ii) passion; 1. 2. 65

WILL (vb.), (i) request; 3. 1. 18; (ii) be determined to; 4. 2. 102; (iii) may (be); 5. 3. 47

WILLING, deliberate; 3. 1. 49

WIN OF, get the better of; 5. 1. 58

WIT, intelligence; 2. 4. 47; 3. 1. 72, 177 (Hol.); 5. 4. 47

WITH, in addition to; 3. 2. 6; 'I shall be with you'=I'll trounce you; 5. 4. 29

WITHAL (adv.), in addition; 3. 2. 164

WITHAL (prep.), with; 3. 2. 130

WORK (sb.), fortification; 5. 4. 58

Work (vb.), take effect; 3. 2. 37

Working, effective; Prol. 3

Worship, high rank; 1. 1. 39

Worthily, deservedly; 2. 4. 97

Wot, know; 3. 2. 122

Would, (i) wish (that); 1. 2. 65; (ii) require to, ought to; 1. 2. 48; 2. 2. 7

Wrenching, rinsing (arch. and dial.); 1. 1. 167

Yet, still; 2. 4. 204

Young, recent; 3. 2. 47